DATE DUE			

International Library of Psychology
Philosophy and Scientific Method

WHAT IS VALUE?

International Library of Psychology Philosophy and Scientific Method

GENERAL EDITOR: C. K. OGDEN, M.A. (*Magdalene College, Cambridge*)

Philosophical Studies . . . . *by* G. E. Moore, Litt.D.
The Misuse of Mind . . . . *by* Karin Stephen
Conflict and Dream* . . . . *by* W. H. R. Rivers, F.R.S.
Tractatus Logico-Philosophicus . . . . *by* L. Wittgenstein
Psychological Types* . . . . *by* C. G. Jung, M.D.
Scientific Thought* . . . . *by* C. D. Broad, Litt.D.
The Meaning of Meaning . . . . . *by* C. K. Ogden and I. A. Richards
Individual Psychology . . . . *by* Alfred Adler
Speculations (*Preface by Jacob Epstein*) . . . . . *by* T. E. Hulme
The Psychology of Reasoning* . . . . . . *by* Eugenio Rignano
The Philosophy of "As If" . . . . *by* H. Vaihinger
The Nature of Intelligence . . . . *by* L. L. Thurstone
Telepathy and Clairvoyance . . . . *by* R. Tischner
The Growth of the Mind . . . . *by* K. Koffka
The Mentality of Apes . . . . *by* W. Köhler
Psychology of Religious Mysticism . . . . . . *by* J. H. Leuba
The Philosophy of Music . . . . *by* W. Pole, F.R.S.
The Psychology of a Musical Prodigy . . . . . . *by* G. Revesz
Principles of Literary Criticism . . . . . . *by* I. A. Richards
Metaphysical Foundation of Sciences . . . . . *by* E. A. Burtt, Ph.D.
Thought and the Brain* . . . . *by* H. Piéron
Physique and Character* . . . . *by* Ernst Kretschmer
Psychology of Emotion . . . . *by* J. T. MacCurdy, M.D.
Problems of Personality . . . . . . *in honour of* Morton Prince
The History of Materialism . . . . *by* F. A. Lange
Personality* . . . . *by* R. G. Gordon, M.D.
Educational Psychology . . . . *by* Charles Fox
Language and Thought of the Child . . . . . . *by* J. Piaget
Sex and Repression in Savage Society* . . . . . *by* B. Malinowski, D.Sc.
Comparative Philosophy . . . . *by* P. Masson-Oursel
Social Life in the Animal World . . . . . . *by* F. Alverdes
How Animals Find their Way About . . . . . . *by* E. Rabaud
The Social Insects . . . . *by* W. Morton Wheeler
Theoretical Biology . . . . *by* J. von Uexküll
Possibility . . . . *by* Scott Buchanan
The Technique of Controversy . . . . . . *by* B. B. Bogoslovsky
The Symbolic Process . . . . *by* J. F. Markey
Political Pluralism . . . . *by* K. C. Hsiao
History of Chinese Political Thought . . . . . *by* Liang Chi-Chao
Integrative Psychology* . . . . *by* W. M. Marston
The Analysis of Matter . . . . . . *by* Bertrand Russell, F.R.S.
Plato's Theory of Ethics . . . . *by* R. C. Lodge
Historical Introduction to Modern Psychology . . . . *by* G. Murphy
Creative Imagination . . . . *by* June E. Downey
Colour and Colour Theories . . . . . *by* Christine Ladd-Franklin
Biological Principles . . . . *by* J. H. Woodger
The Trauma of Birth . . . . *by* Otto Rank
The Statistical Method in Economics . . . . . *by* P. S. Florence
The Art of Interrogation . . . . *by* E. R. Hamilton
The Growth of Reason . . . . *by* Frank Lorimer
Human Speech . . . . *by* Sir Richard Paget
Foundations of Geometry and Induction . . . . . *by* Jean Nicod
The Laws of Feeling . . . . *by* F. Paulhan
The Mental Development of the Child . . . . . *by* K. Bühler
Eidetic Imagery . . . . *by* E. R. Jaensch
The Concentric Method . . . . . . *by* M. Laignel-Lavastine
The Foundations of Mathematics . . . . . . *by* F. P. Ramsey
The Philosophy of the Unconscious . . . . . *by* E. von Hartmann
Outlines of Greek Philosophy . . . . *by* E. Zeller
The Psychology of Children's Drawings . . . . . *by* Helga Eng
Invention and the Unconscious . . . . . . *by* J. M. Montmasson
The Theory of Legislation . . . . *by* Jeremy Bentham
The Social Life of Monkeys . . . . *by* S. Zuckerman
The Development of the Sexual Impulses . . . . *by* R. E. Money-Kyrle
Constitution Types in Delinquency . . . . . . *by* W. A. Willemse
The Sciences of Man in the Making . . . . . *by* E. A. Kirkpatrick
Ethical Relativity . . . . *by* E. A. Westermarck

* *Asterisks denote that other books by the same author are included in the Series.*

WHAT IS VALUE?

AN ESSAY

IN PHILOSOPHICAL ANALYSIS

by

EVERETT W. HALL

Kenan Professor of Philosophy in the University of North Carolina

NEW YORK

THE HUMANITIES PRESS INC

LONDON: ROUTLEDGE & KEGAN PAUL LTD

First published in 1952
by The Humanities Press Inc

Reprinted 1961 by special arrangement
with Mrs. Everett W. Hall
and the
Research Council of the University of North Carolina,
both of whom have made possible
this reprint edition by subsidies
to the publisher.

Printed in the U.S.A.

NOBLE OFFSET PRINTERS, INC.
NEW YORK 3, N. Y.

The process of sound philosophizing, to my mind, consists mainly in passing from those obvious, vague, ambiguous things, that we feel quite sure of, to something precise, clear, definite, which by reflection and analysis we find is involved in the vague thing that we started from, and is, so to speak, the real truth of which that vague thing is a sort of shadow.—BERTRAND RUSSELL

PREFATORY REMARKS

A GLANCE at the section-headings of the ensuing essay will show the reader that, like the title, they all have the form of questions. It is not assumed that this device will materially increase the sale of the present work. Although the whole literate world is vitally interested in bringing to a settlement the current strife of various incompatible systems of values, only a very few people will, or perhaps can, take the time to make the logically prior investigation as to what value—any value whatever—is. To those few, however, who are concerned with this prior issue, the question-form of its headings is meant to indicate immediately that the present essay is a genuine inquiry, not a recondite formulation of one of the received, dogmatic positions. Its author is more anxious to raise certain extremely central issues than to settle them. Not that the essay does no more than this. It is concerned to call attention to a possible answer which, though perhaps somewhat novel, yet seems to be worthy of serious consideration. But the author is not at all sure that the answer suggested is the correct one. Indeed, he is not overly confident that it even points in the right direction. Moreover, he is keenly aware that he has not as much as formulated his answer. He has had to be satisfied with setting down some remarks, in quite incorrect language, that may suggest to the reader in some fashion what the author thinks might be an answer if only he could put it down. And so if the reader wants, as he may feel he has a right to demand, a straightforward and unhesitating reply to the simple question, What is value?, he had best put aside this book as a waste of time.

However, if the author is not too sure as to what he is doing or whether it can be done, he is quite sure as to some things he is not doing. (It does not follow that he is convinced that any of these things can be done!) He is not trying to answer the question, What things are valuable? It may be that pleasant experience is valuable, perhaps it is the only thing that is. Or again, it may be that personal integrity, or individual self-expression, or the acquisition of knowledge are valuable. Perhaps the world is just chock full of valuable things: that is beside the point so far as the present inquiry is concerned. Nor is the author trying to answer the question, What are the main sorts or varieties of value? Is value properly subdivisible into cognitive value, aesthetic value, and moral value? Or is all value moral? These are interesting questions, but are not taken up in this essay. Finally, and this is particularly to be stressed, this book is not concerned with the exceedingly important and difficult issue as to whether assertions of value can be verified and if so how this can be done. Perhaps some of the things here said will have a bearing on this issue. If so, that bearing must await another occasion for its exploration. It cannot be stressed too much that the present essay is nothing but an attempt to analyse value, to try to find out what it is.

Has this extremely limited inquiry any importance? It seems to me that it has. In some sense, answers to all the other questions about value are determined by one's answer to this question. Indeed, I think the very significant trend toward general scepticism concerning value—I do not mean the challenge we see to the traditional values in certain contemporary "transvaluations of all values," but the serious and honest doubt whether there is any such thing as value at all—is due in large measure to the absence of any satisfactory answer to our question. I think it is especially important to those who would like to believe that there are values that certain false analyses of value (or, to use the newer language, of value-sentences) be cleared away. And particularly I think it important to show that the view that value is a property, whether a quality or a relation (to put it linguistically, that the view that value-expressions function as predicates), rests on an incorrect analysis. Yet any other view might seem entirely implausible. Nevertheless I am going to present an extremely odd proposal to try to extricate us from the serious difficulties inherent in the traditional view that value is some sort of property, some "tertiary quality." To prepare the way, I have felt it necessary to overthrow that view quite decisively. This explains the amount of energy I have devoted to that unpleasant task. I hope the reader will excuse it as a necessary evil and press on to the positive proposal I have to make and, when he has done so, not be too weary to wade through hesitations, qualifications, and circumlocutions.

To that reader who wants to know beforehand where it is all coming out, I recommend that the "Concluding Remarks" be read first. Not that they will have much meaning by themselves, but they may furnish some sense of direction to a pursuit which, though relatively straightforward in the author's eyes, seemed to one reader not dissimilar to following the trail of a rabbit "through all the twists and turns of the underbush and briar-patch." And to him who, though willing to follow this "rabbit-trail," would yet appreciate some anticipation of its main directions, let me address the following rough characterization. The main turn may be said to occur between sections 4 and 5. Before that the argument is mainly negative in purport; thereafter there is an increasingly positive tendency. That is, in sections, 2, 3, and 4 my chief concern is to show the untenability, in its various forms, of the view that value is a property, whereas in sections 5, 6, and 7 I am venturing, most hesitantly and without final success, to formulate a view that makes value a different sort of thing, something having a status more like that of fact. But this characterization is misleading. Not only is there no sudden turn taken as one goes from section 4 to section 5, but in the earlier sections the forms of the position rejected are found to be less objectionable as one proceeds, and likewise in the later sections though complete success in stating an acceptable alternative is never attained yet definite progress is made.

This leads me to add a final word in justification of the large amount of space devoted to the statement and criticism of other views. Why did I not go directly to work stating the position I wanted the reader to consider? No doubt a completely candid answer would include the confession that the present author, like so many other philosophers, is subject to the occupational disease of his vocation. But I feel convinced that this would be a partial answer only. Another part of the answer would relate to difficulties of communication. One can state one's insights, so far as they involve something new, in a language peculiar to oneself and one's cronies. It is then fairly easy to achieve brevity, precision, and disdain for other positions. But to be understood requires a different form of statement than the oracular. It demands some give-and-take in the courts of philosophy. Indeed, without meaning any sacrilege, I am not sure that the Oracle always completely understands his own cryptic utterances. Perhaps some adjustment to, some recognition of, the views of others might actually clarify him. No oracle myself, I have found this procedure necessary both to the clarification and the communication of my ideas. But in adopting it I have had to sacrifice brevity and forthrightness of exposition, I have found it necessary to use the ideas and expressions of others as approximations, needing qualification to indicate the sort of view I am trying to formulate clearly to myself and communicate understandably to others.

ACKNOWLEDGEMENTS

Several people have read the manuscript of this book and given me the benefit of both criticism and encouragement. Without mentioning their names individually, I want to thank the graduate students at the State University of Iowa for the stimulus which their careful reading of the essay has furnished me. My gratitude is also due to Professor Charner Perry, editor of *Ethics*, for his interest in, and critical comments upon, the work. Above all, I wish to thank two men who devoted many hours to a painstaking reading of the manuscript and a detailed criticism of certain aspects and portions of it. I refer to Professors C. J. Ducasse of Brown University and Charles Baylis of the University of Maryland. That I have not accepted all their criticisms will be evident to the reader when he comes to those passages in which their views are specifically mentioned. This should not, however, obscure the fact that I have modified many statements in the light of their valuable comments. I am indebted to Mr. Romane Clark and Mr. Thomas Thompson for reading the proof and to an unknown editor for changing my spelling from the American to the English form. In conclusion, if there are still serious infelicities of expression, as I am sure there are, it is in spite of the very considerable help in their elimination given me by Mr. Donald Eichert, who also checked the references and constructed the index of proper names.—E. W. H.

CONTENTS

I

IN WHAT SENSE CAN VALUE BE ANALYSED?

THE present essay is meant to be an instance of philosophical analysis. Just what is meant by 'philosophical analysis' can best be indicated by actual examples. The author hopes the following essay furnishes such an example. But a few preliminary remarks may help to indicate the sort of problem being raised.

It is just foolish to attempt complete analysis, at least in any one essay. By this I mean that analysis must be carried on with conceptual tools that, in the given undertaking, are not themselves analysed.[1] What these tools are must be gathered by alert attention to their actual use. I leave this, in the present instance, to the reader.[2] But I do wish to point out at the very start that I am assuming throughout that in some sense there are values. Unless one accepted this, there would be nothing, in the area here chosen for investigation, to be analysed. Thus the present essay is based on the assumption of the objectivity of values in one very broad yet not wholly trivial sense. This sense of 'objectivity of values' should not be confused with a species of it: that there are values

1 The refusal to admit this bit of common sense leads to the involutions of the "analysis" of the neo-Wittgensteinians, a symptom of which is the inability to stop the analysis once the initial inhibition to undertaking it, which is usually great, is overcome. A case in point is John Wisdom's "Other Minds," *Mind*, vols. xlix and l, 1940 and 1941.

2 It will be noted that I use a mixture of linguistic and metaphysical terms, shifting to suit the context. I think I could have kept consistently to linguistic terminology, avoiding the many pitfalls awaiting the user of what Carnap called "the material mode of speech." The cost however would have been not only an insufferably affected style, but worse, the illusion that language constituted the subject-matter of analysis, not merely, as is the case, the tool thereof. Moreover, I shall shift back and forth, no doubt disconcertingly, between correct and incorrect linguistic formulations. This is partly the result of indolence—actual on my part and assumed on the reader's. But it also seems to be involved in the very nature of the case that we must set up our problem and state criteria for its solution in incorrect, common-sensical language. Then we must come to see this incorrectness and try to attain a more nearly correct formulation. I have a duty, in this connection, of explaining my use of quotation marks. On the one hand, they are used in accordance with the ordinary rules of punctuation for direct quotation, although with a slight

outside human experience.[1] I shall not raise at all the question of the locus of values. An analogy may help to clarify this distinction. One may hold that there are colours without committing oneself to the view that there are colours outside human experience; without raising this latter question, one may seek to answer various questions about the nature of colours, quite apart from the question where colours are and what sorts of things are coloured. I am attempting to do something like this for values.

Let me be even more explicit. There is a weak and a strong sense of the proposition, 'there are values.' Compare, 'there is a property, redsquare.' Suppose by 'redsquare' in this last sentence is meant a complex property exemplified by patches that are both square in shape and red in colour. Then one might reasonably say that one accepts 'there is redsquare' but that redsquare is not ultimate. One could even say that redsquare is analysable into two components (and a form of union). Likewise one could

extension. Not only are actual quotations put within pairs of double inverted commas, but also expressions that are used in a way which is peculiar to or indicative of a specific point of view. Along with this, however, is a technical semantical usage. When a linguistic expression is "mentioned," *i.e.*, when it is used to refer to itself, I put it within a pair of single inverted commas. This gets a little complicated when I am mentioning an expression which itself contains the mention of an expression. Here the use of single quotation marks is continued for each such occurrence (as contrasted with an alternation of single and double marks as in ordinary quotation). By adhering strictly to this programme I think some confusions may be avoided; moreover, the reader is warned whenever there is a shift from the "formal" to the "material mode of speech" or *vice versa* (to recur to Carnap's terminology). By this punctuational commitment, however, I am forced to use expressions that may seem improper. For example, speaking linguistically I can use the expression, ' 'Red' is a predicate,' but to put the same thought objectively I must use the sentence, 'Red is a property'; *i.e.*, I am prohibited from using such expressions as, ' 'Red' is a property' or ' "Red" is a property.'

[1] James Ward Smith, in "Senses of Subjectivism in Value Theory" (*Journal of Philosophy*, vol. xlv, 1948), distinguishes three senses of 'subjectivism,' the first two of which are the contradictories of the senses of 'objectivism' I differentiate in the text. This distinction likewise correlates roughly with A. C. Ewing's first and third meanings of 'objectivity of ethical judgments' on the first two pages of his book, *The Definition of Good*. Although the objectivism of this essay does not involve the assertion that there are values outside human experience, it does involve a double commitment. This may perhaps be best indicated by stating that it is opposed to both of two forms of naturalism, *viz.*, the naturalism which would refuse to allow to value-expressions any extra-linguistic reference, and the naturalism which requires that the extra-linguistic reference of value-expressions be limited to matters of fact or sensibly observable properties. It is opposed, that is, both to naturalisms that deny outright that there are, strictly speaking, value-expressions and to those that make all value-expressions redundant, *i.e.*, properly replaceable by descriptive expressions. There is value and it is unique.

say that red is not so analysable into components, that it is simple. Holding this, one might say 'there is redsquare' is weak whereas 'there is red' is strong. Now I accept 'there is value' (for some value) in this strong sense. That is, there is some value which is not analysable into components, such as, for example, being pleasant and being desired. Or again, there is for me at least one value-term which is indefinable. It goes without saying that I am speaking of what has traditionally been referred to as "intrinsic value." The phrase, 'extrinsic value' has, quite generally, been used to characterize something as being a cause or part-cause of something else that is valuable. Thus it is a complex notion one of whose elements is precisely value in the non-complex form which is the subject of the present inquiry.

This, however, does not commit me to the position that value is a quality, or that there is a value-quality. Beyond the simplicity of some value, it is still an open question what such a simple value is—a question for analysis. But did I not just say that value is unanalysable? True, but 'analysis' is used in different senses. One cannot analyse something simple by pointing out component elements, for it has no component elements. But one can characterize it. One can, for example, say that purple is simple, that it is a quality, not a relation, that it is more like red than like green. And this sort of characterization can be called, without too much conflict with common usage, "an analysis of purple." Such a view raises many serious problems for analysis—do qualities have properties? etc.—without ever going outside the assumption that purple is simple in the sense of not being composed of elements or constituent parts (such as red and blue).

I propose to give an analysis of value in a sense of 'analysis' closer to " 'yellow is a colour not an odour' or 'yellow is a quality not a relation' are analyses of yellow" than to " 'redsquare is simply the property of being red in colour and square in shape' is an analysis of redsquare." In asking, What sort of thing is value?, I shall to some degree have to ask, What is a property? What sorts of properties are there? What sorts of things can properties characterize? If there is something not a property which can in some sense be displayed or exhibited by other things, what is it and how can it be described or referred to? But in the main these questions will be left to the reader to deal with as best he may, for they divert me from my analysis to a consideration of the tools with which it is carried on, and so must be reserved for other essays in analysis.

2

IS VALUE A FIRST-ORDER PROPERTY?

By 'first-order property' I mean a property of particulars or individuals, thus not a property of properties. By 'property' I mean any entity that is capable of being exemplified by something, a test of which is that the name of such an entity can properly occur in the predicate-place in a sentence. There are, I assume, two general sorts of first-order properties, namely qualities (such as sour) and relations[1] (such as simultaneous with). A quality can be exemplified by a single particular. A relation requires for its exemplification two or more particulars each of which must perform its special exemplificational function.[2]

2*a*. *Is value a quality?*

It would seem that value is not a quality. For one thing, it does not appear to be a sensory quality, like bitter or magenta. This strikes one as so obvious upon any thoughtful inspection of experience that the point probably does not need arguing. However, a very elementary clarification may be inserted. The above denial does not rest on any physiological considerations, such as the absence of any appropriate physiological receptors. The position that there are sensory qualities and that among them is no value is epistemologically prior to any statement about physiological mechanisms, not in the sense that requires a phenomenalism, but in the sense that such a position is categorial rather than empirical

[1] It is regrettable that the term 'relation' is used so very loosely, that it is used to refer, for example, to higher-order properties and to features of fact and of language that are not properties at all, as well as to first-order properties.

[2] These last two sentences are obviously categorial, not empirical. That is, they attempt to elucidate the natures of qualities and relations, not to formulate an observable uniformity. It may not be irrelevant to the present context to state that I question the exhaustiveness of the current classification of propositions into analytic and empirical. Categorial propositions are not tautologies (in the sense of being true by virtue of their form alone), yet they are not confirmable by particular observations. It is hoped that the present essay may incidentally help to show what they are.

(in the ordinary sense). Various colour-qualities have an affinity to one another, marking them off as a class from taste-qualities. So, in general, sensory qualities have an affinity to one another such that it seems appropriate to treat them as a class. And in this class is found no simple quality of value.

No one, to my knowledge, has maintained that value is a colour or an odour. But may it not be a simple quality not falling within any sense modality, a unique quality? Again, it would seem not. Speaking for myself, I do not so find it in my own experience. Nor, apparently, do others, to go by what they say.[1] Indeed, the outstanding proponent of the view that there is a simple value-quality, namely G. E. Moore, qualified the doctrine by characterizing this quality as "non-natural." Although it is difficult to make out just what this qualification meant, it at least indicates that Moore himself was aware that he used 'quality' in a rather special sense when he said that good is a quality.[2]

Moreover, if good (positive value) be a quality, what of bad (negative value)? It would seem only reasonable to suppose that

[1] To mention only a few ethical objectivists who deny that value is a quality, there is H. W. B. Joseph, *Some Problems of Ethics*, p. 75, and "Is Goodness a Quality?" *Aristotelian Society Supplementary Volume xi*, 1932, pp. 132 ff.; A. E. Taylor, *ibid.*, pp. 146 ff.; C. D. Broad, *Five Types of Ethical Theory*, p. 283 and *passim*; A. C. Ewing, "A Suggested Non-naturalistic Analysis of Good," *Mind*, vol. xlviii, 1939, pp. 1 ff., and *The Definition of Good.* In fact, G. E. Moore was singularly unsuccessful in getting adherents to his view that good is a simple quality.

[2] From the first, this qualification meant more than an insistence upon the uniqueness of this quality—as though, for example, it were the only quality in a certain sense mode. In *Principia Ethica* (p. 41) Moore held that a natural property was one which could exist by itself in time, not merely as a property of something, and that it is more properly described as a part of what exemplifies it than as a mere predicate; if all of an object's natural properties were taken away there would be nothing left. Thus by saying that good is not a natural property he meant to deny to it that relative substantiality he ascribed to most qualities. In his contribution to the symposium, "Is Goodness a Quality?" (*Aristotelian Society Supplementary Volume xi*, 1932), Moore tells us that what he meant in *Principia Ethica* by speaking of good as a quality was that it "*was* a character and was *not* a relational property: that and nothing more" (p. 126). In his essay, "The Conception of Intrinsic Value," Moore wrote that natural intrinsic properties "seem to *describe* the intrinsic nature of what possesses them in a sense in which predicates of value never do" (*Philosophical Studies*, p. 274). This is developed in *The Philosophy of G. E. Moore* to the position that "in ascribing to a thing a property which is not a natural intrinsic property, you are not describing it *at all*. . . ." My purpose is not so much to point out the vagueness in Moore's treatment of good as a quality (C. D. Broad has done this admirably in *The Philosophy of G. E. Moore*) as to indicate that in it he uses 'quality' in a peculiar way. Apparently good does not have a positive qualitative nature, such as we find in pain or middle C. As seems indicated in his contribution to "Is Goodness a Quality?" referred to above, one of the

it, too, is a quality, unless one wished to hold the view that strikes all but theologically inclined neo-platonists as bizarre, namely, that badness is just absence of goodness. But if good and bad are both qualities, how are they related? Like sweet and sour or other Aristotelian contraries; that is, sufficiently like one another to be classed together, but being the most dissimilar in their class? This would require other value-qualities. And in any case we would seem to need a sort of contrariety or opposition here not furnished by positive qualities however dissimilar.

Furthermore, good, or at least some form of positive value, seems to include intentionally, *i.e.*, as a non-asserted feature of its meaning, the element of occurrence, as is felt in such phrases as 'ought *to be*' or 'it is good *that* such and such *is the case*,' and contrariwise for negative value.[1] This reference to existence is part of the very nature of positive value and thus makes it quite unlike a quality.

For these reasons, I reject the view that there is a (first-order) value-quality.

chief reasons leading Moore to speak of good as a quality may have been his desire to use the method of imaginative isolation as the test of its presence. Only if the thing experienced as good retains its goodness when we think of it all alone, as though only it existed, is its goodness intrinsic. I think that this test involves several confusions (*e.g.*, of exemplification with causation and of end with inner nature), but, even granting its legitimacy, it is compatible with several characterizations of good: not only as a quality, but as a "relation" between a particular and a property, or as a property of a state of affairs.

[1] Interesting enough is the fact that Moore himself at one point seems to admit this: "But when we assert that a thing is good, what we mean is that its existence or reality is good . . ." (*Principia Ethica*, p. 120). True, this might be interpreted to mean "Good is a quality, but a quality of facts not of particulars" (rather than " 'Good' is elliptical for 'it were good that so and so exist' " as I am here suggesting). However, in any case the admission is incompatible with saying that good is a first-order quality. I think that one important element in the opposition of many ethical objectivists to Moore's view is precisely that it leaves out this peculiar intentional inclusion of existence in such concepts as ought, obligation, and duty (compare with W. D. Ross, *The Right and the Good*, and William Frankena, "Obligation and Value in the Ethics of G. E. Moore" in *The Philosophy of G. E. Moore*).

This contention, that positive value bears inherently a reference to existence, clearly goes back at least to Meinong, as was pointed out by Urban when he tried, rather unsuccessfully, to re-emphasize it in an article on "Value and Existence" in *The Journal of Philosophy* for 1916. He wrote: ". . . value is not a 'what' at all, either quality or relation. It is a that. . . . It adds no new quality to the object (it is indeed because of its qualities or relations that it is valued): by this predicate its 'what' is raised into the sphere of value, as by the existential judgment it is raised into the sphere of existence. . . . This is Meinong's position when he says that it is objectives, not objects, that are valued. I desire not the object, but *that* the object shall exist or not exist. I value not the object, but *the fact that* the object exists or does not exist" (pp. 458, 460–1, 463).

2*b*. *Is value a (first-order) relation?*

The parenthetical qualification in the question above is important. It is meant to rule out, in the present stage of our analysis, a certain type of view that could be and has been characterized as a relational theory of value.[1] I refer to the view, suggested by C. D. Broad and developed by A. C. Ewing, that the basic value-predicate is 'fitting' or 'appropriate.' They themselves characterize these terms as "standing for a relation." Sometimes this relation is described as a relation that may hold between an action and a situation.[2] But again, it is also described as a relation between an attitude or desire and its object.[3] Now it seems to me that a "relation" of appropriateness between a desire and its object is not a first-order relation. Though a desire and its object may both be particulars and in fact be related by first-order relations (for example, a desire may occur before its object becomes actual), yet appropriateness or fittingness is not such a relation. If fittingness holds between a desire and its object, it holds between them not in that they occur as particulars, but in that the desire is directed toward that object and that that

[1] A good example is furnished by Ewing. People, he writes, "misled partly by the fact that 'good' is an adjective, look for some other *quality* and cannot find it and then become more and more inclined to adopt the naturalistic view. But what they should have looked for is perhaps a relation. And they could hardly deny that there is such a relation as fittingness on which the concept of 'ought' is based, the action which I ought to do being the action which fits the situation" (*Mind*, vol. xlviii, 1939, p. 21). The tacit assumption here, that if a fundamental value-term does not refer to a quality it must refer to a relation, is explicitly made by Broad: "With regard to any ethical characteristic it may be asked whether it is a pure quality, like *red*; or a pure relation, like *between*; or a relational property, like *loved-by-Jones*" (*Five Types of Ethical Theory*, p. 263). It is one of the chief purposes of the present essay to challenge such an over-simplified statement of the possibilities.

[2] Broad speaks (*Five Types of Ethical Theory*, p. 219) of an act's "fittingness or unfittingness to the total course of events as modified by it. . . ." Likewise, Ewing writes, "If I ought to do something there must be a certain relation between the action and its environment such that the action is fitting, appropriate, suitable, and its omission unfitting, inappropriate, unsuitable" (*The Definition of Good*, p. 132). And again, " 'Fittingness' stands for a relation between an action and its environment . . ." (*ibid.*, p. 133).

[3] Broad suggests (*op. cit.*, p. 283) that 'X is good' could "be defined as meaning that X is such that it would be a fitting object of desire to any mind which had an adequate idea of its non-ethical characteristics." Ewing carries this suggestion out: "We may therefore define 'good' as 'fitting object of a pro-attitude! . . ." (*op. cit.*, p. 152).

object is the object of just that desire. The fittingness is in short a property of the direction or intention of the desire. It is a semantical or quasi-semantical property. Whether value is such a property will be considered below;[1] the question is irrelevant here.

However, it might seem that when fittingness is treated as a relation between an act and its environment we really have in it a first-order relation. I think that this is not the case. We sometimes say that an act fits the situation in which it occurs. And 'fits' in this usage may seem to be the same sort of word as 'fits' in the sentence 'This peg fits that hole.' I doubt whether this is so, or, if it ever is so, whether it is in any such usage that 'fittingness' is urged as the basic value-term. 'This peg fits that hole' does not imply nor need it suggest that it would be a good thing, that it would be appropriate, to put this peg in that hole. But 'fittingness,' as used, *e.g.*, by Ewing, does have such a value-significance as attached to the *occurrence* of an act that is appropriate to its situation.[2] This is revealed in the more usual expression, not, 'the act fits the situation' but 'it is fitting that that act occur in that situation.' To make the grammatical structure of this last expression clear, let us put it, "That that act occur in that situation is fitting." Thus we see that 'fitting' is used adjectivally to modify a substantival clause. If then it refers to a property, it must be a property of what is referred to by a clause; *i.e.*, it must be a property not of a particular or of a set of particulars, but of a (possible) fact or state of affairs. Essentially the same remarks apply when Ewing speaks as though 'fitting' designated a property of the occurrence of the object of a "pro-attitude."[3] That this object exists would then be that which is, or could be, fitting. If there be such a property as 'fitting' used in this manner would serve to designate, it is not a first-order relation and its discussion must hence be postponed.[4]

There is a view, however, that may be properly described as

[1] In section 5b.

[2] For example, in speaking of the fittingness of admiration Ewing gives the impression that he means fittingness "to feel it," *i.e.*, the fittingness of the occurrence of admiration. *Cf. The Definition of Good*, p. 158.

[3] "To apply 'good' to something is to say of this that it is fitting, other things being equal, to bring it into existence" (*The Definition of Good*, p. 152). This perhaps should be interpreted: The act of bringing the object into existence is fitting. But it might be interpreted to mean or imply the following: That the object exists is fitting.

[4] See below, section 4.

holding that value is a first-order relation.[1] It holds that the fundamental value-term, by means of which all others can be defined, is 'better.' 'Better' refers to a relation that can hold between two particulars. Thus it may be that one act is better than another, one picture better than another, or one person better than another. The question of course arises whether it is possible, *i.e.*, meaningful, to hold that *any* two particulars whatever may be so related, whether, for example, a person can be better than a picture or an act than a building.[2] If it be held that only as particulars have certain other properties in common can one of them be said to be better than another, one wonders if this view does not really reduce to the following: a particular is better than another not *in toto* but in some respect. If so, it would seem difficult to distinguish it from a form of the position that value is a characteristic of states of affairs. If this is not the case and if better is such a relation that it would make sense[3] to assert of *any* two particulars whatever, taken *in toto*, that one is better than the other, then 'better' seems to be used in an odd way, not consonant with everyday custom.

It may be argued in favour of this view that it allows a simpler and more plausible definition of other value-terms than the view which starts with a quality, say good, as ultimate. For example, it is not necessary to add another undefined term to have a place for negative value. We can simply take 'worse' as the converse of 'better.' Also we may say that anything has value if it stands in the relation of 'better than' to anything else. The crucial term of course is 'good.' It is suggested[4] that 'good' be defined in use

[1] I have in mind a view something like that briefly outlined (but never systematically developed) by A. P. Brogan, "The Fundamental Value Universal," *Journal of Philosophy*, vol. xvi, 1919, pp. 96–104. (It is schematically outlined in "Logical Analysis of Intrinsic Value," *ibid.*, vol. xii, 1915, pp. 105–6. See also references immediately below.) As subsequent footnotes will indicate, I am not at all sure that Professor Brogan means to accept the view here discussed,-yet I am not sure that he does not. Hence it had better be conceived as simply a hypothetical position.

[2] Professor Brogan would apparently answer this question in the negative: "I know of no valid proof that every object is in the scale of intrinsic value" ("Urban's Axiological System," *Journal of Philosophy*, vol. xviii, 1921, p. 203). See his whole criticism of what he calls "Urban's Law of Universality" from which this quotation is taken.

[3] It might of course be false in any given case of a pair of particulars.

[4] " '*A* is good' means 'the existence of *A* is good' or 'that *A* exists is good.' Now this is defined as meaning 'the existence of *A* is better than the non-existence of *A*,' or 'that *A* exists is better than that *A* does not exist.'" (*Journal of Philosophy*, vol. xvi, 1919, p. 98.)

so that '*A* is good' means 'It is better that *A* exist than that it not exist.' Such a definition however immediately commits one to the position that better is a property of facts or states of affairs, rather than of particulars.[1] If one wishes to avoid this commitment and retain 'better than' as referring to a first-order relation, how can 'good' be defined? There are several alternatives. One could say that a thing is good if it is better than at least one other thing, or if it is better than some chosen thing taken as the point of orientation (the neutral point) of one's value system.[2] A difficulty, however, still remains. It is the same as that pointed out in connection with the view that value is a quality. I refer to what I called the intentional or non-asserted inclusion of existence in value. Just as '*A* is good' is elliptical for 'It is good that *A* exists' so '*A* is better than *B*' is elliptical for 'It is better that *A* exist than that *B* exist.' This interpretation may seem a little forced until one recalls that we are here saying not that *A* is better than *B* in some respect, that is, in some property exemplified, but that it is better simply and *in toto* or as a particular. If of course we never do mean to assert that *A*, just as a particular, is better than *B*, but when we seem to do so we really intend to assert that some

[1] Professor Brogan himself urges this: "In discussing the definitions of good and bad we must notice that these qualities like all intrinsic value universals, apply only to 'facts.' . . . What is good or bad is a fact, and a fact is whatever can be denoted by a complete judgment" (*ibid.*). That Mr. Brogan does not keep consistently to this view, in the sense at least of not seeing its implications if not in the further sense of explicitly shifting to the position that 'better than' refers to a first-order relation, seems obvious to the reader of his "Urban's Axiological System" (*Journal of Philosophy*, vol. xviii, 1921, pp. 197–209). He there characterizes his position as follows: ". . . value judgments will be true or false in the same general way that other judgments are true or false. But they will differ in that they refer to the value relation rather than to such relations as time or causality" (p. 208). And although he again verbally admits that the complete objects of a value-judgment may be an objective, in Meinong's sense, he not only insists that "Value is a relation, not an objective" (p. 208) but fails to see the point of the Urban–Meinong position, namely, that value-judgments internally embrace a reference to existence ('It is good that *x* exist' or 'It is good that *x* exemplify *Y*'). His whole treatment of the relation of value to existence reduces to the trivial remark that we may make value-judgments concerning that which does not actually exist. Moreover, his criticism of Urban's use of 'ought' or 'ought rather' as basic value-terms and his urging that they be replaced by 'better than' fails to grasp Urban's chief reason for choosing them which is that 'ought' bears inherently a reference to existence (it is elliptical for 'ought to be'), and so cannot be a quality or a relation. Says Urban: ". . . value is not a 'what' at all, either a quality or a relation. It is a 'that' " (*Journal of Philosophy*, vol. xii, 1916, p. 458). "I value not the object, but *the fact that* the object exists or does not exist" (*ibid.*, p. 463).

[2] *Cf.* Brogan, *International Journal of Ethics*, vol. xli, p. 291.

fact about *A* is better than some fact about *B*, than, as I have already pointed out, we are not taking better to be a first-order relation. And so likewise if '*A* is better than *B*' is elliptical for 'it is better that *A* exist than that *B* exist' then again better is not a first-order relation.

But, finally, suppose we do seriously and consistently treat better as a first-order relation, quite like simultaneous with or to the right of: then the serious question arises why there is so little agreement between people as to instances of it. Its occurrences should be directly experienceable. This however does not seem to be the case. I do not directly see an act to be better or worse than another act in the way in which I directly see my pencil to be to the right of my pen. And I am no more making a physiological observation about my perception of relations than I was about my perception of qualities. I am saying that in reviewing the relations I immediately experience I do not find 'better than' to be among them.[1]

[1] It perhaps is only fair to point out here that, translated into quite a different theoretical context, I do find a possible usefulness for Brogan's suggestion that expressions containing 'good' be replaced by expressions containing 'better than.' *Cf.* below, p. 182, footnote.

3

IS VALUE A SECOND-ORDER PROPERTY?

I MEAN by 'a second-order property' a property of a first-order property. I shall not discuss the possibility that value may be a property of an even higher order than the second since any plausibility in the view that value is a property of a property diminishes as we go up the hierarchy of types. However I do wish to deal with a recently advocated possibility to the effect that exemplification (of a property by a particular) is itself a property and that value may be a property of it. Perhaps such a view should not be characterized as making value a second-order property, but for the sake of convenience I shall so classify it, distinguishing it however from the view that value is a property of ordinary first-order properties.

3a. *Is value a property of ordinary first-order properties?*

An affirmative answer to the question formulated above involves the acceptance of second-order properties, a commitment some philosophers would wish to avoid. I suppose no one would question the existence of second-order properties in one sense, that in which they serve as bases of classification of first order properties. Classing colour-qualities together, distinguishing them as a class from odours, certainly has some foundation in the very natures of the qualities so classed. And, as the basis of grouping particulars into different classes is the properties exemplified by the particulars, so we may say that, since we can classify properties, they must in turn have properties.[1]

[1] This is obvious on the extreme view that a property just is the class of entities that in ordinary terminology are said to exemplify it. Then, *e.g.*, the colouredness of red just is its membership in the class, colours, a class whose members are classes, *viz.*, classes of particulars each of which classes constitutes a specific colour. This view has a decided advantage over all others in giving 'property of' a single unequivocal meaning at all type-levels. However, this view is so out of accord with ordinary language and so "unintuitive" in relation to direct experience that it need not here be seriously weighed, especially as it would seem to have nothing in particular to offer on our problem of the

But now it may be that the basis of classification of properties is, in other respects, so different from first-order properties as to make it far more clarifying to deny than to affirm that there are second-order properties. It would certainly seem, on appeal to direct experience, that there are no simple, positive, second-order qualities, like colours and odours. To me, at least, it seems almost equally plain that there are no second-order relations as positive characters directly experienceable.[1] It may be that all we need as a basis for classifying first-order properties, all of which are completely determinate, is these very properties in a less determinate form, *i.e.*, a set of determinables, to use W. E. Johnson's term.[2] Even should one wish to ascribe to determinables some sort of ontological status of their own over and above that of the determinates falling under them, it seems clear that they are not properly described as "properties" of the latter. The colouredness of red seems plainly not to characterize red as red characterizes my blotter. It has no distinct nature of its own, which, along with other such natures, characterizes red. It just is a less determinate form of red. Moreover, that a particular exemplifies a certain property is always an accidental fact.[3] But what determinable a determinate falls under is no accidental fact. Moreover, we do not in ordinary speech use determinables to characterize determinates but only to classify them. We do not say 'Red is coloured' but 'Red is a colour.' Contrariwise, we do say of a red thing, that it is coloured. Thus popular speech suggests that a determinable is of the same type-level as its determinates. It

status of value. Of course if properties just are the classes of things which in ordinary speech are said to exemplify them, then to say that value is a property implies that value just is the class of things ordinarily said to have value. Although this does not logically require the relinquishing of objectivism (since this class may be held to be unique), yet psychologically its adoption would tend to alienate one from objectivism, for one of its consequences is that a value-judgment, being just an assertion of class-membership, is essentially the same in character as a descriptive proposition.

[1] I would deny that sameness and difference are relations. There are affinities of various closeness obtaining between first-order properties. These however cannot be abstracted from the specific properties involved, which suggests that they are nothing in their own right over and above the various complexes of properties between which they "obtain."

[2] See the very excellent statement, both historical and analytical, of Arthur N. Prior, "Determinables, Determinates and Determinants," *Mind*, vol. lvii, 1949, pp. 1–20 and 178–94.

[3] If there is any necessary determination of first-order properties, it holds between properties (as exemplified by a particular), not between a particular and a property.

thus seems improper to speak of a determinable as a property exemplified by the determinates falling under it. The case is not so good for relations. We do, for example, say, 'The relation, simultaneous with, is symmetrical.' We do not say 'Simultaneous with is a symmetry.' Yet something like the "relation" between a determinate and its determinable in the case of qualities seems involved here. For that simultaneous with is symmetrical seems to be no accidental fact about that relation.

This is not the place to argue the issue whether there are properties with distinctive ontological status above the first order. It is sufficient to show that he who would have value a second-order property commits himself on this highly controversial issue. However, to get on with the discussion, let us suppose there are second-order properties and inquire whether it is reasonable to suppose that value is to be found among them. As may be anticipated my answer is in the negative. But first it is helpful to make a distinction.

If first-order properties do exemplify properties it would seem natural to suppose that these second-order properties are of one or both of two kinds. On the one hand, there are the properties first-order properties have by virtue of the latter's being exemplified or exemplifiable.[1] Being a universal would be such a property —it is in fact a complex one, including being capable of characterizing and plurality (of subjects of such possible characterization). Let us call these "exemplificational properties." On the other hand, there are the properties first-order properties have by virtue of the latter's being just the positive natures they are. Being a colour or a temporal relation would be such a property. Let us call these "characteral properties." The difference may be brought out rather strikingly by the example of violet. We may say that violet is at the farthest remove (in the spectrum or in terms of wave length) from red, but that it is between red and blue (in quality). The first is an exemplificational property of violet, the second a characteral property.

Platonists furnish the outstanding example of those who would have value an exemplificational property of properties. The universality and immutability of properties is taken either to be valuable[2] or simply to constitute value itself. That a property is

[1] For example, Wilfrid Sellars speaks of "the property of having exemplifications," *Cf. Philosophy of Science*, vol. xv, 1948, p. 298 and *passim*.

[2] In this case value would be a third-order property. There is however no need to explore this as a separate possibility.

not restricted in space and time and does not share the vicissitudes of fortune that fall to the lot of particulars exemplifying it seemed to Plato (if we can ascribe the doctrine of ideas to him) to establish the superlative value of properties. Properties reside in a higher realm than particulars. Plotinus's hierarchy of being seems to equate degree of universality with degree of value. Now there seems to be a rather basic confusion here. This is revealed by Socrates' embarrassment in the *Parmenides* when the venerable Eleatic asks whether there are not ideas of hair, mud, and filth. Value seems not to be merely an exemplificational property. Characteral features of properties are also relevant. Moreover, the uniform ascription of positive value to universals and negative to particulars breaks down at another point. Certain particulars can achieve at least to a degree the value supposedly peculiar to universals. In the contemplation of universals the soul can become so united with them as to absorb their value-character (as universal and immutable).[1] To me, this indicates pretty clearly what Plato was really after: a changelessness of certain particulars as having certain properties. It is supposed that a certain state of affairs (a soul in complete harmony) is good, and that it is moreover good that this condition be persisted in. It may be that to achieve this end contemplation of universals is a necessary and even sufficient means, but the status of such a good is to be a property of a state of affairs, not of ideas or properties (*i.e.*, universals). There can be no literal transfer of a property of properties either to a particular or to a state of affairs.[2]

Platonism never made much of an impression upon the popular mind. There are however expressions in everyday use that might be interpreted as implying that value is a second-order property, though a characteral, not an exemplificational, property of properties. I have in mind such expressions as 'blue is lovelier than pink,' 'mercy is better than justice,' 'pleasure is the supreme good.' Taken out of their contexts not merely of everyday language

[1] I have in mind the well-known passages in the *Phaedo*, *Phaedrus*, and *Symposium*.

[2] A similar confusion is revealed in the Cambridge Platonist, Ralph Cudworth. Though not holding that value just is the immutability of any property, he does contend that, being a property, value is immutable. From this however he easily slips into the position that what things or acts have value is an immutable fact. Thus he fails, in this line of argument upon which he placed such high hopes, to refute Hobbes, who could admit that goodness just is immutably the being an object of an appetite, though what things are actually objects of appetites is a most mutable fact.

but of accompanying behaviour, these and similar expressions can certainly be given such an interpretation. It might seem, for example, that when in everyday conversation one says that blue is lovelier than pink he means that the property blue stands to the property pink in the relation of lovelier than. In context, however, such expressions are far more plausibly interpreted as elliptical. Instead of asserting that properties themselves have certain value-properties, they are loose ways of saying that all particulars having certain properties also exemplify certain value-properties[1] (they are what might be called value-laws). Thus the expressions instanced could be rendered 'blue things are lovelier than pink ones,' 'merciful acts are better than just acts,' 'pleasant experiences are supremely good.' It is true that we value things because of certain properties we take them to have, but it seems plain that what we value are not the certain properties as such but the thing which we take to possess them (or possibly the fact, as we suppose, that it does).[2]

Moreover, value-expressions, as already argued, seem to have intentionally or non-assertively present in their meaning the element of occurrence. What is taken to be good is some possible occurrence. Thus value is not ascribed to properties *qua* properties. It is the exemplification of the properties said to be valuable, the existence of something having them, that is taken to be good.[3]

3*b*. *Is value a property of an ontologically peculiar property?*

The possibilities so far discussed have not taken seriously what I have called the intentional inclusion of existence in the basic character of value. The views to which we shall now turn would

[1] The discerning reader will see that this type of interpretation as here formulated presupposes first-order value-properties, previously held to be implausible. Let it be remembered, however, that I am not yet in a position to give what I think is the most plausible interpretation (all things considered), and so I am forced to resort to pointing out, for the sort of expressions discussed and at this stage, a more plausible interpretation than that under criticism.

[2] We would consider a theologian to be somewhat deficient in intellectual honesty who would admit that mercy is better than justice but would excuse an unmerciful God on the grounds that it doesn't follow that merciful acts are better than just acts. And we would certainly condemn, on the principle that pleasure is the supreme good, actions that obviously tend to decrease the amount of pleasant experience in the world, nor would we be assuaged by the argument that after all 'pleasure is good' does not imply 'pleasant experiences are good.'

[3] The person who said 'Yes, I think blue is distinctly lovelier than pink', and yet purchased pink articles and painted objects pink in preference to blue wherever possible would be deemed to belie his words in his actions.

remedy this defect. The simplest would make value directly a property of existence or of exemplification. We must here however confine our attention to the possibilities that 'existence' and 'exemplification' refer to properties and that one or the other of these properties is that which is characterized by value. If it were the existence of a particular or again the exemplification of a property by a particular that had value we would be involved in the view that value is a property of facts, which is to be discussed later.

That existence is a property is a position which at the moment probably no self-respecting philosopher dares defend. I do not wish to defend it. However, there seems to be no inherent illogicality in such a view. The trouble is rather that if consistently developed it requires that 'existence' be used in ways that simply do not square with everyday language. For example, consider the following argument: "When we ascribe an attribute to a thing, we covertly assert that it exists: so that if existence were itself an attribute, it would follow that all positive existential propositions were tautologies, and all negative existential propositions self-contradictory; and this is not the case."[1] The unpleasant consequence here urged is not itself self-contradictory. It is unsatisfactory simply because in everyday discourse we do mean to convey information when we say that something exists. We could have a language in which any name or description that was allowed must refer to something existent. Then the very adoption of that language would be the way in which the user made his existential assertions; all existentional sentences could be eliminated. Also be it noted that the unpleasant consequence arises not merely from taking 'existence' as a predicate but also from assuming that "when we ascribe an attribute to a thing, we covertly

[1] A. J. Ayer, *Language, Truth and Logic*, 2nd ed., p. 43. *Cf.* also John Wisdom, *Interpretation and Analysis*, pp. 62–3. The argument needs "unpacking." What Ayer wishes to say is that we covertly assert that a thing exists in *both* cases, *viz.*, when we affirm an attribute of it and when we deny that attribute of it. If then existence is the attribute in question, we covertly assert it *both* when we overtly assert it and when we overtly deny it. Wisdom's argument is perhaps a little different. It amounts to saying that if we were to treat existence as a property, then all propositions asserting existence would be universal propositions and thus properly expressed as hypotheticals. Thus " 'Horses exist' treated on these lines becomes 'If there exists anything which is a horse, it exists'. . . . And 'Horses do not exist' treated on these lines becomes 'If there exists anything which is a horse, it does not exist' " (*ibid.*). The difficulty with this form of the argument is that it does not appear to be relevant to assertions of existence expressed in singular or particular sentences, such as 'There is at least one such galaxy that actually exists' or 'Homer never existed.'

assert that it exists." If this were denied the consequence in question would not follow.[1] It does of course seem odd (and this seems to be the real point of Kant's argument[2]) that when we add to a certain concept, say the concept of a hundred dollars, the idea of existence, we do not thereby increase the content of the concept. If existence be a property, it seems to be a particularly pallid one, having no positive nature of its own. Moreover, it has a peculiar way of attaching to other properties, allowing us, when it is present with another property, to say that there is something having that property. These peculiarities of 'existence' as popularly used seem to indicate that it would be clarificatory to deny that 'existence' designated a property.

If, however, treating existence as a property were to help us solve our present problem of the status of value, it might well be worth the risking an appearance of oddity. But I do not think that it does, since no one seriously holds that sheer existence as such has value. It might seem as though St. Thomas furnished an exception. He held that God is pure actuality, existence itself, and that God is good. But for St. Thomas the existence which is God is not a property but an individual.[3] I do not understand positively what this means, but negatively it seems clear that the existence which is perfection is not some character or form that could be common to a number of existent beings. In any case, receding from these high realms of theological speculation to everyday traffic with value, humans do not seem to value sheer existence, but rather the existence of this or that thing, with such and such other properties. Hence, even granting that existence is a property, it would seem that value was not a property of it, but of its exemplification by certain things.

Thus all roads seem to lead to the position that value, if a property, is a property of the exemplification of properties by particulars. But how is this to be interpreted? One, to my mind the least plausible, interpretation is to say that 'exemplification' refers to a property, a property which itself exemplifies value.

[1] The proposal of a language in which this assumption is not made is advanced by W. V. Quine, "Designation and Existence," *Journal of Philosophy*, vol. xxxvi, 1939, pp. 701–9, reprinted in *Readings in Philosophical Analysis* by Feigl and Sellars, pp. 44–51; *A Short Course in Logic* (mimeographed by Harvard Cooperative Society, 1946) especially pp. 115 ff.; and "On What There Is," *Review of Metaphysics*, vol. i, 1948, pp. 21–38.

[2] *Cf.* Transcendental Dialectic, ch. iii. sec. 4.

[3] See *Summa Contra Gentiles,* ch. xxvi.

In the first place, this interpretation would commit one to the view that exemplification is itself a property—a relation (between the referent or referents of the subject and the referent of the predicate of any true proposition).[1] Thus, unlike first-order relations, it holds between entities of different type-levels. Yet as a relation it would seem that when it obtains it is itself exemplified by its terms.[2] If so, we seem immediately hustled off into a Bradleian regress. Suppose that my pencil is yellow. Then my pencil stands to yellow in the relation of exemplification. Clearly then exemplification is itself exemplified (by the pair—my pencil, yellow). This second exemplification would itself be a relation and, since it must actually obtain, on our supposition, it must in turn be exemplified (by the pair—exemplification and pencil-yellow). Such a series involves no logical contradiction but it does involve the empirically embarrassing consequence that necessarily accompanying every observed fact is an infinite hierarchy of actual yet unobservable entities.

Furthermore, the treatment of exemplification as a property though not inherently self-contradictory does involve a conflict with everyday usage similar to that noted in the case of existence. Supposing, as is only natural, that every affirmation and every denial of an exemplification of a property (including relations under this term) covertly asserts that the subject exemplifies something, it follows, when the property in question is *exemplifies something*, that both its affirmation and its denial covertly assert it for any subject whatever. It thus becomes self-contradictory to say that something we can properly name, *i.e.*, whose name can be a subject-term in a sentence, does not exemplify any property at all, a consequence we would certainly wish, in ordinary usage, to avoid. For example, it would be most inconvenient to have to admit that 'Red exemplifies no property whatever' was self-contradictory. Such things could still be said, but only indirectly, by not allowing certain entities to be designated by names that could occur to the left of 'exemplifies.'[3] It might also be noted

[1] Such a view seems suggested, though it is apparently not explicitly adopted, by C. A. Baylis; "Facts, Propositions, Exemplification and Truth," *Mind*, vol. lvii, 1948, pp. 459–79.

[2] It might be held that when exemplification obtains between a particular and a first-order property it is not itself exemplified. I do not see what this could mean and in any case it would require that exemplification be so unlike any first-order relation that calling it a "relation" would be extremely misleading.

[3] Similar remarks could be made concerning 'characterizes,' which is the converse of 'exemplifies.'

that both existence and exemplification would be remarkable properties. They would be present whenever any other property was exemplified. Such necessary ubiquity would seem to argue against referring to them by the same term, 'property,' as was used to designate entities whose compresence is a matter for empirical determination.

Let us however waive these general objections to treating exemplification as a property (a relation). There are others that specifically apply to the view that value is a property of such a property. Although, as already noted, it would seem that we attach value not to properties as such but to their exemplifications, it does not seem to be the case that we value the exemplification as such. If exemplification be a property, then like other properties, it would not seem to be valued as such but only in its instances or occurrences. In fact, as a property it seems a peculiarly pale and empty one to exemplify value. There may be some plausibility in saying that pleasantness is good (though I have argued that it is far more consonant with ordinary views to hold that an experience's being pleasant is good). There seems to be no plausibility whatever in saying that the sheer *being* (so and so) in, say, an experience's being pleasant, is good. Moreover, if value were a property of exemplification as such, it would seem that all instances of exemplification would have to embrace or include exactly the same value (that of the property, exemplification, that they all exemplify—for only in this indirect way would they exemplify value). But it is notorious that various instances of exemplification are characterized by different values. At least it is plausible to hold that the exemplification of pleasantness by an experience is good whereas the exemplification of painfulness by an experience is bad, though supposedly, on the view here criticized, the property of exemplification is precisely the same in the two cases.

Now of course it may be said that whether the relation, exemplification, exemplifies a certain value is determined in each case by the relata between which it obtains. I know of no one who explicitly accepts such a view. In any case, it would be difficult to keep distinct from the position that value is a property of states of affairs or facts (*i.e.*, not merely of exemplification, but of the whole: this-as-exemplifying-that). So I turn directly to the latter and far more plausible standpoint.

4

IS VALUE A PROPERTY OF STATES OF AFFAIRS?

CERTAIN recent statements of objectivists in value-theory indicate willingness to accept an affirmative answer to the question we are now asking. There seems, indeed, to be a feeling that such an affirmative answer is implicit in the writings of such objectivists as Moore and Ross and, moreover, that it effectively meets objections of the sort raised earlier in the present paper. Thus Professor Charles A. Baylis writes: "Granted that value is not a property of either a substance or a predicate, may it not be a property of a concrete state of affairs denoted by . . . a propositional statement? Thus one might properly say that the state of affairs . . . pleasantness-qualifying-my-present-experience is good and other things of that sort."[1]

That this view can meet many of the objections raised against other forms of the position that value is a property is immediately evident. Let me recall the most fundamental and general objection only. It is that value-terms include in their meaning a reference to the (possible) occurrence of some property. This, as Professor Baylis's example of 'pleasantness-qualifying-my-present-experience is good' makes clear, is met in the present case by the device of restricting the use of value-terms as predicates to those sentences whose subjects designate states of affairs. And if, as will be the case, I devote more space to the criticism of this view than to those previously discussed, it is because I consider it the most plausible attempt to treat value as a property.

[1] From a personal letter to the author. Professor Baylis adds: "Such a proposal seems to me off hand to avoid the difficulties that you mention" (in "A Categorial Analysis of Value," *Philosophy of Science*, vol. xiv, 1947, especially pp. 335–40). The way in which it does meet these difficulties is more fully stated by Professor Baylis in *Mind*, vol. lvii, 1948, pp. 462–3.

Similarly, G. E. Moore, commenting on this same passage, has written to the author: "You say, quite rightly, that 'fitting', as used *e.g.* by Ross (and 'good', in at least one of its fundamental senses) don't express properties either of individuals or of properties; and you infer that they can't express properties at all. But why shouldn't we say that they express properties of *states of affairs*?"

In considering this view I shall organize my remarks under five questions. (a) Are there states of affairs? (b) If so, what are they? (c) Have they any properties? (d) If so, what sort of properties are they? (e) Can value be treated as a property of states of affairs?

4a. *Are there states of affairs?*

If we were to answer the first of these questions in the negative there would be no point in going on to the others, all of which presuppose an affirmative answer to it. I do not propose to dispose of the view under consideration in this fashion, yet I do wish to state why I believe we must allow that there are states of affairs, since I think the reasons for answering (a) in the affirmative have a definite bearing on our answers to (b), (c), (d) and (e).

That there are states of affairs or facts, as distinguished from particulars and properties, is tantamount to saying that descriptive, declarative sentences show something about the world not revealed by a mere vocabulary, however extensive.[1] As Russell has said, sentences come in pairs, one true and one false for each fact.[2] Names, on the contrary, are solitary, one for each entity

[1] This would seem obvious in the case of a vocabulary composed of names of particulars. A difficulty appears to arise in the case of predicate-terms. (An exactly analogous difficulty is present in the case of names of particulars, but is ordinarily overlooked, probably because of the extraneous ontological assumption that particulars can exist in their own right.) Predicate-terms ordinarily perform a double function: they designate a certain character and they indicate a certain syntactical place (the predicate place in a sentence) to which they are restricted. This leads Russell, for example, to say, "To understand 'red,' for instance, is to understand what is meant by saying that a thing is red" (*Monist*, xxix, 1919, p. 34). (Russell does not see that, correspondingly, to understand 'John' is to understand what is meant by saying that John has some property.) It should be clear that in order to perform this syntactical function predicate-terms must also name, and name in precisely the same sense as a proper name names a particular (though what is named is different in categorial status). We might mark this out by using the substantival form, *e.g.*, 'redness.' Even here however we are not safe, as Cook-Wilson's distinction between the "characteristic being of a universal" (*e.g.*, 'red' as referring to the colour-quality) and the universality of the universal (which is indicated by the suffix 'ness' in, *e.g.*, 'redness') makes clear (*cf. Statement and Inference*, vol. ii, pp. 677–9). So when I refer to a vocabulary or to names it is to be understood that I am referring to simple symbols in their capacity of designating only, that is, as abstracted from any syntactical features such symbols may also have.

[2] *Op. cit.*, p. 39. It should be obvious to the informed reader that I am essentially accepting Russell's position as outlined in his lectures, "The Philosophy of Logical Atomism," published in the *Monist* for 1918 and 1919, especially lectures i and ii. So far as this involves the "Wittgensteinian position" (I am

named.[1] A false sentence is significant, but a name that names nothing is a *contradictio in adjecto*. Or again, in sentences, we have the contrast between assertion and denial which is simply absent from a vocabulary. It is probably this that Gilbert Ryle has in

not here interested in trying to determine the extent to which this characterization is correct, *i.e.*, to what extent the view was really originated by Wittgenstein and not by Russell) that a correct language mirrors the world, I shall say something in its defence below (*cf.* pp. 195–7 and 207–11). But I do want to dissociate myself from certain views that Russell, in these lectures, quite unnecessarily incorporates in this position. Foremost of these is the principle of acquaintance. In the form here relevant this principle requires that names be so restricted that there can be names only of those entities with which the speaker is directly acquainted. The argument seems to be that only in these cases could the speaker know, exactly and completely, what he refers to by the name. I agree with Professor Max Black ("Russell's Philosophy of Language," *The Philosophy of Bertrand Russell*, edited by Paul Schilpp, reprinted in *Language and Philosophy*) that such a restriction is quite unnecessary, although I think my reason is perhaps quite different from Professor Black's. He makes out Russell's argument to be circular, that Russell has tacitly defined 'meaning' in such wise that a speaker would not be able to know the meaning of a name unless he were acquainted with that which is named. I would rather say that the requirement is psychologistic, or, if it is epistemological—and it may be interpreted as a meaning–criterion—, the argument for it (that we can understand a whole only if we are acquainted with each of its parts) is psychologistic. It may be a sound restriction, but if so, it springs from the way we name-users think and understand, it does not spring from any linguistic requirement. Semantically considered, a name must designate something in the world, but anything will do. And the name is united (ultimately) with what it names by a rule of designation, whose sole function just is so to unite them. No knowledge of the psychology of name-users and how they are to understand what a name designates is relevant. To state this linguistically, Russell has apparently confused names with demonstratives (*cf.*, Wilfrid Sellars "Acquaintance and Description Again," *Journal of Philosophy*, vol. xlvi, 1949, pp. 496–504). A demonstrative designates only *via* the context of its occurrence. Thus, linguistically a sentence containing a demonstrative is elliptical, and requires for its completion a pragmatical meta-linguistic sentence about some occurrence of the demonstrative (along with the occurrence of its designatum), whereas we must have names in the lowest-level empirical language, thus in sentences that do not contain demonstratives.

Secondly, I do not see that the Wittgensteinian position, at least in the form in which I am accepting it, requires the acceptance of ultimately simple entities in the world. Sentences assert facts; facts cannot be named. Sentences must include names. Thus our sentences (in a correct language) show that facts are complex, that they are in some sense made up of entities named. The latter cannot be facts, and so are not complex in the way facts are, but it does not follow that they are simple in any other way. They may be made up of parts having the same status, ontologically, as the whole; *e.g.*, particulars may be made up of particulars, universals of universals. And there may well be other alternatives such that although analysis never issues in the discovery of the absolutely simple, yet we never grant to entities that can be named the sort of complexity that is characteristic of facts.

[1] This is strictly true. No single entity can have more than one name, since a name, *qua* name, just is a specific designative capacity.

mind when he says that a mere list can never constitute a sentence.[1]

Perhaps the contention may be formulated in a less oracular manner as follows. Suppose we have a complete vocabulary, *viz.*, one that has a name for each nameable entity. Let us represent this by the following fragment: 'white' 'brown' '*A*' (naming this chalk I now hold) and '*B*' (naming the table I now touch). Anyone with "a robust sense of reality" will want to distinguish the assertion '*A* is white and *B* is brown' from '*A* is brown and *B* is white.' They will moreover say that a universe in which the former is true is different from one in which the latter is. But since the vocabulary of the two sentences is the same, it follows that the difference between these two universes is a difference not in the entities in them which our vocabulary names, but in the facts which our sentences assert. But may this not just indicate a deficiency in our vocabulary? Let us have names for the facts asserted, *e.g.*, 'white_a' for *A*'s being white and 'brown_a' for *A*'s being brown. This will not do. For in the universe in which *A* is white, 'brown_a' would name nothing, it would not be a name. Of course in that universe we could just omit it, but then we could not deny that *A* is brown, nor say that '*A* is brown' is false (and consequently we could not *assert* that *A* is white nor claim that '*A* is white' is true). Such a price is too high to pay. Common linguistic decency compels us to admit that there are facts.

4*b*. *If there are states of affairs, what are they?*

So we turn to our second question. What is a state of affairs? Clearly we must already have presupposed an answer to it in answering our first question. This answer is, a state of affairs is any case of a quality's being exemplified by a particular or a relation's being exemplified by a set of particulars.[2] What question

[1] *Philosophy*, vol. xxiv, 1949, p. 71.

[2] This formulation not only presupposes that sentences are irreducible to names. It also assumes that all sentences have names as constituents and that, as constituents of sentences, names perform two rôles, the substantival and the adjectival. See footnote [1], p. 22. I need not point out that these remarks are intended to characterize a clarified common-sense language. It might be thought that 'being exemplified by some particular' itself can properly function as a predicate, *i.e.*, can name a property—a "relational property" to use a term favoured by some British philosophers. This, I think is incorrect if we wish to avoid the sort of paradox outlined in section 3*b* above. For example, it would require that anyone holding the view that every quality actually is exemplified by some particular treat any sentence asserting of a given quality

then is left as to the nature of a fact? There should be none. We should be able to say simply that a state of affairs is just uniquely this sort of thing. And such indeed is my position. Unfortunately there seems to be a need of clearing away certain confusions. One of these would amount to treating a state of affairs as a particular. This would be attractive since it would undercut questions as to how states of affairs can have properties and would simplify the task of making out that value is a property of facts.

There are two sorts of confusion that easily lead to this result. One is very elementary and need not detain us. It is the failure clearly to distinguish 'characterizes' from 'is part of.' The parts of a particular are themselves particulars, *e.g.*, the barrel and bladder

that it has this property (the property of being exemplified by some particular) as a tautology, and the negation of such a sentence as a contradiction. That is, on such a point of view no sentence having this predicate could be empirical (nor categorial, if one admits categorial sentences). Moreover, it should be pointed out that such a property could not be used to define the class, facts ("a fact is whatever exemplifies this property"), for it would be a property of properties, although it conceivably might be used to define a certain class of properties (*viz.*, those that exemplify the property of being exemplified by some particular). It seems to me we are even worse off if we try to treat 'some quality's being exemplified by some particular' as a proper predicate and attempt to define the class, facts, in terms of predicates of this general kind [I see no reason for dealing separately with 'some relation's holding between some particular and some other particular']. Suppose such a predicate did designate a property. What sort of property would it be? Obviously not a quality. Nor does it seem it could be a relation or a relational property. If it were either of these latter, that of which it is properly predicated would need to exemplify it, but clearly nothing can *exemplify* it, though something may *be* it, or more accurately, may be a case of it. I am of course supposing that 'is a case of so and so' is not to be restricted to the usage 'exemplifies so and so.' Thus though 'This surface is an instance of sky-blue' is probably correctly translated by 'This surface exemplifies sky-blue,' it may be incorrect to translate 'Sky-blue is a case of blue' by 'Sky-blue exemplifies blueness.' So I would contend that 'The fact that this surface is sky-blue is an instance of a quality's being exemplified by a particular' is incorrectly translated by 'The fact (that this surface is sky-blue) exemplifies the relational property of a quality's being exemplified by a particular.' The "relation" in this case is not between something (a fact) and a property thereof, but between something determinate and something less determinate, or, more correctly, between a more and a less determinate reference to something. And, in this case, where the thing is a fact, the reference is, determinately, by means of a sentence ('This surface is sky-blue') and, less determinately, by means of the form of a propositional function ('A quality's being exemplified by a particular'). I think this can be brought out by asking what a rejection of such a sentence as 'The fact that this surface is sky-blue is an instance of a quality's being exemplified by a particular' could be based on. I think its grounds would not be any failure to observe some property of the fact involved, but could only be a rejection of certain categories (or of the propriety of certain syntactical forms). For a further discussion of this distinction see pp. 42ff, below.

of my pen. The properties characterizing a particular are not particulars, *e.g.*, the weight and shape of my pen. Two particulars that are parts of a whole stand in a relation by virtue of this fact; let us call it the relation of being co-parts in a whole. Thus the bladder and barrel of my pen are co-parts of my pen. Since a quality and the particular it characterizes are somehow constituents that make up the fact of that particular's exemplifying that quality, it is an easy mistake to suppose that they are co-parts of the fact and thus that the fact is itself a particular.

The other confusion leading to this result turns in part on a failure to distinguish the adjectival from the substantival use of 'particular.' The mistake goes beyond mere grammar, in the ordinary sense, but it involves grammar, and so we may start at the grammatical level. 'Particular' may be used as a common noun, as indeed I have been using it,[1] as when one says, 'My pen is a particular.' But it may also be used adjectivally, *e.g.*, to mean specific or concrete, as when one says, 'The particular red I have in mind is the red of yonder rose.' It is quite legitimate to say of some—or for that matter of all—facts that they are particular. This could mean simply that the properties that are constituents of them are fully specific, are determinates not determinables. It would indeed be a very crude error to go immediately from this to the supposition that these facts are themselves particulars (now using 'particulars' substantivally). But the transition is aided by a view to the effect that particulars exemplify only specific properties, and that higher-type properties are more abstract. Particulars are then wholly concrete, as are also first-order facts.[2] Moreover, it may be held that a particular just is the concrete totality of all the particular facts in which it is a constituent, and that these facts are separable only by abstraction. By some such transition—involving at least two meanings of 'concrete,' or of 'particular' used adjectivally, *viz.*, concrete in the sense of determinateness of properties and in the sense of completeness in the totality of properties—by some such transition facts become identified with particulars.[3] Such a transition, however, is illegitimate.

[1] I no doubt have also used it as an adjective.

[2] I have so defined 'fact' or 'state of affairs' as to rule out any but first-order facts. This definition would have to be modified if one were to accept higher-order facts.

[3] Something like this seems involved in the first few pages of Professor Baylis's "Facts, Propositions, Exemplification and Truth" (*Mind*, vol. lvii, 1948,

That a fact cannot itself be a particular seems to me to be established by the very argument for the existence of facts outlined above. It is precisely the uniqueness of facts as the sort of things that cannot be named but must be referred to through assertion or denial that leads to their admission. Particulars, on the contrary, can be named.

Another view that seems to me to rest upon confusions is that states of affairs are themselves properties. The contention that states of affairs exemplify properties must then be treated as a species of the position that there are properties of properties. This, though not quite as uninvolved as the view that properties of facts are properties of particulars, still does place the essentially strange idea of properties of states of affairs in a more familiar and thus apparently more acceptable classification. Of what are states of affairs properties? The tendency is to answer —and here implausibility becomes obtrusive—that states of affairs are all properties of the universe, as though the universe were the only *real* particular (each state of affairs would of course involve its own apparent particular).

This I believe rests on confusions. But there are at least two quite different sets of confusions giving rise to it, which I want to outline very briefly. The one is illustrated by F. H. Bradley. What we have spoken of as a "state of affairs," *viz.*, a particular's exemplifying a quality or a set of particulars standing to one

pp. 459–79), although it is incompatible with Baylis's admission of a double hierarchy of types (p. 477; see also the discussion below). Otherwise I cannot understand the following: ". . . there are certain hard facts about the entities we experience. In the case of ordinary empirical knowledge these facts are fully concrete and particular. Going out into a rainstorm, for example, we become acquainted with some few aspects of the highly complex fact of fully particularized rain falling in a completely particularized way. Though we notice, and perhaps talk about, only certain features of this complex particular event, we believe that it has an indefinitely large number of characteristics. . . . Such facts furnish the basis for accepting propositions about particulars as true or rejecting them as false" (*loc. cit.*, p. 459). Now it would seem to me that a "complex particular event" that exemplifies "an indefinitely large number of characteristics" is a particular. It is not a fact about anything; it is that about which there are facts. Indeed, the very properties that Mr. Baylis cites as instances of the indefinitely large number of completely particularized properties of a concrete fact—such as rain falling in a completely particularized way—seem clearly not properties that such a fact exemplifies but rather properties contained in it, properties of particulars whose exemplification by those particulars just *is* the fact. So I am inclined to think although I may be wrong, that Mr. Baylis has confused concrete fact with particular through the intermediation of the concept of concreteness, though this was no part of his conscious intention.

another in a relation, is, if taken by itself, "riddled with contradictions." What contradictions? Essentially they reduce to one form: The particular is and is not the quality; the terms and their relation are and are not different from one another. And the source of these contradictions seems to be simply the confusion of the predicative and the identity–'is,' and obversely the confusion of predicative denial with assertion of difference.[1]

However, the real world cannot tolerate contradictions. Bradley does not conclude that there are no states of affairs, but rather that they must be transmuted. Into what? Into interdependent attributes of the one substance or individual, the Universe. The argument is that the reason contradictions break out in states of affairs is that they are taken as independent and coexisting, and that the contradictions can therefore be eliminated if states of affairs are taken as all attributes of the one individual.[2] The tacit assumptions without which this argument completely fails of cogency are that difference is a relation and that to predicate a relation between terms is to assert that they are (in whole or in part) identical. Thus this whole line of reasoning leading to the view that states of affairs are properties is based on confusion—the confusion of predication with identification (assertion of identity) and the confusion of denial of identity (assertion of difference) with predication of a relation.

The other set of confusions leading to the conclusion that states of affairs are themselves properties is illustrated in the recent

[1] There is of course no need to summarize Bradley's charming dialectic. Whenever he meets a predication he translates it into a (partial or complete) identity and whenever he meets a denial of a predication he translates it into an assertion of difference (or non-identity) and then is pleasantly surprised to discover that a contradiction arises! He even generalizes this procedure. Speaking of the predicative 'is' (or 'has') he says, "If you predicate what is different, you ascribe to the subject what it is *not*; and if you predicate what is *not* different, you say nothing at all' (*Appearance and Reality*, p. 20), in which, it will be noted, each 'is' is an identity–'is' and the dilemma is constructed on the attempt to translate predication into the affirmation or denial of identity.

Similarly in dealing with relations Bradley tacitly assumes difference (non-identity) to be a relation. So the dialectic is at heart simple: any entities in relation are different from their relation, thus must be related to their relation by another relation, and so on (*cf. ibid.*, ch. 3).

[2] The argument can be conceived as the obverse of the earlier one. Suppose several states of affairs. They must be different, therefore related. If related they must be one, not merely different. Their diversity thus becomes adjectival, substantially they are the same. "We cannot therefore maintain a plurality save as dependent on the relations in which it stands. . . . The plurality then sinks to become merely an integral aspect in a single substantial unity . . ." (*ibid.*, p. 143).

Carus Lectures of C. I. Lewis. Professor Lewis assumes, contrary to the general custom, that propositions are terms. In line with one very respectable tradition, however, he gives all terms both denotation and signification (or connotation in the older phraseology).[1] To give this view plausibility in the case of propositions, he identifies the denotation of a proposition with its extension and its significance with its intension, taking 'extension' and 'intension' from current logical discussions.[2] This appears however to rest on a shift in the meaning of 'extension' whereby extensionally equivalent propositions are said to have the same extension, as though they had the same denotation,[3] and so *a fortiori* had some denotation.

To add to the plausibility of his view that propositions are terms, Lewis points out that propositions (or rather participial phrases that present the content of propositions without their element of assertion) can serve as subjects or predicates of sentences. It should be noted, with reference to this argument, that Lewis's examples are all of one sort, *viz.*, sentences with cognitive or attitudinal verbs. Such sentences present grave problems which cannot here be disposed of, but it would seem that they are

[1] Lewis distinguishes four modes of meaning (*An Analysis of Knowledge and Valuation*, p. 39). The other two, however, have no bearing upon the present issue.

[2] At least this is my reading of *ibid.*, pp. 49–50. It is the writer's conviction that, in a subtle fashion, the same confusion permeates Rudolph Carnap's *Meaning and Necessity*. In both cases there seems to be a false analogy operating between the concept, on the one hand, of an extensional occurrence of a sentence such that in that context any truth-functionally equivalent sentence may be substituted for the given one without affecting the truth-value of the whole and the concept, on the other hand, of the extension of a term as its denotation, as that, in short, to which it refers or of which it holds. To get two such disparate concepts together under one classification the heroic measure of making the truth-value of a sentence its extension or denotation is resorted to. Added to this is the realization of the non-extensionality of modal sentences. If these are spoken of as "intensional" there is an easy transition to the notion of the intension (connotation or signification) of a sentence.

I am not arguing *at this point* against the view that sentences are terms with both denotation and signification. I am arguing here against the supposition that any support for this view is furnished by the distinction between extensional and non-extensional contexts in which sentences occur.

[3] An analogous shift is to be found in Appendix F of *Mind and the World Order*. Here Lewis identifies analytic propositions with intensional propositions and empirical generalizations with extensional propositions. An intensional proposition asserts that the property (or concept) referred to by the subject includes that referred to by the predicate. An extensional proposition asserts that the class denoted by the predicate includes that denoted by the subject. Lewis fails to see that all propositions can be read either in extension or in intension, and that this has nothing to do with the question whether a proposition is analytic or synthetic.

distinctive in that they can be true where there is nothing named by the participial phrase, that is, where that phrase, were it to occur as a separate proposition, would be false.[1] Thus we run again into the now familiar objection that propositions cannot be names upon pain of making their falsity impossible.[2] At least in such non-extensional contexts as involve cognitive and attitudinal verbs it may be necessary to deny that propositions themselves occur and to assert that only the names of these propositions do.[3]

For our present purpose, the important feature of Lewis's contention that propositions are terms is that he assigns states of affairs as their signification.[4] Thus, on his account, states of affairs must literally be properties, and the interesting question arises, Of what are states of affairs properties? To apply his general view as to the relation of the signification to the denotation of a term, they must be the properties of the denotations of the propositions whose significations they are. In determining what this is,

[1] This is clear for the example given by Lewis, 'We believe that Mary is making pies' (*op. cit.*, p. 50). This sentence can be true when 'Mary is making pies' is false. It might be thought that the same cannot be said of another of his examples, 'The gratifying fact is that Mary is making pies.' This whole sentence may be interpreted as a value-judgment. If so, its analysis cannot be undertaken at the present point. But suppose it is simply descriptive. Then the two elements in it—the assertion that there is gratification and the assertion that Mary's making pies is a fact—can be separated. Gratification (as all motor-affective states) is directional but does not require that the thing with which one is gratified be there, it only requires that one so believe. Hence Lewis's sentence can be translated into: 'It is a fact that Mary is making pies and the belief that Mary is making pies is gratifying.' And in this, 'The belief that Mary is making pies is gratifying' can obviously be true when 'Mary is making pies' is false.

[2] Carnap would say that the difficulty only arises in a semantics based on the name-relation, *i.e.*, that a semantics based on a dual meaning-relation (extension and intension) can avoid it. Lewis no doubt would say something similar. This is criticized below.

[3] And certainly this is a possibility. That is, merely because in such sentences sentences appear to occur as subjects or predicates we are not forced to conclude that they are subjects or predicates and therefore terms.

[4] Carnap makes the proposition expressed by a sentence the intension of the sentence (Sec. 6–2). However, though this is analogous to a property as the intension of a predicator, I do not find that Carnap literally identifies a proposition with a (certain sort of) property. Max Black, in a review of Carnap's book, (*The Philosophical Review*, vol. lviii, 1949), makes the criticism, "And it seems to me that to identify the relation between a sentence and the proposition it 'expresses' with that between a predicate and the property named by it is to obliterate important differences" (p. 263). I think Carnap would speak of the two as analogous. Yet the same criticism could be put: Are they sufficiently analogous for an assimilation of one to the other in formal semantics to be philosophically enlightening?

he appeals to another principle usually accepted in the tradition that distinguishes connotation from denotation. This principle is based on the law of excluded middle and interprets that law as follows: every entity falling within the denotation of a given term must fall within the denotation of any other term of the same type-level or of its negative correlate (contradictory). For example, anything denoted by 'red' must be denoted either by 'square' or by 'not-square.' Thus no limited state of affairs could be the denotation of a proposition; its denotation must be the whole actual world, for only the whole world can determine the truth or falsity of every other proposition of the same type, *i.e.*, can determine whether the denotation of a given proposition falls within that of another of the same type or within that of the other's contradictory.[1] Thus, concludes Lewis, every empirical proposition attributes as a property to the whole actual world that state of affairs which it signifies.[2]

This view has the same highly paradoxical consequence as has that of Bradley, though it is not as frankly faced by Lewis. The only particular having any properties is the whole universe, or, to state it more weakly but more strictly as a consequence of Lewis's position, the only particular of which any property may be predicated in any proposition is the whole universe. A proposition does not predicate anything of its ostensible subject, for that subject just is an aspect of a complex property being predicated of the

1 "If, then, what 'Mary making pies now' denotes should be the limited state of affairs, Mary making pies now, this same state of affairs should likewise be denoted by 'It being hot' or by 'It being not hot'; . . . and so on, for every pair of contradictory propositions. But that fails to be the case. Mary making pies now, neither includes its being hot nor its being not hot. . . . What could be so denoted by 'Mary making pies now', and likewise denoted by one or other of every pair of contradictory propositions, is the kind of entity we call a world. Nothing short of the whole of reality could determine simultaneously for *every* proposition, the truth or falsity of it" (*op. cit.*, p. 52). This argument, be it noted, assumes that the denotation of a proposition determines the truth of the proposition. A similar statement does not apply to Carnap's concept of the extension of a sentence, for this concept is that the extension of a sentence just is its truth-value, and obviously truth and falsity do not, as such, determine which sentences are true and which false.

2 Thus for Lewis the extension of all true empirical propositions is the universe and of all false propositions is zero. So his view has the gratifying consequence: "Thus all true propositions are equivalent in extension, and all false propositions are equivalent in extension; and the important extensional property of any proposition is simply its truth-value" (*ibid.*, p. 53). This passage reveals rather clearly, it seems to me, the tendency in Lewis to confuse 'extensional' in the sense of truth-functional with 'extensional' in the sense of having to do with extension (denotation).

universe.[1] Such a consequence, I submit, must be repugnant to anyone with "a robust sense of reality." And this, no doubt, is the ultimate basis of my rejection of the view giving rise to it.[2]

But there are other considerations. One is that even were one to pay this high price of infidelity to common sense, the goods that Lewis has in mind would seem not to have been purchased thereby. He wants to have propositions function as terms (clearly he means as predicate-terms, despite his argument that propositions sometimes occur as subjects of propositions). But as he has developed his view, propositions become very peculiar predicates. In the case of all other predicates, on the traditional doctrine, it is an accidental and highly atypical case if any pair (whose denotations are not null) have the same denotation. This it might have been the case that 'red' and 'square' had the same denotation (every red thing being square and every square thing red). This however would be an odd accident, and would moreover require that 'green' and 'square' should not have the same denotation, and similarly for 'red' and 'round' (where it is assumed that 'green' and 'red' are incompatible, as also are 'round' and 'square'). But in the case of every pair of true propositions (*i.e.*, every pair of propositions whose denotations are not null) the denotation of each member is, and must be, the same as that of the other on Lewis's account, *viz.*, the whole actual world.[3]

[1] Of course Lewis might claim that there is a double predication in every proposition—the predicate is asserted of the subject and this whole state of affairs thus asserted is predicated of the universe. But it would be difficult to make this appear acceptable. How can a predication be predicated? And even if this be granted, would not the only plausible form of such a view be to say that when a predication is itself predicated, it must be predicated either of the proposition itself (though I fear this would turn out to involve a confusion of predication and assertion of identity) or of the user of the proposition?

[2] Professor Baylis, though agreeing that propositional expressions are terms having denotation and signification, tries to avoid the common-sensically unacceptable romantic consequences Professor Lewis's account draws from this by distinguishing between concrete and abstract states of affairs and assigning the former as the denotation of (true) propositions and the latter as their signification. See *Mind*, vol. lvii, 1948, pp. 470 ff. I shall criticize this below.

[3] On Carnap's view a corresponding difficulty arises. Every true sentence has the same extension as every other (*viz.*, truth). But not every predicator (predicate-term) has the same extension (*viz.*, the class of entities exemplifying the property which is the intension of the predicator). This serious breakdown in the analogy of sentences to predicate-terms both in Lewis and in Carnap is due, so it seems to me, to a too facile transition from the concept of extensionality to that of the extension of a sentence.

Moreover, this point of view would seem to involve Lewis in serious difficulties as regards any empirical meaning-criterion.[1] As to non-propositional predicates, this clearly requires that, unless complex, they must have denotation or we cannot admit that they have signification.[2] But should we say this of propositions, considered as predicate-terms, we would run afoul of a large class of them, for who would deny that there are many simple propositions, *i.e.*, propositions containing neither operators nor connectives, such as 'The temperature in this room at the present time is below freezing,' which are false and yet meaningful? Lewis would have to say of them that they have signification but no denotation.[3]

Most basically, the whole dual meaning-tradition seems to me to involve a confusion. It is the confusion of reference with characterization. A predicate-term[4] has both a semantical and a syntactical function. It refers to an entity (say a quality) and it assigns to that entity the status of being a property, that is, of being the sort of thing that characterizes (in the case of quality the status is that of a first-order property that characterizes particulars). The reference is just reference, and *in this respect*, a

[1] Lewis has himself contributed signally to the clarification of the concept of an acceptable empirical meaning-criterion, especially in the idea of 'possible verification' (*cf.* "Experience and Meaning," *Philosophical Review*, vol. xliii, 1934, reprinted in Feigl and Sellars, *Readings in Philosophical Analysis*, pp. 128–45). But despite the distinctly liberalizing trend of Lewis's remarks, it is clear he still wishes to retain a meaning-criterion in a sense sufficient to give point to the criticism of the text. As he himself puts it: "The requirement of empirical meaning is at bottom nothing more than the obvious one that the terms we use should possess denotation" (*ibid.*, p. 140).

[2] 'Redsquare' could have signification with null denotation but only if 'red' and 'square' each had non-null denotation. It will be noted that I do not bring into the argument the requirement of the observability of the entities forming the denotation of a predicate. This would be a work of supererogation.

[3] The only plausible way Lewis could deal with this objection, so far as I can see, would be to say that in the case of predicate-terms that are propositions the meaning-criterion does not demand that in order to have signification they must themselves have denotation but only that the terms in them have denotation. But this again shows that the analogy between propositions and terms breaks down. On Carnap's account, false propositions do have extension (falsity). But in his system we must not formulate the meaning-criterion in terms of a relation between extension and intension. *E.g.*, we must not state it: to have intension a term must have extension. For although this might work for predicators it would not for sentences. Before we can determine whether a sentence has extension we must know that it is true or false, that it is a sentence, that, in short, it meets any required meaning-criterion.

[4] The remark in the text also holds, *mutatis mutandis*, for subject-terms. *Cf.* footnote [1], p. 22.

predicate-term, like a subject-term, is just a proper name. The notion of the denotation of a predicate-term comes from characterization. In various sentences a predicate-term is used to assert that the entity it names characterizes various (ultimately named) particulars. When this is generalized (for all particulars whose names could occur as subjects of true sentences with the predicate in question) we have the basis of the idea of denotation, which, besides the semantical notion of naming or designating, uses the device of generalization and makes a supposition about the world (that some entities characterize others), reflected in the syntactical function of the predicate.[1]

It would seem, then, that it is owing to some set of confusions that philosophers have held either that states of affairs are a certain set of particulars or again that they are a certain sort of property. That they can be neither, that they involve some further and unique aspect appears to be indicated by the basic feature of clarified everyday language: facts cannot properly be named but are asserted, they are not the referents of terms but the objects of sentences, particularly of true declarative sentences

[1] Actually a further abstraction is involved whereby one uses the generalized predication simply to pick out the individually unnamed particulars of which it holds. This is not the place to develop this theory of meaning. It is interesting to note that Carnap, who proposes to substitute the extension-intension method of analysis of meaning for the method of the name-relation, really bases the former on the latter (thus not furnishing a substitute but only a more complicated version) without apparently realizing the fact. Thus in his basic rule of truth (*op. cit.*, Sect. 1–3) for atomic sentences he writes: "An atomic sentence in S_1 consisting of a predicate followed by an individual constant is true if and only if the individual to which the individual constant *refers* possesses the property to which the predicate *refers*" (italics mine). It is on this that he bases his rule of truth for '$\equiv$' which in turn allows him to define 'equivalence,' the basic term in his method of extension-intension.

Since the above was written, there has come to my attention Professor Black's review of Carnap's book (referred to in footnote [4], p. 30). Though formulating it differently, I think Black intends to make a very similar criticism to the effect that Carnap's method of extension-intension is not a substitute for that of the name-relation since it involves the latter. His criticism relates to Carnap's introduction of neutral terms to avoid the apparent multiplication of entities involved in distinguishing extension and intension, *e.g.*, 'Human' in place of 'the property of being human' and 'the class of things which are human.' Writes Black: "The natural thing to do would be to ask—as Carnap, himself is unable to ask—whether the new term 'Human' *names* anything, and if so, what? And it would seem that, insofar as such terms are not ambiguous, they do name *intensions*, not extensions" (*loc. cit.*, p. 264). And again: "Not the least puzzling feature of Carnap's account is the resurgence, even in the neutral metalanguage, of relations of designation. . . . Now I find it very hard to tell 'designation' and naming apart" (*ibid*, p. 260).

in the indicative mood. But once this is clearly seen, the notion that they can themselves exemplify properties of any sort—to say nothing of value-properties in particular—immediately becomes highly paradoxical. If they cannot be named, how can we ever predicate properties of them? This consideration of course at once plunges us into a discussion of our third question.

4c. *Do states of affairs have properties?*

Our present question must, of course, be kept clearly distinct from the question, Do states of affairs *include* properties? '*Have* properties' is to be taken as equivalent to 'exemplify properties in their own right.' The rose's being red includes the property red, but does it have any properties itself? I shall argue that an affirmative answer to this question is, if not completely untenable, at least very unacceptable.

First, this seems already forced upon us by our consideration of the nature of states of affairs. If states of affairs are *sui generis*, and in particular are the sorts of things that can be asserted in declarative sentences but never named, we surely have a basis for denying that they exemplify properties. As already argued, though sentences can be named[1] *their* names are not the names of any facts they assert. However, it might be thought that indirectly we might be able to construct a name of a fact by using a name of a sentence asserting that fact. Suppose I write, 'the fact asserted by *S*' where '*S*' is the name of a sentence. Then I would apparently be able to predicate a property of a fact, for I could write, 'The fact asserted by *S* has the property *P*.' But a moment's reflection shows that in 'the fact asserted by *S*' we have not a name but a description. And as Russell's analysis of description shows, descriptive phrases should, in a clarified language, be replaced be sentences.[2] The reason is that a description may obviously be meaningful when there is nothing answering to it. This is clear

[1] A thorough investigation of this problem might result in establishing that though the vehicles of sentences (whether particulars, *i.e.*, tokens, or universals, *i.e.*, types, need not here concern us) can be named, sentences as linguistic elements cannot.

[2] *Cf.*, *e.g.*, "On Denoting," *Mind*, xiv, 1905, pp. 479–93, *Principia Mathematica*, Intr., ch. 3 or *Introduction to Mathematical Philosophy*, ch. 16. For logical purposes, the statement of the text is not strictly correct. A correct statement would be: Descriptions are incomplete symbols and can be eliminated. But I think the statement of the text gives the epistemological significance of Russell's analysis. What I have in mind is stated by Russell himself in a discussion of lecture i in his "The Philosophy of Logical Atomism" (*Monist*, vol.xxviii, 1918, p. 509). He says, "You can apparently name facts, but I do not

in the case of the proposal here criticized. In the sort of description here referred to, '*S*' may name a false sentence. In such a case there is no fact answering to the description, 'the fact asserted by *S*.' Hence the description is not to be taken as a name. It is in fact just the sentence *S* itself. Thus it must not be taken as the subject of another sentence, if we wish to avoid prejudging its truth by this very use.

It might be objected that the sentence, 'The fact asserted by *S* has the property *P*,' is perfectly permissible if the description in it, 'the fact asserted by *S*,' is eliminated in accordance with Russell's method. Then the sentence becomes, 'There is one and only one *x* such that *x* is a fact and *x* is asserted by *S*, and this *x* has the property *P*.' If we allow such a sentence as this latter, then it becomes possible in a correct language to state that a fact exemplifies a property, so the objection runs. However, I find difficulties in the way of admitting that the proffered sentence is correctly formulated. Consider the propositional function it contains, '*x* is a fact.' This would seem to do two things. On the one hand, it characterizes *x*, it says that *x* belongs to the category of fact (not, *e.g.*, to that of particular or universal). This, I think, can be dropped from present consideration, for it is also done by '*x* is asserted by *S*.' On the other hand, it asserts the existence of *x*. This is the important matter, for here there is no redundancy (we must not allow '*x* is asserted by *S*' to imply that *x* exists upon pain of denying the meaningfulness of *S* where *S* is false). How are we to put this? On the one hand, we could suppose there is a property of factuality, and thus that '*x* is a fact' is properly rendered '*x* exemplifies factuality.' Remembering that our concern is not with any characterization or categorizing that may be involved in '*x* is a fact,' we see at once that this rendition is just a form of '*x* exemplifies existence.' We are thus committed to the position that existence is a property, a position for whose rejection we have already seen reasons which need not be repeated here. On the other hand, we may suppose that '*x* is a fact' is properly rendered '*x* is a member of the class, facts,' where the class in question is defined by enumerating its members. This,

think you can really: you would always find that if you set out the whole thing fully, it was not so. Suppose you say 'The death of Socrates.' You might say, that is the name for the fact that Socrates died. But it obviously is not. You can see that the moment you take account of truth and falsehood. Supposing he had not died, the phrase would still be just as significant although there could not be then anything you could name."

however, runs into the absurdity of prohibiting assertions to the effect that given sentences of the sort under consideration are false but meaningful unless it is possible to enumerate the members of the class, facts, and this possibility would seem to be denied all humans, at least in this life. I see no other plausible way of rendering 'x is a fact.' So I conclude that 'x is a fact' is not permissible and consequently a sentence including it is not in correct form. Although it is not necessary I might add as a sort of footnote that the 'there is' in the sentence under criticism is not to be taken as that which carries the existential assertion. If it were so taken, 'x is a fact' would be completely redundant in the sentence. Moreover, 'there is' in this sort of context (where it is part of what the logicians call the "existential operator"—'there is an x such that') involves no assertion of existence in any ontological sense (as is clearly revealed in such sentences as 'There is an x such that $x=\sqrt{4}-1$' or 'There is an x such that x was the father of Ulysses').

It might be retorted that the argument just given is sound enough, but is merely linguistic. That is, it might be held that, by the nature of language, we find ourselves unable to predicate anything of facts. Still it may be the case that facts have properties without our being able, in a correct language, to say so.

This is, of course, a real possibility, and a careful consideration of it would involve a thorough study of the relation of language to the world—a laudable enterprise but one which cannot be undertaken here. Two relatively superficial remarks must suffice for rebuttal. First, such a standpoint would be most inconvenient for an objectivist in value-theory. It would require that all value-judgments be relegated to the limbo of incorrect language. A traditional way of defining objectivism—*viz.*, the view that there are true value-judgments—would have to be discarded. This would not prove fatal, but it would seem to require that objectivism reliquish any attempt to assign to linguistic analysis any fundamental rôle.

Second, not only would value-judgments have to be confined, on this view, to unclarified language. The same fate would be in store for any formulation of this view itself. Granted the argument given above, 'fact' cannot function as a general name. Since individual facts cannot have proper names, the class of all such facts cannot be named by the method of enumeration of its members. Nor can it be named by the device of designating a defining property of its members. The only promising candidate for such a defining property would be the property of being a fact. But that there can be no such property, or rather, that the admission of such a property involves consequences highly unacceptable to common sense, can be established by arguments similar to those given above (Section 3b) against the view that existence is a property or again that exemplification is a property. Thus it would seem that 'fact' cannot function as a general name. Hence to say that facts can have properties even though we cannot correctly say so is to say something that is obviously incorrect. As I have already suggested, something that can only be stated in unclarified language may yet be the case. But argument here is fruitless since any clarification is, by hypothesis, ruled out.

However, the argument may not be granted. It may be held that in a perfectly correct and clear language it may be possible to say that facts have properties. The question we are asking then is this: Can there be a fact about a fact? Now it might seem that there can be and indeed that we frequently assert that there is. In discussing Lewis above, we dealt with apparent assertions of of facts about facts. In his examples, however, involving cognitive or attitudinal verbs, we found that it was possible and plausible to substitute sentences for facts, so that we could translate his sentences asserting facts of facts into sentences asserting facts of sentences. That is, we treated apparent sentences that were included in others as really names of the sentences apparently so included. But there are other cases, not involving attitudinal or cognitive verbs, where this procedure is no longer plausible. Consider the sentence, '*A*'s being red is incompatible with *A*'s being blue' (where '*A*' names a surface). It might at first seem unobjectionable to render this, ' '*A* is red' is incompatible with '*A* is blue.' ' But one might legitimately hold that the latter follows from the former but is not equivalent to it. The former sentence seems in its ordinary use to say something about the world, not merely about sentences. Let us grant this much. It does not follow that the former asserts a fact of facts. For what would be the facts? *A*'s being red and *A*'s being blue? Clearly not; since it is asserted that they are incompatible, they cannot both be facts. Then is it of only one of them that the sentence asserts a fact? Clearly not, for incompatibility is symmetrical. Moreover, it is a relation requiring two terms; to assert it of one alone would be meaningless. I am not sure what is the proper way to clarify our sentence—perhaps by translating it, 'If *A* were red it could not be blue and if it were blue it could not be red.'[1] But this does seem clear: The sentence in question is about the world (not merely about sentences), yet it cannot be asserting that a certain relation (incompatibility) holds between facts.

By using incompatibility in my example my case has been easily made. I think it can however be generalized to cover all cases of supposed objective (*i.e.*, non-cognitive) relations of facts. Take causality, as in the sentence, '*A*'s being hot caused *B*'s becoming red.' Here we seem to be asserting both that there are two facts and that they are causally related. But what is meant by the latter clause? I think it would be almost unanimously agreed that we are not asserting a relation, similar to the relation of inside of, which could be observed to hold or not to hold just in the individual case.[2] We would suppose some tacit generalization to be involved. This may be rendered by a subjunctive conditional, as before, such as: 'If anything like (in certain ways here unspecified) *A* were hot then anything like *B* would become red.' This, we would want to say, holds even in the contrary-to-fact situation where, *e.g.*, it is false that there is something sufficiently like *A* that is hot, etc. Thus when we assert that *A*'s being hot caused *B*'s being red at least part of our assertion holds of contrary-to-fact situations, in which, obviously, we are not meaning to contradict ourselves by both asserting and denying some fact about facts. Part of what we assert is no doubt the facts—*A*'s

[1] There are a few remarks on subjunctive conditionals below.

[2] A notable exception is furnished by C. J. Ducasse ("On the Nature and the Observability of the Causal Relation," *Journal of Philosophy*, vol. xxiii, 1926, pp. 57–68). He holds that causation is an observable relation, just like *immediately before* or *contiguous to* (I am not sure that he does not hold that it is a complex of which the latter are elements), that it can be generalized but that generalization is no integral part of its own character. Thus there are causal facts, *i.e.*, some particulars stand in causal relations. These particulars he speaks of as "changes" or "events." It seems to me quite clear that these particulars between which causal relations obtain are not facts, they are not exemplifications of other properties, but concrete occurrents. It is not, using an example of his, the brick's hitting the window which stands in a causal relation to the window's being broken, but the total concrete event, of which one property is that it is a case of a brick's hitting of the window, which stands in the causal relation to another total event, one of whose features is that it is a case of a window's being broken (*cf. ibid.*, p. 67 and *passim*). That is, I take it he holds that the causal relation is of the same type level as the relations of hitting and being broken. If so, as I say, he is holding that the causal relation is a relation not between facts but between particulars (though of course 'fact' and 'particular' are not terms he uses).

being hot and *B*'s becoming red. But it seems plausible to deny that we are asserting any fact of these facts. Thus the most acceptable view seems to be that a clarified language will not allow sentences that assert facts of facts, that is, that it is improper to say of any fact that it exemplifies any property whatever.

There are, moreover, other serious difficulties in the view that states of affairs themselves exemplify properties. One of these is the multiplication of type-hierarchies that would seem to be required.[1] On the one hand, there is the familiar hierarchy: particular, property of a particular, property of a property of a particular, and so on. But if facts can have properties, then there appears to be added to this the hierarchy: first-order fact (*i.e.*, a particular's exemplification of a property), property of such a fact, property of a property of such a fact, and so on. Moreover, if a fact may exemplify a property, it would seem that this exemplification must itself be a higher-order fact. Thus still another hierarchy seems involved, namely, first-order fact, fact about a first-order fact, and so on. And this in turn proliferates new hierarchies, such as, second-order fact, property of a second-order fact, property of a property of a second-order fact, and so on. In short, admitting that facts themselves have properties seems to commit one to an infinite set of type-hierarchies, a result that would seem highly undesirable from any common-sensical standpoint.[2]

Various methods might be adopted to soften this unattractive consequence. Perhaps the most radical would be to identify properties, of various orders, of facts, of various orders, with properties of appropriate orders in the ordinary hierarchy (whose base is formed by particulars). For example, lowest-order properties of lowest-order facts might be identified with properties of properties of particulars. Wherever one makes the identifica-

[1] I am assuming in what follows that a state of affairs is *sui generis*, *i.e.*, neither a particular nor a property, but just the exemplification of a property by a particular or set of particulars.

[2] Professor Baylis, *loc. cit.*, p. 475, apparently admits only one new hierarchy besides the customary one, *viz.*, fact, fact about a fact, etc. But on his own view, he should maintain the difference between a property of a particular and a property of a fact (the former is a quality or relation, the latter a proposition). Thus he should admit the hierarchy: fact, property of fact, etc. And although for him exemplification is itself a property, yet it is not the property exemplified. Thus a property of a fact must be distinguished not only from a property of a particular but also from the fact about a fact which is the exemplification of a property by a fact.

tion, however, the same objection would seem to apply. A property of a fact, if there be such, must be different from any property, at least any characteral property (as contrasted with an exemplificational property), of a property. For a property of a fact just is a property of an exemplification of a property. That is its nature, which thus bears within it some feature or features of exemplification.[1] This is not so for a characteral property of a property. For example, suppose that 'between,' in 'orange is between red and yellow,' refers to a relation of qualities. As a characteral property of properties this relation does not contain any feature of exemplification; it is, in its nature, independent of all fact. Not so for a property of a fact. If my pencil's being yellow itself exemplifies a property, it is clearly a property whose very nature relates, in whatever degree of specificity, to exemplification. Were there no such thing as exemplification or factuality the very character of any property of a fact would be absent from the world.

A less radical attempt to cut off the proliferation of type-hierarchies involved in the admission that facts have properties would be to stop the various hierarchies at some relatively low level. Many philosophers with nominalistic proclivities have denied ontological significance to types, in the ordinary hierarchy, above the first or even the zero-level. So our advocate of properties of facts might claim ontological status for a property of a first-order fact (an exemplification of a property by a particular) and thus for second-order facts (facts about first-order facts) but for nothing higher. He could thus deny ontological significance to 'properties of second-order facts,' to 'third-order facts,' and so on up.

This would seem to be legitimate providing it avoids sheer *ad-hoc*ness. It would still require theoretical complexity, as contrasted with the view that there are only particulars, properties of particulars, and exemplifications of properties by particulars. For it would require properties of facts and exemplifications thereof, *i.e.*, it would require two levels of properties and two of facts (as against one of each). The most serious objection, however, would relate to its arbitrariness. He who stops the hierarchy of

[1] If this were denied, the whole contention that states of affairs have properties would lose its significance, particularly when that contention is used to support the view that value is a property not of particulars nor of properties but of facts.

types at properties of particulars clearly has an empirical basis for doing so. He can plausibly say, I experience properties of particulars, such as red, sweet, before, but not higher-level properties. But if one admits that the having of a property by a particular itself in turn exemplifies properties, why stop at this level? If there are second-order facts why not third-order facts, etc.?

This leads directly into a further difficulty. Properties of facts and again facts about facts are not observed entities. I can, in terms of my direct experience, locate certain positive natures referred to by first-level property-terms, but I cannot do the same for terms purporting to refer to properties of facts. I can locate other facts (including other first-level properties) that are caused by or associated with a given fact (*e.g.*, my experiencing pleasure upon observing certain colour-combinations), but this of course would not be a fact about a fact (*e.g.*, the being an experience of a certain colour-combination as itself being pleasant).

4*d*. *If states of affairs have properties, what sort of properties are they?*

I think, then, that there are rather good grounds for denying that states of affairs have properties. This conclusion, it seems to me, is strengthened if we seriously attempt an answer to the question, Supposing that states of affairs do have properties, what sort of properties must these be? It would seem clear that they cannot be properties exemplifiable by particulars. It would be absurd to suppose that my pencil's being yellow was itself yellow—or blue, or sour; or that the pencil's being longer than the pen was itself longer than the blotter's being longer than the paper clip. Every instinct of good sense urges us to deny that the very properties that are constituents of facts can be exemplified by those facts. Likewise, if properties have properties, particularly if they have characteral properties, it would seem that such properties could not be of the sort that could characterize facts. Yellow is a colour, but my pencil's being yellow cannot be a colour. Temporally before is transitive; who would consider holding that Tuesday's coming before Wednesday is transitive?

Thus if there are properties of facts they must be unique. How are we to describe or identify them? Professor Baylis has made the radical suggestion that the properties of states of affairs are propositions.[1] By 'propositions' he refers not to any linguistic expressions, such as sentences, but to certain real entities he describes as "abstract states of affairs" which are to be contrasted with concrete states of affairs.

Professor Baylis argues that there is an analogy between characters (I take it he means first-order properties) and propositions. This parallelism is revealed in the linguistic expressions for these entities.[2] But his basic argument is not linguistic. It is rather that

[1] *Loc. cit.*, and in correspondence with the writer. It should be pointed out that the main concern of Professor Baylis is to develop an exemplificational theory of truth, yet he does explicitly claim that his position solves certain puzzles as to the nature of value-predicates (*cf.* pp. 462–3), and the notion of propositions as properties of concrete states of affairs is integral to his main objective. Thus there seems to be no essential falsification involved in referring to his views in the present context.

[2] He writes, "That it (the parallelism between characters and propositions) is extensive is indicated by the well-known fact that Boolean algebra applies not only to classes and class concepts but to propositions as well" (*ibid.*, p. 467). That there is such a parallel cannot be denied. But I cannot see how it helps in the least to make plausible the view that a proposition can be a property (or a class—I do not here raise the issue whether 'class' and 'property' should be taken to refer to different entities). There is a strict parallel between points on a straight line and moments of time, but it does not follow that we can treat moments as a subclass of points and thus can say, *e.g.*, that moment *a* is to the left of moment *b*. I think Baylis may here have committed a fallacy I shall call "the fallacy of mixed interpretation." Suppose we have the expression '$a<b$.' This can be interpreted to mean "Class *a* is included in class *b*." Likewise it can be interpreted to mean, "Proposition *a* implies proposition *b*." But of course we must not mix the two and interpret it as "Proposition *a* is included in proposition *b*." If we could give this latter, hybrid interpretation, we would be warranted in saying that propositions are really a set of classes (or properties). But that propositions stand in some sort of relation paralleling some other relation in which classes stand gives no basis for saying that propositions are classes. We might of course on the basis of this isomorphism wish to deny that there are both propositions (standing in implicative relations) and classes (standing in relations of inclusion); we would then say that one of these is enough. But we would not mix them. Baylis does not say there are only propositions, or again that there are only properties. He wishes to have propositions a subclass of properties. This the parallelism he points out does not make plausible. Rather, it makes it most implausible. Mr. Baylis might say (in fact, he has said to the author) that he did not mean that propositions are themselves properties but that both propositions and properties are entities that can characterize. But something like the fallacy suggested above still seems to be at work. It will be noted that the isomorphism indicated by the two interpretations of Boolean algebra is read in one way: propositions are like properties, therefore it is plausible to say they can characterize other entities. But surely the same kind of argument could be used to show that it is plausible to say that properties (not be it noted their exemplifications, which linguistically would appear as sentences) can imply other properties. Nor is Mr. Baylis interested in showing that implication and characterization are just different forms of some more generic relation.

propositions "are like characters in being abstract, in being capable, if not self-inconsistent, of characterizing."[1]

Before we can decide whether we are to accept this contention we must note what Baylis means by 'being abstract.' But here we are beset with difficulties, for he seems to mean several things. I think I can distinguish the following in his usage: (1) To be abstract is to be omissive of something that actually obtains, *i.e.*, of some fact. A proposition is abstract in that it does not include every exemplification of a property by a particular that actually is the case as regards the particular concerning which the proposition makes some assertion.[2] (2) To be abstract is to be an indeterminate form of something completely determinate. This is often expressed linguistically by the use of a (real) variable. It has two forms: that which is indeterminate or referred to by a variable is (2a) a particular or set of particulars exemplifying some property (2b) a property or set of properties characterizing some particular.[3]

That propositions are abstract in senses (2a) or (2b) might easily be countered by pointing out that linguistic expressions containing (real) variables are not sentences, hence that their real counterparts (if they have any) cannot be propositions; there are no such things as indeterminate propositions. This however would be a rather doctrinaire triumph. Surely Baylis is getting at something analogous, at least, to propositions as ordinarily understood (for example, something true or false) by

[1] *Op cit.*, p. 468. In a letter to the writer Professor Baylis makes it clear that he does not mean to argue that since propositions are more abstract than concrete states of affairs that therefore they characterize the latter and even less that 'is an abstraction from' means just the same thing as 'characterizes.' His contention, he says, simply is that since propositions are abstract they are capable of characterizing. His assumption, I take it, is that what is wholly concrete (*viz.*, particulars and concrete states of affairs) cannot characterize, whereas whatever is abstract can.

[2] Mary making pies is abstract since Mary "might be wearing a red apron, or a blue apron, or no apron at all" (*loc. cit.*, p. 469).

[3] Usage (2a) is rather obviously involved in his expression "the abstract nature of propositional functions" (p. 467) such as that signified by "$\hat{x}$ being blue" or "$\hat{x}$ being taller than the Woolworth Building." It is perhaps also involved in the following passages, though they more obviously illustrate (2b): "For this abstract state of affairs ('A rose being red in my dining-room now') could be realized by there being as a matter of fact in my dining-room now, one or more of a large variety of roses with the colour of any one of a large variety of shades of red" (p. 468). " 'Being taller than' signifies a relational character that is clearly abstract. There are many different degrees of being taller than [(2b)], and for each many possible instances [(2a)]" (p. 468). A rather clear case of (2b) is found in the claim that Mary making pies is abstract, since "Mary might be making lemon pies or apple pies or mince pies or assorted pies" (p. 469).

such an expression as 'Mary making pies,' even granting that as a concrete fact she must be making some specific sort of pies. But it is substantial to point out that there are many propositions that are wholly determinate in senses (2a) and (2b). Baylis apparently would still contend that they are abstract. He could do this by shifting to (1). This does, it seems to me, furnish grounds for a really serious objection. Since propositions can be abstract in any one of the three senses without being abstract in either of the other two, is it at all plausible to say that by showing that a proposition is abstract in any one of these senses we have shown it to be capable of characterizing? To be capable of characterizing would apparently require having some *one* feature in common, but this is not to be established by showing that all propositions are abstract, for 'abstract' is ambiguous.

It is interesting to ask, Just what feature do properties have in common whereby they are all capable of characterizing? Perhaps this question cannot be answered save circularly (by saying that is just is their capacity of characterizing which alone is common and peculiar to them).[1] But I think an indirect test at least[2] is possible. That which is capable of characterizing is such that its name can properly appear as a predicate in some descriptive sentence. Here 'properly' does not require that the descriptive sentence be true; it simply means "in accordance with (logically clarified) everyday usage." Now, as I have already argued, propositional expressions or sentences cannot function as predicates. If they could, it would be possible to have a language composed wholly of terms (*i.e.*, of a mere vocabulary). There is no need to repeat this line of criticism here. There are in addition other difficulties.

It should be observed that there are ways in which propositions are decidedly not analogous to properties. Every property is at least capable of being exemplified by several particulars.[3] The

[1] Of course if the class of all properties is finite and legitimate (gives rise to no logical paradoxes) we could construct a common feature by the device of enumeration. But it is just this sort of technical device that furnishes solutions to philosophical puzzles without casting any light upon them at all.

[2] I believe it is more than a test, that it reveals something about the nature of properties.

[3] G. F. Stout at one time denied this (*cf.* "The Nature of Universals and Propositions," *Proc. of the British Academy*, 1921–2, reprinted in *Studies in Philosophy and Psychology*). I am willing to admit that being capable of characterizing a plurality of entities is not necessary to being a property—*i.e.*, to being capable of characterizing. In other words, the concept of a property that could only characterize a single entity is not self-contradictory. Yet I think every property is capable of a plurality of characterizings, and in this, I think I am in the main stream of the philosophic tradition.

analogous statement cannot be made for propositions. On Baylis's view, singular propositions can be exemplified by only one fact—the concrete fact that makes them true, if they are true, or the fact that if it were to occur would make them true, if they are false. Thus, the proposition expressed by 'Mary making pies now,' granting that it is singular—*i.e.*, that 'Mary' is strictly a proper name and 'now' is an unambiguous particle—can by its nature be exemplified by no more than one concrete fact.[1] Indeed, even in the case of universal propositions it would seem that a plurality of exemplifications is impossible. For it is just the unique set of facts (actual and possible) about the particulars forming the range of values[2] of the universal quantifier with its limiting description that can exemplify the proposition. No smaller set, no larger one, no differently constituted one could exemplify the universal proposition. Thus the proposition expressed by 'All cats are blue eyed' can be exemplified by only one entity (Baylis speaks of it as a fact): the set of all facts about cats.[3] Thus it would seem that only in the case of particular propositions (propositions whose linguistic expressions include

[1] To be true to Professor Baylis's actual statement we should add 'limited' to 'concrete' in qualifying 'fact.' Baylis holds that facts can contain other facts, and that a proposition exemplified by a given fact is also exemplified by all the facts containing the given fact (*cf. op. cit.*, pp. 473–4). I shall not argue this beyond pointing out that therei s an analogous relation to 'containing' for particulars, namely, 'having as a part.' It would thus be parallel to Baylis's position as to facts to hold that a property of a given particular is also a property of the wholes of which it is a part. Hence the paradox is not much mitigated. Professor Baylis writes, "For where a propositional expression contains a singular term, locational or otherwise, no fact which fails to include the entity, if any, denoted by the singular term can exemplify . . . the proposition signified" (p. 474). The proposition expressed by 'Mary making pies now' can only be exemplified by one limited fact and each of the facts containing it. But red, and other properties of particulars, are not restricted to characterizing only one particular and the various wholes of which that particular is a part.

[2] I use terminology suggestive of Quine's to the effect that the values of a variable are not names but entities named. This is not necessary to the point.

[3] Professor Baylis does not literally say this, but I take it his view involves it. What he does say is ". . . a generalization expressed with the aid of a universal quantifier is true if and only if it is exemplified by a fact which contains every entity denoted by the quantifier and its limiting description. . . . Thus 'All cats are blue eyed' and the generalization this expression signifies is true if and only if every cat is part of a fact characterized by cat-being-blue-eyed. Material generalizations . . . are *true of* the facts which exemplify them" (*ibid.*, p. 474). The unique fact Baylis here refers to is of course that which actually exemplifies the proposition expressed by 'All cats are blue-eyed,' supposing the latter true. To determine what could, by the nature of this proposition, exemplify it,

the existential quantifier) is it possible that more than one fact exemplify the same proposition.[1]

Another important way in which propositions are not analogous to properties, as ordinarily understood, is that propositions are true or false, properties are not. A property just is the nature (the positive *what*) that it is, and characterizes whatever it does characterize. It is itself never true or false save in a metaphorical sense (as in 'That hue is not a true red'). This is all the clearer if being abstract is the sufficient condition of being capable of characterizing, *i.e.*, of being a property. For an abstraction is not, as such, true or false. 'Higher than' is abstract (in sense (2b)) in relation, for example, to 'five-feet higher than,' but who would say it is true or false?

Now of course this argument involves a tacit appeal to ordinary usage. It could thus be easily rejected by Professor Baylis if he cares to present his view as a proposal for changing ordinary usage in a certain way. However it may be to the point to indicate how radical a change is involved in such a proposal.

As we ordinarily use it, 'characterizes,' (and its various synonyms and their converses) is a predicate of the second degree or, if you please, a two-termed relation; it requires two names to form a sentence.[2] Thus 'Blue-eyedness characterizes' and 'characterizes all cats' are both recognized to be incomplete. But 'true'

supposing it to be false, we must ask, what fact that does not obtain would have to obtain if the proposition were to be true? It seems clear it would be an entity described exactly as above: "a fact which contains every entity denoted by the quantifier and its limiting description"—in the instance given, a fact which contains all cats. Thus for a universal proposition there is only *one* entity that ever could exemplify it—the single fact it is true of, if it is true, or the single fact it would be true of were it to be true.

[1] Professor Baylis would add another type. "There are two principal kinds of first-order propositions which are not generalizations." One is the singular proposition. The other "is illustrated by the unrestricted propositional meanings signified by 'Rain falling' or 'Communists infiltrating' or 'War breaking out.' Such propositions are true of any actual states of affairs, one or more, which exemplify the meanings signified. They are false and their contradictories true of all actual states of affairs which they do not characterize" (*op. cit.*, pp. 472–3) It seems to me, however, that such propositional meanings are not propositions but propositional functions, that they cannot, as they stand, be true or false. To become true or false they would have to be modified in a way conveniently indicated by saying that a proper name or a quantifier and apparent variable would have to be added to their linguistic expression. This criticism entails a rejection of Baylis's concept of 'true of,' for which see below.

[2] As will be indicated below, I think it is highly misleading to state the matter thus. However, a translation of the present point into less misleading terminology is easily made.

and 'false' are predicates of the first degree; each requires only a single name to make a complete sentence. Thus, supposing that '*p*' names some particular proposition, '*p* is true' and again '*p* is false' are recognized as being complete. To assimilate propositions to properties Baylis finds it necessary to propose a change, amounting to the suggestion that we use 'true' and 'false' as predicates of the second degree. Thus '*p* is true' becomes incomplete, to make it complete we must reformulate it, '*p* is true of *f*' where '*f*' names some fact.[1] A similar remark holds for 'false.' Now, accepting the ordinary logic of predicates of the second degree, this has a most startling consequence, which is explicitly recognized and accepted by Professor Baylis. The same proposition can be both true and false (just as the same person may be both taller than and shorter than). Thus, suppose 'f_1' and 'f_2' name two different facts. Then the following becomes logically possible: *p* is true of f_1 and false of f_2.[2]

[1] *Cf. loc. cit.*, p. 472 and *passim.*

[2] Writes Professor Baylis: "it is not the case that first-order propositions —other than universal ones—are true simply, true at all times, at all places, and under all circumstances. Rather they are *true of* limited states of affairs. . . . Thus Nero-fiddling-in-burning-Rome was exemplified in Rome at a past time, but does not characterize the state of affairs in Mary's kitchen to-day. It was *true of* the states of affairs there then but is not *true of* the state of affairs here now. Its contradictory, not-(Nero-fiddling-in-burning-Rome) did not characterize the state of affairs there then and was not true of it, but it does characterize the state of affairs here now and is true of it. No contradiction is involved here" (p. 472).

The last sentence in this passage is correct only if the law of contradiction is reformulated. No longer can that law be stated, 'The same proposition cannot be both true and false.' At least for first-order propositions it must be stated something as follows, 'The same proposition cannot be both true and false of the same fact.' But now a serious anomaly from the standpoint of ordinary usage appears. (Professor Baylis does not point it out, but he might have been aware of it, as indicated by the limitation of his discussion of contradiction to first-order propositions.) Suppose 'f_1' to name a limited, concrete fact. Then on Baylis's view '*p* is true of f_1' cannot be both true and false. Here we have an instance of the law of contradiction in its traditional form. This is startling, for it indicates that, applied to propositions above the first order, 'true' and 'false' are predicates of the first, not of the second, degree. We are not to say that '*p* is true of f_1' is true of F_1 but may also be false of F_2, where 'F_1' and 'F_2' designate facts about facts, even though for Baylis a fact's exemplification of a fact is itself a (higher-order) fact, and therefore f_1's exemplification of *p* is itself a fact (which might be designated 'F_1'). To save the law of contradiction we must say '*p* is true of f_1' is simply true or simply false and not both. Thus though Baylis accepts a hierarchy of facts (*cf. ibid.*, p. 477), it would seem that he should deny above the lowest level that facts exemplify propositions (or at least that 'true' here means "exemplified by"). Of what nature then are the properties of higher-level facts?

Now this consequence is not only in conflict with ordinary usage, requiring modification of the law of contradiction and other changes in everyday language, but it involves a type of reference we have found reason for rejecting. It requires that facts be named. Thus the sentence 'p is true of f_1 but false of f_2' contains 'f_1' and 'f_2' as names of facts. It seems clear that this is inherent in Professor Baylis's position, and is not a mere accident of exposition. Suppose we try to put a proposition in place of 'f_1.' The only proposition that would meet the situation would be that named by 'p,' so that we would have to replace 'p is true of f_1' by 'p is true of p.' This is either nonsense (as I suspect) or a sheer tautology, in which case it would seem there can be no empirical statements concerning the properties exemplified by facts.

Indeed it would seem that if the properties of facts are the propositions which are true of the facts, then all statements predicating such properties must be *a priori*.[1] Suppose that f_1 exemplifies p, that is, that p is true of f_1. *This* truth, that p is true of f_1, is not contingent; it is a necessary truth. There seem to me to be just two possibilities of its contingency. One is that it is contingent upon the nature of f_1 and that f_1 might have been different from what it is. The other is that it is contingent upon the existence of f_1 and f_1 might not have existed. Consider the first possibility. How could f_1 have been different in nature from what it is? Let us remember that f_1 is a fact, not a particular. It is the exemplification of a property by a particular.[2] We can suppose then that if it had been different it must have been different either in its constituents (the particular and property making it up) or in the properties it exemplifies. But it could not have been different

[1] One of the arguments Professor Baylis uses for his exemplificational theory of truth (*op. cit.*, p. 479 and in correspondence with the present writer) is that it makes truth an empirical relation capable of observational determination. This seems to me quite wrong; it reduces all truth, or at least all factual truth, to tautology.

[2] This is my own formulation. There is reason to suppose that Professor Baylis would use 'concrete fact' in such a way that it would be correct to say that a given concrete fact is an indefinitely large number of exemplifications. This I think does not affect the argument, since if a proposition is true of a concrete fact, that fact must, even on Professor Baylis's account, have as one of its constituent exemplifications that one which makes the proposition true. Hence for what follows in the text we need only suppose we are talking of this constituent in the fact to make the language agree with that used by Professor Baylis.

in the former fashion and still be f_1. This is no barren tautology, such as 'f_1 is f_1.' It is significant to say that a particular, *a*, exemplifying properties *A*, *B*, *C*, might have been different if we mean that it might have exemplified *A*, *B*, *D* instead. But in this case we suppose there would still have remained *a*, that it would have been *a*, not *b* or some other particular, that would have exemplified *A*, *B*, *D* rather than, as is the case, *A*, *B*, *C*. It would not, I feel, be significant to say of *a* that it could have been different if we meant that apart from the properties it exemplified, and just in itself as a particular, it could still have existed yet have been different. So with the fact, f_1; it just *is* the exemplification of a property, say *A*, by a particular, say *a*. If *this* exemplification had not occurred, then, quite independently of whether *a* had exemplified *B* or *b* had exemplified *A*, it would be meaningless to claim that we still had f_1, though different in nature. Very well then, the only way f_1 could have been different in nature would be that it had exemplified different properties. But its properties just are the propositions true of it. These could not have been different if f_1 (*e.g.*, *a*'s exemplifying *A*) had in its own nature been no different.

Consider the second possibility. If it is said that the truth of '*p* is true of f_1' or 'f_1 exemplifies *p*' is contingent upon the existence of the fact designated by 'f_1,' we need only note that 'f_1' is here functioning as a name. If there is nothing named by it it cannot be a name. In this case the whole expression, '*p* is true of f_1' ceases to be a statement. Thus it is incorrect to say that the truth of '*p* is true of f_1' or 'f_1 exemplifies *p*' is contingent upon the existence of f_1. What should be said is that whether 'f_1 exemplifies *p*' is *meaningful*, is a statement at all, is contingent upon whether 'f_1' is a name. It does not follow that all statements of the form 'f_1 exemplifies *p*' are true. What follows is that all true statements of this form are necessarily true, true *a priori*, and all false statements of this form are false *a priori* by the nature of the language itself. I would suppose that such a consequence is quite undesirable to anyone wishing to claim that facts have properties.

There are, then, serious difficulties involved in the attempt to treat propositions as the properties that facts exemplify. Of course no success, however complete, in disposing of one view as to the nature of properties of facts itself goes very far in establishing the untenability of all such views and, thereby, the unacceptability of the whole position that facts have properties. Yet since this position itself, as we have seen, is open to serious objections, we are warranted in remaining sceptical of it at least until such time as someone develops a plausible suggestion as to the nature of properties of facts. Moreover, we must still face the issue immediately relevant to our present subject. To that we now turn.

4e. *Can value be treated as a property of states of affairs?*

Were we to say, in line with the view just discussed, that the sort of property a state of affairs can exemplify is a proposition or abstract state of affairs, we would, I am sure, be inclined to answer the present question in the negative. It would seem strange indeed to have to speak of good and bad as propositions. It would be only slightly less odd to characterize them as abstract states of affairs. It would seem that only as concrete states of affairs themselves are values or in some fashion incorporate values can the abstract states of affairs that characterize them be or incorporate values. That is, it would hardly seem plausible to hold that merely being more abstract constitutes value. Now of course one could hold that there are unique value-facts, or even that all facts are values, and that the value-features of facts are somehow explicated in certain abstract facts. But on such a view the abstraction does not constitute the value but only separates it out, and our analysis of what value is would have to turn from the (abstract) properties of facts to the nature of the concrete facts as such. Moreover, this position would require that we give up what we have found to be so central a consideration in this whole matter, namely, value's independence of fact.

This last consideration, however, is fatal not only to the specific view just criticized but to any view whatever that would have value a property of facts. Suppose we put aside for the moment all objections against saying that states of affairs can have properties. I think we should still want to deny that non-occurrent states of affairs ever exemplify properties. In ordinary speech, singular propositions whose subjects refer to nothing are taken to be either false or meaningless. That is, such propositions tacitly involve an assertion of the existence of the referents of their subject terms.[1] Moreover, it is at least highly plausible to reconstruct common speech so that all generalized propositions are built from singular ones; and, in any case, some singular propositions would seem to be indispensable if we are to say what is said in everyday language. This usage, I would suppose, ought to be carried over if one were to allow propositions with subjects that apparently designate states of affairs. That is, at least some of them must be singular and involve a tacit assertion of existence of their subjects. Common usage, then, would seem to require that (apparent) propositions of the form '*f* is characterized thus and so' or 'The state of affairs . . . is characterized thus and so' be deemed either false or meaningless if there is no state of affairs named by '*f*' or answering the description 'the state of affairs . . . .'

Now, as we have repeatedly observed, we often wish in everyday life to assert the value of some state of affairs that we do not take to be actual, and we treat as irrelevant to an argument as to the goodness or badness of some state of affairs evidence as to whether that state of affairs exists. This is surely beyond controversy in the case of ought-sentences, that is, sentences containing 'ought' as an auxiliary verb. When we say that a certain state of affairs ought to be we are not necessarily assuming that that

[1] I am not unaware of the suggestion of W. V. Quine ("Designation and Existence," *Journal of Philosophy*, vol. xxxvi, 1939, especially pp. 701–3; *A Short Course in Logic*, Cambridge, 1946, especially pp. 109–16, 123–8; "On What There Is," *Review of Metaphysics*, vol. i, 1948, especially pp. 26–8.) that 'proper name' be defined wholly syntactically, and thus that the occurrence of a proper name in a sentence involve no assumption as to the existence of anything named by it. On this suggestion any assumption of existence of that which is named must occur as a separate proposition, *e.g.*, 'Socrates exists' or 'There exists such a thing as Pegasus.' In this form, however, such existential propositions fall into a serious difficulty. If there is nothing named, *e.g.*, no Socrates or no Pegasus, then the existential proposition is not false but meaningless. A reconstruction is necessary that will avoid this. This can be accomplished if we can dispense with proper names by the use of descriptions. This is in general possible by the device of a predicate formed from the proper name, such as 'socratizes' or 'pegasizes.' We can then speak of the something which socratizes or assert that there exists something which pegasizes, and so on.

I am in no position to criticize this *tour de force* as a technical device in logical syntax, specifically as a device for eliminating proper names. If however it is meant to clarify ordinary usage I fear I must dismiss it as just absurd. In everyday life the mere use of a proper name is taken to commit one to the existence of something named. Fiction presents no special problem: it is not a serious use of names nor of any other linguistic elements. (Of course there are non-fictional statements embedded in every work of fiction, and whether or

state of affairs is,[1] thus our statement is not to be analysed as an assertion that that state of affairs has the property of oughting-to-be (to coin a solecism).[2]

It has been suggested that this whole line of objection may be obviated by the use of subjunctive contrary-to-fact conditionals.[3]

not a book is to be dubbed 'fictional' as a whole is frequently a question that must be answered by an arbitrary decision.) Fiction retains all and exactly the features of language as seriously used except that it is fiction. It is something to be enjoyed not believed. To try to account for its peculiarities by separating out one or more parts of speech and finding some special problem in them would be mere pedantry.

[1] If in such sentences we are assuming that the state of affairs does not exist, my case is all the more easily made out. Actually I think common usage is not consistent on this point. See below, pp. 180--1.

[2] Ought-sentences of the sort referred to might be analysed as follows: An abstract state of affairs (*i.e.*, a possible property of concrete states of affairs) itself has the property of oughting-to-be-exemplified-by-a-concrete-state-of-affairs. *E.g.*, to say 'There ought to be a world-organization with effective police power' could be analysed as, 'The abstract state of affairs, being-a-world-organization-with-effective-police-power, has the (exemplificational) property of oughting-to-be-exemplified-by-a-concrete-state-of-affairs.' I am not aware that anyone has ever formulated, much less held, such a view. It clearly does not fall under our present heading, for it would make value (or at least the ought-form of value) not a property of facts, but a property of a property of facts. It clearly would allow value to be independent of fact in the sense we have seen to be required. The chief difficulty in it, as it strikes me, is that it ascribes value to abstractions, to properties, whereas common sense would permit only concrete entities to be valuable.

[3] It seems to me this is involved in certain statements of G. E. Moore in a letter to the writer. In criticizing the contention that it seems difficult to hold that value is a property, he suggests that such terms as 'good' and 'fitting' may designate a property of states of affairs. He writes: "I think you have made it more difficult for yourself to see that this is a possibility by talking only of propositions of the form 'it *would be* fitting that you should do so and so', 'it *were* good that you should shut the door', and failing to notice that we can also make propositions of the form 'that you did that action *was* fitting', 'that this was the case *was* a good thing', 'that this *is* the case *is* a good thing'. It seems to me that in such cases we can properly say that we mean by good and fitting properties of actual states of affairs; and that where we say 'it *would be* fitting that you should do that', 'it *would be* a good thing that so and so should be the case', these are equivalent to 'if you did that, the state of affairs that *would* then exist *would be* fitting', 'if that were the case, the state of affairs that would then exist *would be* good'."

I think that W. D. Ross has in mind a similar mode of solving this problem when he writes: ". . . if we do not judge that *A* is happy, we cannot say '*A*'s happiness is good' but only '*A*'s happiness would be good'. The judgment that a thing is good presupposes the judgment that it exists; and the judgment that it would be good presupposes the supposition of its existence. We can, of course, make the judgment that it would be good if it existed, without knowing or even judging that it exists, or even that it is possible. But that in no way tends to show that value is independent of existence. Actual value presupposes actual existence, and conditional value supposed existence" (*The Right and the Good*, p. 114).

Thus when I say that a certain state of affairs ought to be, I am, on this analysis, saying that if that state of affairs were to exist it would exemplify the property of goodness (or fittingness or rightness or whatever may be the appropriate value-property). That this escape is quite illusory, at least in the case of ought-propositions, has been decisively shown by H. A. Prichard.[1] To say that a state of affairs ought to be is not to say that if it were to be it would have some value-property. For the former is a simple, unconditional statement; it asserts a value not contingent upon the occurrence of the state of affairs, and thus it cannot be reduced to the latter which, being hypothetical, makes actual value contingent upon the actual occurrence of the valuable state of affairs. To say that *f* ought to be (in the future) is to say something not contingent upon whether *f* does occur. To say that *f* ought to have occurred, though it did not, is to say something about the actual past, not about what would have been the case had *f* occurred.

This, as I have said, seems to me to be unassailable as far as any ought-form of value is concerned. The case is not as clear-cut for such value-terms as 'good,' 'worthy,' etc. When we say that something *is* good, we may ordinarily be supposed to imply that it exists; and when we wish to avoid this, we usually have recourse to the subjunctive conditional; we say that something, were it to exist, would be good. In connection with such (non-ought-) forms of value it might, then, with plausibility be contended that value is a property of facts, and that where value is asserted of that which is non-actual, the assertion is properly formulated as a subjunctive conditional, thus showing that value, in these forms, behaves exactly like any other property (or at least any other property whose exemplification is subject to laws).

A consideration of this possibility requires a brief glance at subjunctive conditionals and their analysis. It should be pointed out first that a subjunctive conditional is not necessarily contrary

[1] I am generalizing beyond his highly moralistic formulation, and abstracting from his contention that ought, in the form of moral obligation, must be a property of the agent. With this in mind, consider the following: "To say that we ought to do an action is to make a statement about ourselves. The obligation exists whether or not we do the action. If we don't do it, then there is no action to have the quality" (Lectures on the Nature of Moral Obligation, from notes by Wilfrid Sellars). See also the passage quoted below, footnote[2], p. 85.

to fact.[1] For example, it is perfectly correct to say, "If by chance he were to come, he would be able to tell us what happened," where one does not mean to assert the falsity of the antecedent. However, many, perhaps most, subjunctive conditionals are contrary to fact, *i.e.*, they are meant to assert the falsity of the antecedent along with the connection between antecedent and consequent. And it is indeed just this sort of subjunctive conditional that furnishes the most interesting problems, both in general and as applied to our specific issue.

There has recently been considerable discussion of the contrary-to-fact conditional.[2] To a great extent this discussion has turned on the question whether a purely extensional or truth-functional logic can render the sense of a contrary-to-fact conditional. To translate a contrary-to-fact conditional into a material implication in the indicative obviously will not do, since the contrary-to-factness of the antecedent would make every such statement true, vacuously, whereas some contrary-to-fact statements, we would suppose, are false and surely some at least of those that are true are not true *a priori* or by their mere form.[3] Likewise, to translate contrary-to-fact conditionals into indicative, universal generalizations or laws (perhaps plus singular instantial or subsumptive statements in cases where the contrary-to-fact conditional is singular) is unacceptable. The contrary-to-fact conditional is stronger than an ordinary indicative generalization; it seems to involve a necessary connection which, if not as

[1] Stuart Hampshire has made this mistake. He writes, ". . . the subjunctive form *explicitly implies* that the condition specified is contrary to fact, the antecedent unfulfilled . . ." ("Subjunctive Conditionals," *Analysis*, vol. ix, 1948, p. 11).

[2] Besides Stuart Hampshire (*loc. cit.*), see for example Roderick M. Chisholm, "The Contrary-to-Fact Conditional," *Mind*, vol. lv, 1946, pp. 289–307, reprinted with some alterations in Feigl and Sellars, *Readings in Philosophical Analysis*, pp. 482–97; Frederick L. Will, "The Contrary-to-Fact Conditional," *Mind*, vol. lvi, 1947, pp. 236–49; and K. R. Popper, "A Note on Natural Laws and So-Called 'Contrary-to-Fact Conditionals,'" *Mind*, vol. lviii, 1949, pp. 62–6.

[3] Consider as an example, 'Had Hitler invaded England in 1939 he would have won the war.' This it would seem can be analysed into a contrary-to-fact element and a hypothetical or conditional element. The former could be put, 'Hitler did not invade England in 1939 and he did not win the war.' Now if the latter or hypothetical element be rendered by an ordinary material implication, 'Either Hitler did not invade England in 1939 or he won the war,' it is seen to follow tautologously from the contrary-to-fact element. This would destroy the hypothetical element, as distinguished from the contrary-to-factness, entirely. Yet it surely seems consistent to accept 'Hitler did not invade England in 1939 and he did not win the war' but to reject 'Had Hitler invaded England in 1939 he would have won the war.'

strong as logical necessity, is yet not merely accidental fact.[1] There is, it seems fairly obvious, an element of objective connection expressed in contrary-to-fact conditionals that escapes any wholly truth-functional language.[2].

So far as this is the case, however, it would seem to be a source of embarrassment to anyone using contrary-to-fact conditionals to account for value's independence of fact while also holding that value is a property of fact. I do not mean merely that such a person must deny the adequacy of a purely truth-functional language and accept non-accidental, objective connections. I mean that, so far as contrary-to-fact conditionals are taken by their very nature to express a necessary connection, such a person is committed to the view that we can only say that some value obtains though the corresponding fact does not when we mean to assert a necessary connection, *i.e.*, when we mean to assert that the occurrence of the fact would require the fact's exemplification of the value.[3] It would, for example, be meaningless to

[1] Thus, *e.g.*, to borrow an example from Popper, we can distinguish between a strict law, such as 'All planets move in ellipses,' and an accidental generalization, such as 'All my friends speak French,' by noting that the former can, but the latter cannot, be translated into a contrary-to-fact conditional, such as 'For any *x*, if *x* were a planet it would move in an ellipse, and 'For any *x*, if *x* were a friend of mine he would speak French.'

[2] Popper denies this. His argument turns on reducing all contrary-to-fact conditionals to statements of identity. This however involves an even greater break with ordinary usage, since most contrary-to-fact conditionals are clearly predicative in character. Thus, *e.g.*, he holds that we hesitate to render 'All my friends speak French' by 'For any *x*, if *x* were a friend of mine he would speak French' since this latter might mean 'For any *x*, if *x* were added to the class of my friends, he would speak French.' It would be all right, however, if it were taken to mean, "For any *x*, if *x* were identical with one of the friends I now have he would speak French.' Now the same remarks, *mutatis mutandis*, can be made about the translation of 'All planets move in ellipses.' Thus, Popper claims, there really is no distinction between necessary and accidental universal propositions, marked out by the capacity of the former and the incapacity of the latter to be rendered by contrary-to-fact conditionals. As already indicated, this analysis flagrantly sins against the sense of many contrary-to-fact conditionals. 'For any *x*, if *x* were a planet it would move in an ellipse' is meant, in ordinary usage precisely to assert a connection between exemplifications of properties—between being a planet and moving in an ellipse. It is a trivialization that common sense would reject to treat it as an assertion of identity: 'For any *x*, if *x* were identical with one of the planets (all of which actually move in ellipses) it would move in an ellipse.'

[3] This would not, perhaps, be any source of embarrassment to G. E. Moore, who accepts the synthetic *a priori*. I believe in fact that Moore's involved discussion of intrinsic value (in "The Conception of Intrinsic Value," *Philosophical Studies*, pp. 253–75) does commit him to synthetic *a priori* knowledge

say 'I think it might have been good had I done so and so,' or 'It would have been just an accident had such or such a state of affairs, supposing it to have occurred, been good.' And if this is accepted for contrary-to-fact values, *i.e.*, for values that are not exemplified since the facts that would exemplify them do not exist, there would seem little basis for not accepting it for values actually exemplified. It would seem, that is, that if one is committed to such a view it must be because he holds that all values are connected with the facts that exemplify them (or would if they were actual) by laws which involve objective necessity. I do not mean that such a view is just untenable, nor, certainly, that it involves inherent contradictions. But it does involve a serious commitment, one which might be difficult to square with common sense. It does not seem implausible to hold that there are accidental values.

Moreover, I am not sure that even with this commitment one is able to solve our problem along the lines indicated. Suppose we say that 'If *a* were *A* it would be good' or '*a*'s being *A* would be good' assert a necessary connection between a fact and a value. Still if we treat the value as having the status of a property of fact, then the value only obtains when actually exemplified. Now it seems to me that we frequently wish to say that some fact ought to be when it is not, or that it would be better were it to exist than (as happens to be the case) not. That is, we wish to say that a value obtains when the corresponding fact does not exist. This is not the same thing as saying that whenever the fact in question exists it requires that the value obtain. We might also wish to say the latter, but that is a further matter. We might express this by saying that 'The fact, whenever it is a fact, of *a*'s being *A* is necessarily, by its nature, good' does not assert the same

of connections between the "intrinsic natures" and the "intrinsic values" of things. And it is, indeed, a view precisely formulated by C. D. Broad (though not derived from the considerations urged above). "Suppose a person regards goodness as a non-natural characteristic, and admits that its presence is always dependent on the presence of certain natural characteristic which are good-making. Suppose, further, that he holds that the connection between a good-making characteristic and the goodness which it confers is *necessary*. Then he will be obliged to admit that there are *synthetically necessary* facts, and that he knows some of them. He will therefore be obliged to admit that he can make *synthetically a priori* judgments" (*The Philosophy of G. E. Moore*, p. 66). This commitment does not seem to bother Broad, but it does me more especially because one would then have to hold that *all* true or valid value-judgments are *a priori* or at least (to meet our problem) that all valid value-judgments as to non-existing facts are *a priori*.

thing as 'It would be good were *a* to be *A* even when *a* is not *A*.' And it seems to me it is something more like the latter than the former which we mean to assert when we say that *a* ought to be *A* and that it would be good if *a* were A.

Recent discussion has brought out another feature of contrary-to-fact conditionals. Even when singular, they seem to have a tacit universality of meaning as indicated by the fact that attempts to translate them into indicative sentences quite uniformly use universal sentences.[1] Thus, 'If that egg had fallen it would have broken' is frequently rendered 'All eggs that fall (through some minimum distance) break.' And if this latter is felt to be insufficient, if it is qualified by some further singular statement (*e.g.*, by 'that egg did not fall through the specified mimimum distance'), still the generalized statement is retained as an irreducible element in the translation of the singular, subjunctive conditional.

This again, if taken as an irreducible element in the analysis of contrary-to-fact conditionals, may well be a source of embarrassment to anyone holding that contrary-to-fact conditionals can show how value is independent of fact. For it commits him to holding that whenever one supposedly is making a singular value-judgment about some merely possible state of affairs one is really intending to make a universal judgment. Thus when one supposes he is saying, 'It would have been bad had Hitler invaded England in 1939,' he is really saying, 'Any invasion, under certain conditions, is bad.' Such a commitment seems difficult indeed to square with common sense.

The above two arguments are not decisive. They could be countered either by boldly making the commitments indicated and saying that one is willing to embrace a view that may seem thus paradoxical to common sense or by denying that any such commitment is involved. By the latter alternative I mean that one could deny that contrary-to-fact conditionals universally involve an element of necessity or an element of universality.[2]

[1] Stuart Hampshire is an exception. Scientists could, he says, dispense with subjunctive conditionals by the use of causal laws, but "judges, juries, historians, and moralists would certainly be embarrassed, if challenged to replace all their singular conditional sentences" in the subjunctive by the use of generalizations in the indicative (*loc. cit.*, p. 11).

[2] There seem even in common usage to be contrary-to-fact conditionals that deny necessary connection (*cf.* Chisholm, *loc. cit.*, p. 298), and others that are irreducibly singular (*cf.* Stuart Hampshire).

However, there does seem to be an argument against the view I am criticizing which, if it is not decisive, comes very close to being so.

Let us recall what is needed. It is held that value is a property of facts. Yet it is recognized that in some sense it is independent of facts, can obtain when the appropriate fact does not exist, and can be asserted without the assertion of the correlated fact. It is to mitigate this paradox that appeal is made to contrary-to-fact conditionals, to sentences of the form 'If *a* were *A* it would be good,' or 'If *a*'s being *A* were the case, that (state of affairs) would be good.' Here 'good' appears to function as a predicate, whose subject is a reference to a state of affairs that does not exist.

Now we must note a peculiarity of this valuative form of contrary-to-fact conditional. In the ordinary declarative contrary-to-fact conditional, the subjects of both clauses are terms referring to particulars, in the simplest case to the same particular. If this reference is by an apparent proper name (or proper name and pronoun whose antecedent is the proper name), and there is no entity thus named, both clauses, and hence the whole conditional, are meaningless. Thus if 'Boysterous' names nothing, then 'If Boysterous had been built to specifications she would have won the series' is meaningless, is not a sentence at all. It is not so clear if the reference is by description and there is no particular answering the description. Suppose we have 'If the man who robbed my house had been a professional he would not have left his fingerprints' and suppose my house was not robbed. It is clear the antecedent here must be false, but it is not false in the way the contrary-to-fact form seems to require. That form, on my analysis of everyday usage, requires the antecedent to be false in its predication, not false in its tacit assertion of the existence of the subject. Thus it seems to me proper to say that the whole contrary-to-fact conditional is false in any such case.

A somewhat more complex type of declarative contrary-to-fact conditional is that in which the antecedent and consequent do not have the same subjects. Suppose the consequent has as subject an apparent proper name which, however, names nothing. Then again, so I apprehend, the whole conditional is meaningless, as in the case of 'If Hitler had not bombed London, George P. Sanders would not have been killed' where 'George P. Sanders' names no one. Similarly I would suppose the whole conditional to be false if there is nothing answering the description serving as the subject of the consequent, as in the case of 'If I had been robbed then my debt to you could not have been paid so promptly,' supposing I had no debt to you. In general, then, it would seem that the contrary-to-factness of ordinary subjunctive conditionals must lie in their predications, *i.e.*, in the predications of their antecedents or in both their antecedents and consequents. When either subject is meaningless (an apparent name that names nothing) or involves a false existential assertion (in cases of subjects which are descriptions) it is impossible for the whole conditional to be true.

The sort of valuative contrary-to-fact conditional needed by the view under criticism is that in which the subject of the consequent refers to a non-existent state of affairs (of which value is predicated). Let us consider first the form, 'If *a* were *A* it would be good,' *i.e.*, 'If *a* were *A* that (state of affairs) would be good.' Here there is no quarrel as to the antecedent—we will suppose its subject names a particular and that the clause is false in that that particular does not exemplify the property predicated. The difficulty arises with the consequent. Its subject is a reference to a state of affairs. Suppose this reference is by means of an apparent name. Then, since there is no state of affairs so named, not only the consequent but the whole conditional becomes meaningless, unless the analogy with ordinary subjunctive conditionals breaks down. Moreover, as already argued, a state of affairs cannot be named. Thus the pronoun 'it' and even the demonstrative 'that (state of affairs)' in the above are misleading. Could they not however be replaced by a description so that we have, for example, 'If *a* were *A* then *a*'s being *A* would be good'? If this is allowed, however, we have again a breakdown of the analogy with the ordinary contrary-to-fact conditional. For in the latter case we saw that if there is nothing answering the description constituting the subject of the consequent the whole conditional is false. Indeed, as we have seen, the whole contrary-to-factness of the ordinary subjunctive conditional must lie in the predications involved. Any meaninglessness or falsity introduced in the subject-reference destroys the possibility of the truth of the whole conditional.

Nor will it help matters if we try to make the subject of the antecedent as well as that of the consequent a reference to a state of affairs. Consider the form, 'If *a*'s being *A* were the case, that (state of affairs) would be good.' I suppose the antecedent here is meant to be an existential assertion. If so, how is it properly formulated? We might try to make the subject a description (of the state of affairs). But then, besides the criticism already made (that such a subject, having nothing answering to it, would make the whole conditional false), there would be another. What would be the predicate? Apparently existence. This, as we have seen, is not to be allowed. Let us attempt a different formulation, one in line with recent analyses. The tendency today is to translate existential statements into the form: 'There is something such that it exemplifies such and such properties.' Now if we were to analyse the antecedent proposed above in this fashion it would require that a state of affairs be a property. To say '*a*'s being *A* is the case' would become 'there is something such that it exemplifies the property of *a*'s-being-*A*.' Likewise 'if *a*'s being *A* were the case' would become 'if there were something such that it exemplified the property of *a*'s-being-*A*.' But a state of affairs, as I have tried to show, cannot itself be a property. This way then seems closed. Indeed the most plausible formulation of the antecedent in 'If *a*'s being *A* were the case, that (state of affairs) would be good' is 'if *a* is *A*' were true,' that is, 'if *a* were *A*,' which is just what we had before.

By way of summary. The ordinary contrary-to-fact conditional says that if some particular or particulars had some property the same or other particulars would have some other property. That is, it says (though it cannot strictly be formulated in this way): if there were some specified fact, there would be some other fact. The view under criticism needs to say: if there were some fact, there would be a fact about that fact, more particularly, there would be a value-fact about it. For the reasons given, such a statement seems quite improper. Moreover, it does not say what is wanted. What we want to say is not merely that if there were some fact that fact would be good. We want to say that, whether or not some fact obtains, just that fact is what is valuable. What is good is not some particular, but some particular's having a certain property. Yet the goodness of this is not a further property only exemplified when and as the particular exemplifies the certain property. This can be expressed by 'It were good that *a* be *A*,' but we must not be misled into supposing this means that when and as *a* is *A* then and only then is there any good. Some other analysis of the way in which value includes fact or existence in its nature while yet obtaining when the fact does not exist is necessary. For the analysis which says that value is a property of facts has, in my judgment, failed.[1]

[1] If exception is taken to the above argument on the grounds that 'good' does not mean 'good to be' or is not elliptical for 'it were good that,' then for the present I fall back on the ought-form of value. It seems clear that 'ought' always means 'ought to be,' that it ineradicably involves reference to fact. Similarly if it be said that 'good' can be used properly only in the case of that which is actual, then again for the present I have recourse to 'ought.' Some things which are not actual ought to be. I shall presently however (*cf.* below, pp. 177 ff.) argue that ordinary value-statements, *i.e.*, sentences in everyday usage having 'good' or an equivalent as predicate, can be properly replaced in a clarified language by ought-sentences.

5

IS VALUE THE REFERENT OF A SEMANTICAL PREDICATE?

IN the preceding sections I have tried to canvass all the more obvious interpretations of the statement, 'Value is a property.' I think I have succeeded in showing that in each of these interpretations the position, if not definitely untenable, is at best highly implausible. Certain special difficulties attach to certain particular interpretations, but there are a few basic and recurrent objections. (1) Value does not seem to be something directly experienceable in its own right, like yellow or before and after. It seems rather to be a way in which other things can be experienced. Thus it would not seem to be a property. (2) Value includes in its nature but without asserting it a reference to some fact, the fact which, were it to exist, would be good or bad as the case may be. This would be anomalous, to say the least, if value were a property. (3) Value in some sense obtains quite independently of the existence of the fact a reference to which is involved in its nature. Thus value cannot be a property of that fact, for if it were it could not obtain in the absence of it. And it would be difficult to make out that it was a property of something other than this fact.

In this quandary we turn to another sort of analysis of value. Perhaps our difficulty has arisen from sticking too closely to a kind of value-expression frequent in common usage. This is to be found in the predicate of a sentence at the lowest or "zero-" level, a sentence making no reference to language. I have in mind sentences like, 'The coffee is good,' 'Getting a college education is a worthy objective.' May we not be aided by a consideration of metalinguistic sentences predicating something of value-terms or value-sentences? I have in mind sentences like, ' 'You ought always to tell the truth' is not valid.' It may be that we can find value as the referent of some metalinguistic predicate. This is, I am perfectly aware, an extremely heterodox suggestion, but the difficulties besetting every view making value a property in the ordinary sense may be sufficient to gain it a hearing.

The sort of metalinguistic predicate that no doubt first comes to mind is the pragmatical.[1] I shall, in connection with other metalinguistic predicates, particularly certain syntactical predicates, have some criticisms to offer of the view that value is the referent of some pragmatical predicate. I do not propose to devote a separate section to the discussion of this possibility, my reason being that it is incompatible with that value-objectivism which furnishes the framework within which the present analysis proceeds.[2] A pragmatical predicate describes some aspect of the occurrence of a linguistic expression, whether on the part of a producer or of a consumer of the expression. Thus it always describes some fact,[3] and a fact, we have seen, cannot be a value if value-objectivism is correct.

Let me give an illustration. A. J. Ayer in *Language, Truth and Logic* says that ethical concepts are really pseudo-concepts—their addition to an ordinary sentence does not change the meaning of that sentence. However, they do serve to express the feelings of the utterer of the sentence.[4] This I think may be stated without

[1] I am of course using the now widely current distinction introduced by Charles W. Morris in *Foundations of the Theory of Signs*, *International Encyclopedia of Unified Science*, vol. i, no. 2. I am personally of the opinion that all metalinguistic predicates are semantical, that pragmatics is formalized psychology and syntactics a study of the construction (by rule) of designs. But this is not sufficiently relevant to be worth arguing here. I think one has to be something of an opportunist in his tools of analysis, which is dangerous only so far as one forgets or denies the fact.

[2] See Section 1.

[3] This is equally true whether the pragmatical predicate occurs in an axiomatized calculus or merely as a descriptive statement in its own right, for the difference here would simply turn on how the sentence in which it occurs is established (whether it is derived from certain axioms or is verified by observations). This is also equally true whether or not one holds that philosophical pragmatics has undefined descriptive predicates in its metalinguistic portion, for if one does, one is committed to the factual significance of these predicates as truly as is the person who would limit such descriptive predicates to the object-language portion of pragmatics. And this has nothing to do with the question whether the task of philosophy is the study (or "reconstruction") of the syntax of such a pragmatics (of course in a meta-metalanguage).

[4] Writes Ayer, "The presence of an ethical symbol in a proposition adds nothing to its factual content. Thus if I say to someone, 'You acted wrongly in stealing that money,' I am not stating anything more than if I had simply said, 'You stole that money.' In adding that this action is wrong I am not making any further statement about it. I am simply evincing my moral disapproval of it. It is as if I had said, 'You stole that money,' in a peculiar tone of horror,

too much distortion of Ayer's meaning as follows. An ethical term cannot properly function as a predicate in a zero-level sentence. When you try to make it do so, you find it predicates nothing. In a proper language, such zero-level sentences apparently containing ethical predicates are replaced by pairs of sentences, one, at the zero-level, presenting the descriptive content of the original, and one, naming this last, and predicating some emotional accompaniment of its affirmation. The predicate of this meta-sentence may be said to preserve, in proper form, all that can be preserved of the original, improper, zero-level ethical predicate. Thus, 'Your stealing that money was wrong,' as said by Mr. Ayer (supposing Mr. Ayer *would* say such a thing) is to be replaced by the pair, 'You stole that money' and ' 'You stole that money' was affirmed by Mr. Ayer with moral disapproval.' It should be noted that "You stole that money" as it occurs in the meta-sentence is not a quotation. It is the name of a sentence, in the sense of 'sentence' that would allow two different sets of words, if by the rules of the language they assert the same thing, to be the same sentence.

No sentence with such a meta-predicate can be synonymous with an object-sentence concerning which it makes a predication. Yet such meta-sentences do describe facts, the facts of the emotive features of the occurrence of other sentences. For our present purpose it is not necessary to decide the question whether such meta-sentences can be properly reduced to zero-level sentences (never of course to those which they mention). If they cannot, then their predicates are irreducibly meta-predicates, yet such predicates would be descriptive, and the sentences would assert fact. It thus seems clear that this approach eliminates value in favour of a certain class of facts.[1] The approach is therefore incompatible with value-objectivism and falls outside the sphere of the present analysis.

or written it with the addition of some special exclamation marks. The tone, or the exclamation marks, adds nothing to the literal meaning of the sentence. It merely serves to show that the expression of it is attended by certain feelings in the speaker" (*op cit.*, 2nd ed., p. 107).

[1] It may be that *all* fact is properly expressed in the form of the pragmatical sentence, that every sentence of the form '*a* is *A*' should be replaced by a sentence of the form 'I believe '*a* is *A*'' or perhaps even 'I believe the sentence, '*a* is *A*' with some emotion.' This will not change the outcome with which we are concerned. For if value is here displaced not by a specific set of facts (of human behaviour) but by a categorial requirement in a philosophical analysis of fact, it is still displaced.

Having thus disposed of the first and most obvious meaning of the suggestion that value may be the referent of a meta-predicate, we turn to the more recondite and apparently less attractive interpretations of this proposal. May we consider value to be the referent of either a semantical or a syntactical predicate? It is with the first of these possibilities that we shall be concerned throughout the remainder of the present section.

I mean by 'semantical predicate' any term that refers to any referential aspect or feature of any other term. 'Referential aspect' is of course itself a very loose expression. It is meant to cover both the designation of names and the truth and falsity of declarative sentences. But of course it cannot be confined to these, or the present proposal, *viz.*, that value, though simple and *sui generis*, is the referent of a semantical predicate, would be ruled out *ab initio*. Perhaps, for the present, the best we can do is to use a device of the neo-Wittgensteinians and paraphrase our question: Is it more illuminating to treat value as the referent of a semantical predicate similar to 'designates' or 'is true' than to treat it as a property designated by a zero-level predicate similar to 'yellow' or 'above'?

An affirmative answer to this question must seem very odd to the reader. Indeed, the writer shares this feeling. It may well be that this whole suggestion is nonsense. Even so, it is just possible that the nonsense will get us on in our analysis, so that it is worth some exploration. At the very outset, however, we are plagued with a further, probably not unrelated, obstacle. It seems impossible to find any clear-cut proponents or even expositors of this sort of view. We might, of course, proceed by means of a purely hypothetical development of this kind of position. It is, however, the author's rather reactionary conviction that one is more apt to drift into sheer nonsense if one leaves entirely aside the labours of one's colleagues than if one probes the latter for various possible leads, though God knows that philosophers have not been eminently successful in avoiding wrong paths.

In this situation I propose to investigate three views concerning value, to see to what extent they can be interpreted as making value a referent of a semantical predicate and to try to discover what insight these views as thus interpreted can give us into the status of value. They are roughly arranged in the order of the plausibility of this interpretation, from the view least plausibly to that most plausibly given this interpretation.

5a. *Is value the being an object of an interest?*

It must seem far-fetched to treat Professor R. B. Perry's view that value is "any object of any interest"[1] as an instance of the position that value is the referent of a semantical predicate. And of course it *is* far-fetched. It will require that we read beyond what he actually says in two ways: that we interpret him as saying things that he actually does not say, and that we ignore things he actually says that are patently incompatible with this interpretation. This seems high-handed, but it is to be remembered that we are not concerned with an accurate historical account; we are not saying that Perry *really* means what he did not say; we are rather using Mr. Perry as a springboard to start us on our own excursion.

Obviously the cue for our interpretation of Perry's position is the word 'object.' This word does have a traditional epistemological significance such that a semantical translation by such terms as 'referent' or 'designatum' seems not wholly inappropriate. A value then may be held to be any referent of a certain sort of reference or designation, the sort we have in what Perry calls an "interest." This requires that we read beyond Perry's obviously and intentionally behaviouristic use of 'interest.' For Perry clearly *intends* to use 'interest' to refer to a certain sort of act or behaviour-pattern; "it is fundamentally motor or conative."[2] In the terminology we have adopted, 'interest' is not a semantical term, it does not refer to any referential aspect of symbols or to any symbols as referring; it is rather a zero-level word, referring to a natural event or sequence of events. And almost the same thing must be said of Perry's use of 'object of interest.' It is true that Perry claims that the object of interest is the object of a judgment, the interest-judgment (which is necessarily involved in the interest and anticipatory of what would satisfy it). But his account of judgment as a whole and of the object of judgment in particular is behavioural. The object of judgment is "that to which the response is directed"—in the

[1] *Cf. General Theory of Value*, particularly ch. 5, also "A Theory of Value Defended," "Value as an Objective Predicate," and "Value as Simply Value," *Journal of Philosophy*, vol. xxviii, 1931, pp. 449–60, 477–84, and 519–26, respectively.

[2] *Journal of Philosophy*, vol. xxviii, 1931, p. 450. This is unmistakable in his definition: "Interested or purposive action is action adopted because the anticipatory responses which it arouses coincide with the unfulfilled or implicit phase of a governing propensity" (*General Theory of Value*, p. 209).

case of interest, a "problematic object," that is, that to which that complete response (of which the interest is the partial, anticipatory phase) would be directed. Now although 'directed to' might be given a semantical interpretation, as involving reference or designation, it can also be read empirically, as meaning "completed by" or "normally terminating in," and it is this reading which is certainly the more natural.

Moreover, Professor Perry gives formulations of his view of value as being an object of interest which are incompatible with the position that value is the referent of a semantical predicate. I am thinking of those formulations which would suggest that value is a property causally produced by the occurrence of an interest. Perry frequently speaks of things as "acquiring" value when interest is taken in them, of value as "springing from" or being "created by" the taking of interest in the thing having value, and of the varieties of value as being "determined by" the varieties of interest or of the interest's object. Such expressions are compatible with the view that value is an ordinary property whose exemplification is causally determined by the occurrence of interest. 'Value is any object of any interest' would then be neither a definition nor an epistemological analysis of the status of value but simply an empirical law. In this case, however, the natural interpretation of Perry's exposition taken as a whole lies in the other direction. He says explicitly that his view may be formulated in the equation, "*x* is valuable=interest is taken in *x*";[1] he speaks of "interest being constitutive of value," and says that he conceives "value as the state of being an object of an interest."[2] Likewise he considers that certain people differ from him although they hold that "interest is a necessary condition of anything's possessing or acquiring the quality of value" because "they refuse to *identify* value with interest."[3] Yet I must hasten to add that though these latter formulations would be compatible with the view that value is the referent of a semantical predicate, still they do not require it, and in fact Perry frequently writes as though being an object of an interest is a natural, first-order relation, quite like temporally after or spatially inside of; thus value, as just being the object of an interest, would have the status of an intra-behavioural relation, a relation between

[1] *General Theory of Value*, p. 116.
[2] *Journal of Philosophy*, *loc. cit.*, p. 456.
[3] *Ibid.*, p. 452.

a terminating phase and an anticipatory phase of that sort of motor-affective behaviour Perry calls "interest."[1]

Not *quite* everything Perry says, however, is against a reading of his view that would logically place it in our present section. For example, he writes, "Value is thus a specific relation into which things possessing any ontological status whatsoever, whether real or imaginary, may enter with interested subjects."[2] The meaning of this statement turns in part upon how we take the phrase, 'whether real or imaginary.' If it be taken as non-restrictive, thus as merely illustrative of 'any ontological status,' the statement is much more plausibly interpreted as making value a semantical property than as treating it as a natural or empirical relation. Natural relations can only hold between particulars, *e.g.*, between events or parts of events, such as earlier and later portions of a behavioural sequence. But all particulars have the same ontological status. If things which have the ontological status of being a quality or a relation or a fact could be terms in the relation which constituted value, then that relation clearly would not be the sort of relation which holds between parts of a total behavioural event. It does not *follow* that value must be a semantical relation, such as a specific form of designation, but it becomes plausible to suppose that it is, since it would make sense to say that one can designate things of every ontological sort.

But even if we take the phrase, 'whether real or imaginary,' as restrictive, as showing the total range of 'any ontological status whatever'—and I confess that this seems to me most probably how Perry meant to use it—we still find it difficult to interpret the whole statement in such a way as to make 'value' refer to a natural relation between behavioural events. It *could* of course be given such an interpretation, namely, if we treated 'imaginary' as referring to a real occurrence of the sort that the extreme behaviourist has trouble in describing but an introspectionist does not have, a sort that may be spoken of as "the having of an image as distinct from the having of a percept." But this is not, I think, Perry's intention or whole intention in using this term. I think he means by 'imaginary,' as contrasted with 'real,' to refer to that which does not exist. This is borne out by the fact

[1] This would seem to be the proper interpretation of: "An object is valuable when *qualified* by an act of interest; relation to interest assuming, in the experience or judgment of value, the role of adjective" (*General Theory of Value*, p. 115 f.n.).

[2] *Ibid.*, p. 116.

that for him the object of interest is "problematic"; it is at most (existentially) simply expected or anticipated. And he would surely say that there can be an interest, and thus a value, when the object does not yet exist or, indeed, if the interest is doomed to disappointment and never runs out to fulfilment.[1] In fact, Perry explicitly admits that "the interest-judgment need not be true in order that the interest, and hence the value of its object, shall occur."[2] Now this admirably accepts the logic of everyday language as to value, but hardly seems compatible with any view that makes value a natural relation. For how can such a relation hold in the absence of one of its terms? To say that a man is truly a father although he never did and never will beget any actual children seems to me a rather odd way to talk. Similarly, to say that there is a value constituted by an interest in an object where the object has not existed and will not exist is close to nonsense *if* the key terms in this statement be given a behavioural interpretation. If 'object' is a semantical term and value is a sort of designation, not an observable relation between particulars, then Perry's admission that there can be value even though the object of interest is never realized makes sense, but in this interpretation of his view we are doing Perry no injustice in treating it as an example of the position that would make value the referent of a semantical predicate.[3]

[1] Perry writes, "interest has the effect, so far as the interest-judgment is true, of transforming the object of that judgment from a problematic into an existent object; while mere judgment unattended by interest, has no such effect" (*op. cit.*, p. 347). "The effect of the interest-judgment is the *realization* of its own object, implying that what *becomes* real as a *result* of the interest-judgment was not real when the interest-judgment itself occurred. Nor is there any paradox in supposing that the event whose future occurrence makes the judgment true now, and which when it occurs will verify the judgment, should be an effect of this judgment" (*ibid.*, p. 349). I think there is a paradox here, and indeed that there is a paradox in saying that a judgment can be true before its object occurs, interpreting 'judgment' and 'object' as meaning events and 'true' as referring to a natural relation between them—for it would be like saying that the relation of father of holds between a man and a child before the child is born. But I leave these lesser paradoxes in order to stress a greater one.

[2] *Journal of Philosophy*, *loc. cit.*, p. 451.

[3] I think that Perry's tacit reading of his own position in a semantical fashion can be quite definitely made out in the following passage (which I take to be critical of the type of view espoused by Nicolai Hartmann): "The irreducibility of value to the categories of existence seems to rest on the fact that: (1) *a* can be valuable without existing; or, (2), *a* can be valuable without its value's existing; or, (3), valuableness can be valuableness without existing. But I do not find anything peculiar about any of these alternatives. They are possibilities that must somehow be provided for in subject-matter other than

Let us, then, proceed with our inquiry by giving Perry's view a semantical interpretation. Is it defensible to hold that value just is the being a referent of a certain sort of reference, that something's being valuable just is its being designated in a certain way or in a certain mode of designation or by means of a certain sort of symbol?

In the first place, bizarre as this view may seem, it does offer certain advantages, if one admits the difficulties pointed out above concerning any view that would make value a property in the ordinary sense. We found it implausible to hold that value is a quality or again that it is a natural relation. One reason was that value does not seem to have a positive, directly experienceable nature in its own right. This would be readily accounted for on the present view. Being a referent of a certain sort of designation would not be anything itself observable. Another reason was that value always attaches to something else, not in the way a property does, namely, by being exemplified (for a property does have some character or nature of its own such that it at least is not just nonsense to wonder whether it could not be in the world even if not

value. Thus, (1) *a* can be believed without existing; (2) *a* can be believed without the belief's existing, as when *a* is the object of a purely imaginary belief; (3) belief can be belief without existing, that is, belief may be a null class or a nature that is not exemplified. The supposed diffculty seems to arise from the supposition that if anything is asserted, existence is asserted" (*op. cit.*, p. 459). It seems to me there are several serious confusions in this passage. I have quoted it however simply to show that here quite obviously Perry must be using 'object' and correlative terms (such as the pseudo-name '*a*') as semantical meta-terms, not as zero-level or empirical words. To say that we do not always assert existence is, though misleadingly cryptic, quite correct. Thus it is appropriate to say that the object we assert need not (even if our assertion be true) exist. But surely this would only darken the mystery if by 'object' were meant an event, and by 'true assertion' were meant another event standing in an observable relation to the former.

I must here again acknowledge my indebtedness to Russell's lectures, "The Philosophy of Logical Atomism." He there (*Monist*, vol. xxix, 1919, pp. 51–5) criticizes the account that James and Dewey and "some of the American realists" (Russell may have Perry in mind) give of sentences with "propositional verbs," such as 'I believe the train leaves at 10:24,' which account would assimilate them to sentences asserting natural relations, such as 'I cut my finger.' The latter sentence is false if 'my finger' has no referent. But the former need not be false even though 'the train leaves at 10:24' is false, *i.e.*, if there is no fact to which it refers. As Russell says, "when you believe that a thing exists and it does not exist, the thing is not there, it is nothing, and it cannot be the right analysis of a false belief to regard it as a (natural) relation to what is really nothing" (p. 53). And all the more strikingly, if what you believe is not that the object of your belief exists it cannot be a correct analysis to say that the belief (whether true or false) is just a natural relation between yourself and the object.

exemplified),[1] but in some more constitutive fashion. Here again the present suggestion fits our needs. Clearly to be a referent of some sort of designation requires that whatever it is that so functions have some additional status; for anything to be referred to, it must be more than just an object of that reference. A further reason for denying that value is a property was that value specifically attaches to the existence of something or to the exemplification of a property by a particular. It was this that made attractive the view that value is a property of fact. The present view makes it possible to hold that it is facts that are valuable, since it is possible to restrict the sort of symbols and the type of reference in terms of which value is defined to those whose referents are facts. Since facts can be referred to, this would seem to avoid the difficulties in the assumption, presupposed in the view that value is a property of fact, that facts can have properties. It is even possible to suggest how one could analyse the frequent but perplexing belief in some value where the corresponding fact does not exist, as when we believe that something that is not the case ought to be the case. We could then point out that the sentence asserting the fact is false. Such a sentence is not meaningless, nor is it to be analysed as just a set of names. To put it misleadingly, it refers to a fact that is not there.[2] We could then say that being a value just is being the object of such a sentential reference or assertion, *i.e.*, value would be the referent of a semantical predicate asserted of ordinary factual or descriptive sentences.

But to say this would certainly, as it stands, be overhasty. It would involve an assimilation of value to fact which would destroy the value-objectivism within which the present investigation attempts to operate. For, as we have seen, the least objectionable way to define 'fact' is 'referent of a (descriptive) sentence.'[3] But this is exactly the way we are now suggesting that 'value' be defined.

[1] A certain empirical meaning-criterion might rule out such puzzling as nonsensical. But then, at a higher level, we can legitimately wonder whether, or at least why, we should accept this meaning-criterion. Another way of putting the matter is to say that we can distinguish between the characteral and exemplificational properties of a property. There seems to be no correlative distinction in the case of value.

[2] This shows that we have here a different sort of reference from that of a name. We perhaps had best stick closely to common usage and not say that a sentence refers to or designates a fact but simply that it asserts a fact. But then we should recognize that 'asserts' is a semantical, not a syntactical nor a pragmatical and certainly not a zero-level, predicate.

[3] Clearly *any* definition of 'fact' is illegitimate because it must treat 'fact' as a predicate, and thus as incorporating a name. This, we have seen, gives

In this predicament Perry himself may offer us guidance. He distinguishes between interest and cognition, and although interest embodies cognition (the interest-judgment), this cognition is not to be confused with cognition that has the interest as its object.[1] This alone, however, is not sufficient for our purposes. Both of these cognitions (one *in* and one *of* an interest) *are* cognitions, and their objects, in the semantical interpretation we have been foisting upon Perry, would both be facts.[2] But our author does attempt to make a more basic distinction between interest and cognition. Though he gives behavioural accounts of each, the accounts differ somewhat. The interest, being connected with a governing propensity of the organism, has a tendency to bring into existence its object, which tendency is absent, or at most weaker, in the mere judgment.[3] Indeed, Perry, though trying to keep within a behavioural framework, makes distinctions as to subordinate acts that make up total acts of interest or judgment that are obviously meant to correspond with traditional distinctions as to syntactical features of sentences, and he uses these distinctions to help him differentiate between judgment and interest.[4]

rise to insurmountable difficulties. And I cannot see that such a meta-predicate as 'referent' avoids them. Strictly, something that is not there, since it cannot be named, is not to be named 'the referent of a sentence.' We must not name it *at all*, at any linguistic level. Yet we must be able to assert it, namely, in a false sentence. But even the sentence I just penned is wrong: What is 'it'? A pronoun? Thus a substitute for a name? If so, there would seem to have to be some (non-existent) fact *there*, to be named, to be the "it."

[1] Perry writes, "although interest cannot exist without cognition, it can and does exist without cognition of itself." "In order that the interest itself shall be cognized it is necessary to introduce a new act of cognition . . ." (*General Theory of Value*, p. 358).

[2] Noting that one is at a higher level than the other would be more of a hindrance than a help. For if one of the two, fact and value, is about the other, it is clearly value, not fact, that plays this rôle, but it is interest, not cognition of interest, that creates value on Perry's view.

[3] "The judgment that there is money in my purse does not of itself tend to create the conditions of its own fulfilment. It signifies a disposition to deal with money *when* I open my purse, but not a disposition to open it. The desire that there shall be money in my purse, on the other hand, signifies that I am disposed to do that of which dealing with money is expected; and, therefore, that in so far as the expectation is true, the dealing with money will occur" (*ibid.*, pp. 346–7).

[4] "In judgment the act of indication releases the act of predication, and induces fulfilment or surprise according as the act of predication is or is not executed. In interest the fact that the act of indication and the act of predication are so connected is a condition of the occurrence of the act of indication. The act of indication occurs owing to the prospective occurrence of the act of predication" (*ibid.*, pp. 344–5).

This is indeed a far cry from saying that interest and judgment are two syntactically different kinds of sentences whose objects must, *qua* objects of such different sentences, be basically different in a way relevant to the distinction we seek between value and fact. But it is suggestive. May we not define value as the object (in the semantical sense—the designatum or that which is asserted) of a certain sort of sentence, the interest-sentence or value-sentence, parallel to a definition of fact as the object of a cognitive or descriptive sentence? I think we have a lead here which, though promising pitfalls, is worth careful exploration.

Before leaving Professor Perry's theory, however, it is important to note a way in which it remains recalcitrant to our treatment quite apart from any objection to translation from a behavioural into a semantical language. The suggestion made at the end of the preceding paragraph involves a parallel between 'interest' and 'cognition': they are both to be translated by 'sentence,' though the sentences involved will be syntactically different. This would involve our viewing value and fact as parallel. Just as fact is the sort of thing that cannot be referred to by a name but must be asserted by a descriptive sentence, so value would be something that could not be named but would have to be asserted by a different sort of sentence. The interest-sentence would have to be capable of falsity or some sort of semantical invalidity without becoming nonsensical: otherwise it would be just misleading to call it a "sentence." This requirement, it seems to me, fits common usage, but not Perry's theory, which allows that cognitions or mere judgments may be mistaken, but never interests. This is obscured by Perry's admission that the interest-judgment or cognition, which is embedded in the interest in the form of an expectation, may be mistaken.[1] But as we have already seen—in connection with the problem how the object of a false interest-judgment may still serve as a term of a natural relation—an interest which is mistaken in this sense is just as good as any other in conferring value; value is the being an object of *any* interest. Thus interest as a whole, *qua* interest, is never mistaken. There

[1] "This cognitive factor which is essential to the interest as such, or which *mediates* the interest as a whole, may be termed the interest-judgment; and its object is the object of the interest as a whole, or the end. It is the fallibility of this judgment which renders all interest fallible. As all judgment is liable to error, so all interest is by virtue of the interest-judgment liable to failure or disappointment" (*op. cit.*, p. 346).

are facts corresponding to true judgments but none corresponding to false ones; but for *every* interest there is a corresponding value. Thus 'interest' should not be translated 'interest-sentence' but 'interest-name' in our semantical terminology.

This anomaly becomes the more striking the longer one considers Perry's theory. In the first place, interest, as we have seen, includes cognition. Thus we would seem to be forced to say that a name (a value-term) can include a sentence (a descriptive sentence). And this inclusion would be literal—the name would include the sentence itself, not a name of the sentence, for interest is not about or directed toward its included judgment of expectation; rather, the latter determines what the former is about, it furnishes the object of the interest in its own object, which is only possible if it is used, not merely mentioned. This result would be most unfortunate: it would require that we undo all that we have achieved in distinguishing the semantical functions of names and sentences.

Moreover, Perry has put interest quite on a par with cognition in a different yet correlated duality, the duality of positive and negative.[1] This duality, though behaviourally stated, would seem to express the positive and negative of syntax, the association of any sentence with a sentence formed by negating it. The significance of this syntactical duality, from our standpoint, is its reflection of the semantical duality ordinarily expressed by the words 'true' and 'false.' This may be put in a falsity-condition: ' '*p*' is false if and only if not-*p*,' which parallels the truth-condition, ' '*p*' is true if and only if *p*,' and which, in conjunction with the latter, shows how the positive and negative of syntax are correlated with semantical truth and falsity. The anomaly then is that although the yes-and-no of cognition is, in Perry's system correlated with truth and falsity, the for-and-against of interest has no similar correlation. If a yes-judgment is true the corresponding no-judgment is false. But if a for-interest is valid (in the sense that the value actually does obtain) the corresponding against-interest is not necessarily invalid (its value failing to

[1] *Cf. op. cit.*, p. 115. Though Perry here says that the for-and-against of interest is not to be reduced to the yes-and-no of cognition, this is not because the former is not another instance of positive and negative nor because the latter is not a true case of behavioural for- and against-tendencies, but simply because, in interest, one can be for or against either a positive or a negative expectation. The positive and negative of interest seems to be at a higher level—to be about—the positive or negative of the included cognition.

obtain); each of the two, a for-interest and an against-interest in the same object, may be valid. This is indeed odd since it would seem to require, in translating Perry's remarks into our semantical terminology, that we replace his against-interest by a negative name. But *there are no negative names*. Thus a for-interest and its correlated against-interests are just different names, exactly on a par with two different for-interests, and they serve to name just two different values.

I think we are now in a position to see how Perry's theory of value may involve an objectionable type of relativism. But first it is well to point out certain other ways in which his theory may be taken to be relativistic. It is quite clear that on his theory the same thing can be both good and bad; a thing has these supposedly incompatible properties when it is the object of a for-interest and also of an against-interest. Suppose that 'being an object of an interest' and equivalent phrases refer simply to a natural relation between something and some interest, both of which are particulars, say events. Clearly then there is no theoretical objection to holding that the same thing may be both good and bad, that is, that it may be related as object of desire to one interest and object of aversion to another.[1] Indeed, there should be no theoretical objection to admitting, on this interpretation, that a given thing is both good and not good—*viz.*, when it is the object of one for-interest and not the object of another.[2] If this gives us pause it must be because we are not giving Perry's theory a wholly empirical interpretation.

There is another way in which Perry's theory may be said to be relativistic, which, though perhaps objectionable, is not objectionable in the sense in which I wish to urge that his theory is objectionably relativistic. I can here be brief because the ground

[1] "A term may always possess relational attributes in opposite senses, provided such relations are sustained toward different terms. The same physical object may be both 'to the right of' and 'to the left of,' both 'above' and 'below' . . ." (*op. cit.*, p. 136). Perry did not note, however, that in one important respect the parallel does not hold. 'Above' and 'below' refer to different relations, but 'object of interest' is the same, whether the interest be *pro* or *anti*. Thus we may say "*a* is both above and below" meaning "*a* is both above *b* and below *c*." But when, on Perry's account, we are permitted to say "*a* is both good and bad" this is to mean "*a* is related as object to both *b* and *c*." This is, perhaps, not unconnected with the fact that *b* and *c*, being here considered as directional (as for and against *a*), are tacitly treated as symbols: to develop this, however, carries us again into a semantical interpretation.

[2] Perry's parallel would be such a sentence as '*a* is both above and not above.'

has been thoroughly covered. Both the sentences, '*a* is good' and '*a* is bad' (indeed, both the sentences '*a* is good' and '*a* is not good') can be true, where '*a* is good' is to be interpreted "the speaker has a pro-interest toward *a*" and '*a* is bad,' "the speaker has an anti-interest toward *a*." (I suppose '*a* is not good' would analogously be assigned the meaning, "the speaker does not have a pro-interest toward *a*.") The objection urged against this relativism is that it renders any two speakers incapable of disagreeing on matters of good and bad.[1] Perry explicitly replies to this objection by distinguishing between the judgment that cognizes a value and the interest that creates a value.[2] Although the cognitions or beliefs (I would say the utterances, since here a behavioural event is in mind), '*a* is good' and '*a* is bad,' or again, '*a* is good' and '*a* is not good,' as spoken by different people or by the same person at different times, cannot *be* the same, they can *be about* the same supposed fact (*a*'s being the object of a certain interest). Thus disagreement is possible.[3] Now there is an objectionable feature still remaining. It is that this sort of relativism would make ordinary speech almost wholly ambiguous in its use of 'good' and other value terms. For everyday language almost never specifies the interest involved. It is as though people used 'above' without ever specifying what it was they were asserting *a* was above when they said '*a* is above,' not even in fact when they argued whether *a* was above or below or again whether *a* was or was not above. This is a serious indictment of common speech, and I would be inclined to demand the credentials of any view issuing in it. But this objection is hardly an objection to a relativistic outcome of the theory or, if it is, it is not to the sort of relativistic outcome to which I wish to object.

The objectionable sort of relativism may be called epistemological and is perhaps most easily grasped in the case of descriptive sentences not involving value-terms. Suppose one says that truth is relative in the sense that any descriptive sentence is true by virtue of the way it is made up, of its asserting what it asserts.

[1] This was formulated by G. E. Moore in his book, *Ethics*, ch. 3. I have suggested that Moore's famous elaboration of this type of objection is just a development of a passage in Bentham. *Cf.*, "The 'Proof' of Utility in Bentham and Mill," *Ethics*, vol. lx, 1949, p. 14.

[2] *General Theory of Value*, pp. 130–1 and *passim.*

[3] Professor Charles Stevenson has stated this much more clearly than Perry in "Moore's Arguments against Certain Forms of Ethical Naturalism" in *The Philosophy of G. E. Moore*, edited by Paul Schilpp.

Truth would then be wholly a function of sentences and not at all of facts. This is objectionable because, first, it gives us a redundancy. To say that a sentence asserting *f* is true is to say no more than to say that that sentence asserts *f*. Second, it takes away a perfectly good usage of 'true' which would have to be replaced in any adequate language (the relativist's language just omits this usage). I refer to the usage whereby 'the sentence asserting *f* is true' requires, when correctly used, that *f* be in the world, not merely asserted in the sentence.[1]

Probably no one has advocated this objectionable relativism in the nakedness in which I have just presented it. But clothed with accessories it often makes its appearance in respectable circles. I think this is the case in many of the writings of the sociologists of knowledge.[2] The accessories here are the socio-psychological facts involved in accepting and acting upon the truth of a sentence, and the changes in the meanings of such key words as 'true' as the social context of their occurrence changes. The pragmatists also furnish an example. A case in point is the contention of William James that we make our ideas true.[3] Here the accessory is the effect, upon the object, of our act of believing (including of course overt behaviour). Thus suppose the sentence is 'You like me.' If I believe this and act in accordance with it, I can make it true.

If these and similar accessories are stripped away, the epistemological relativism to which I am objecting is unattractive indeed. Yet I believe that is is involved in Perry's theory of value if that theory is susceptible of a semantical interpretation. If, that is, we are at all justified in translating 'interest' by 'interest-sentence,' then we are involved in the unpleasant consequence that all we need to know in order to ascertain the truth of an interest-sentence is just that sentence; the truth of an interest-sentence is a function merely of that sentence and not at all of the character of the world, specifically, of the nature of that item

[1] I have stated all this in incorrect language because it is so much easier. Indeed, I have doubts whether what I am saying could be said in a correct language. It would seem to me that a correct language would allow us to say no more than that certain sentences are true, not also that the facts they assert are in the world. This would avoid the vicious relativism I am attacking, but could not deny it, because it could not formulate it.

[2] Karl Mannheim is, I am convinced, guilty of it, despite the fact that he eschews the term 'relativism' in favour of 'relationism.' See his *Ideology and Utopia*, section v.

[3] *Cf.*, "The Will to Believe" in *The Will to Believe and Other Essays.*

which is the object of the sentence (save that it is the object of the sentence). This is no doubt another aspect of the contention that 'interest' really ought to be translated 'interest-name' not 'interest-sentence.' But then we must add, that to know that something is an interest-name we need only know *it*, not what it names. Designation of a value is automatic upon the coining of the word to do it. You cannot go wrong; if the syntactical requirements (whatever they may be) for a value-expression are met, then the semantical requirements for correctly designating or truly asserting a value are necessarily satisfied—more accurately, all semantical requirements are set aside, but the semantical relation (truth or designation) is retained. It seems to me that this is scarcely tenable.

Nor will Professor Perry's distinction between judgment of value and interest-judgment help here. The former judges that something is valuable, which, on Perry's view, means that it judges that some interest has that thing as its object. This judgment, Perry correctly says, may be false. In our semantical translation it is a meta-sentence. It says that some interest-name designates or some interest-sentence asserts the thing in question. This may be false in that there may be no such interest-expression, or, if the judgment of value specifies the interest-expression, it may specify one that does not have the thing in question as its object. This sort of meta-sentence may obviously be capable of falsity where the zero-level interest-expressions which are its objects are incapable of falsity (or have no designative requirements which they must satisfy).[1]

[1] It is necessary to insert a qualification at this point. This is demanded by the apparent contradiction that has arisen in our criticism of a type of relativism that may be involved in Perry's theory. First we say that this relativism lays down no semantical requirements for the basic semantical relation (whether truth or designation), while yet permitting that relation. Then we suggest that it is possible that no interest-expression stands in this relation to a given thing or again that a certain one does not. But this possibility presupposes sufficiently definite requirements that must be satisfied by the semantical relation for it to be possible to determine that it does not obtain in the case or cases in question. The qualification we must introduce to meet this apparent contradiction turns on the distinction between an interest and the interest-judgment it includes. The latter is, as I read Perry, a prediction (an "expectation"), that is, a descriptive sentence that may be true or false. Now it is one of Perry's major contentions that the interest creates a value quite independently of the truth-value of the interest-judgment (*cf.* above, p. 70). Clearly then we must distinguish, on our semantical interpretation, between the interest-expression and the descriptive sentence it somehow contains. Hence I suggest we reformulate our semantical interpretation of Perry's theory as follows.

Now of course it may be completely wrong to give Perry's theory of value a semantical interpretation. Perhaps his theory is wholly behavioural, perhaps 'object of an interest' is intended to refer simply to an event as related in an observable fashion to another event, and not in the least to a referent of a value-expression. I cannot *quite* feel that this is so because of the anomalies it would involve, as already pointed out. But, as I have said, our interest is systematic, not historical. If one were to define value as the being the referent of a value-expression, *any* value-expression without restriction, one would involve oneself in the serious difficulties which our discussion of the semantical interpretation of Perry's theory has brought to light. To get on we must consider the possibility of attaining an acceptable view by restricting the value-expressions permitted, or by setting up some requirement that must be satisfied before a value-expression can be allowed to designate or to be true, as the case may be.

5*b*. *Is value the fittingness of an attitude to its object?*

Reference was made earlier[1] to a recent view making fittingness, appropriateness, or suitability a fundamental value-concept.[2] There seems to be a great deal of ambiguity concerning the status of such a fittingness. So far as it is taken to be a relation between an act or an emotion as an event and its environment, whether merely immediate or as also including remote effects, it is irrelevant here,[3] for it would then be simply a first-order, natural relation. Likewise, when, as frequently seems to be the case, it is

For an interest-expression to stand in a semantical relation to some object, it must contain a descriptive-expression for this object, yet it designates or asserts an aspect of this object (its value) *not* designated or asserted by its descriptive component. Thus an interest-expression may be said to have a specifiable object (and in this sense to have to meet certain requirements) while in the aspect peculiar to it, the value-aspect, to be true or designative quite independently of any semantical requirements but just by virtue of its being (syntactically) an interest-expression.

[1] *Cf.* above, pp. 7–8.

[2] This view has perhaps been most fully explored by Ewing, *The Definition of Good*. However both he and Ross, who adopts it in *The Foundations of Ethics*, got it from Broad, *Five Types of Ethical Theory*. It seems quite clear that in some very broad fashion it derives from the Cambridge Platonists: *e.g.*, from the writings of Samuel Clarke and Richard Price. I think perhaps a case could be made out that these writers in turn were indebted to the Aristotelian doctrine of that which accords with nature, and to the Socratic-Pythagorian concept of the health (the harmony) of the soul.

[3] It was in this interpretation that it was discussed above in Section 2b.

taken to be a property of facts, then again it is no illustration of the view at present under consideration.[1]

But there are occasions when, though these authors are probably quite unaware of it, 'fitting' seems to take on a semantical complexion. I refer to that usage whereby emotions, desires, or even acts are said to be fitting or appropriate *to their objects*.[2] When it is said that an emotion or desire or attitude is appropriate to its object, it seems not wholly implausible to assume that 'object' is to some degree used in a semantical sense, and that such words as 'fitting' and 'appropriate' are meant to qualify the attitude in its function of being directed toward, of tactitly designating, its object. Indeed, though Broad uses 'fitting' indifferently in adjacent passages, one where it must clearly be taken as referring to a natural relation and the other where a

[1] Broad's rather contextualistic phraseology ("It seems to me that, when I speak of anything as 'right', I am always thinking of it as a factor in a certain wider total situation, and that I mean that it is 'appropriately' or 'fittingly' related to the rest of this situation," *op. cit.*, p. 164) might be interpreted in the first way, that is, as taking 'fitting' to designate a relation between a part and a whole, *i.e.*, between two particulars. However, there are hints that he has in mind a relation between various properties as exemplified by the same or possibly by different particulars, *i.e.*, a relation between facts, or again a relation between a particular and a fact or a set of facts ("The fittingness of an act to a whole course of events will be a function of its fittingness or unfittingness to each phase in the series, and its fittingness to any phase in the series will be a function of its fittingness or unfittingness to each factor or aspect of that phase," *ibid.*, p. 220).

[2] This is present even in Broad, though not perhaps as his most characteristic usage. "This [the thought of appropriateness to the rest of a situation] is quite explicit when we say that love is the right emotion to feel to one's parents, or that pity and help are the right kinds of emotion and action in the presence of undeserved suffering" (*ibid.*, p. 165). Here 'in the presence of' might be taken to refer to a merely spatio-temporal relation, though I think there are semantical overtones (pity *toward*, not merely when in proximity to, undeserved suffering); but in 'to feel to' the directedness, the referentiality of what is meant is apparent as soon as one's attention is called to it. Likewise, the prepositions 'towards' and 'at' in the statement, "In any possible world it would be fitting to feel gratitude towards one's benefactors and unfitting to feel pleasure at the undeserved suffering of another" (*ibid.*, p. 282), clearly indicate that we have here to do with objects. But perhaps most striking of all is the following: "I am almost certain that 'right' and 'ought' cannot be defined in terms of 'good.' But I am not sure that 'X is good' could not be defined as meaning that X is such that it would be a fitting object of desire to any mind which had an adequate idea of its non-ethical characteristics" (*ibid.*, p. 283). Here, 'fitting object of desire' can very plausibly be given and indeed almost demands a semantical interpretation though not necessarily an exclusively semantical interpretation.

This usage, somewhat incidental in Broad, becomes perhaps the most characteristic usage in Ewing. It is present in his definition of 'good.' "We may

semantical interpretation is plausible if not demanded,[1] Ewing comes very close to an explicit recognition that these are two different uses of 'fitting,' both being legitimate and perhaps both required in ethical theory. I have in mind passages where Ewing says that the rightness of an action is a matter of the appropriateness of the act to the situation whereas the goodness of an action is the fittingness of an attitude of moral admiration towards the act, and that the fittingness that constitutes goodness may depend upon the different fittingness which constitutes rightness.[2] Now I admit that I am going beyond the letter of Ewing's statement when I speculate that in this distinction of two fittingnesses he is groping for a differentiation between a natural relation (in the case of rightness) and a semantical relation (in the case of goodness). But it is an attractive speculation that will help us on our way.

However, even if it be granted to me that these philosophers sometimes use 'fitting object' and equivalent expressions in ways susceptible of a semantical or partially semantical interpretation, it may be denied that this permits me to use their theory as an example of the position that value is a referent of a semantical predicate. It may be that the semantical dimension is here used simply as a device to pick out those particulars or facts between

therefore define 'good' as 'fitting object of a pro attitude' . . ." (*op. cit.*, p. 152). It appears in his examples of good and evil. "It is more appropriate, or fitting, to feel disgust than pleasure at cruelty, more appropriate to desire reconciliation than revenge, to admire fidelity than clever cheating, to feel aesthetic emotions on contemplating great works of art than not to do so" (*ibid.*, p. 151). It is even present in his definition of 'moral obligation,' particularly in part (2). "We might say that 'A morally ought to do this' means (1) it would be fitting for A to do this, and (2) if he does not do it, it is fitting that he should be in that respect an object of the emotion of moral disapproval, or perhaps simply (2) without (1)" (*ibid.*, p. 168).

[1] I have in mind *ibid.*, pp. 164 and 165.

[2] "To say that an action is right is not the same thing as to say that it is good, for to call it 'good' would mean that not necessarily it but some pro attitude relative to it was fitting; but no doubt all right actions are good in some sense, for in relation to them some pro attitude is fitting. . . ." "For the fittingness of adopting an attitude of moral admiration towards an action depends on the rightness of the action (that is, its fittingness in certain respects) . . ." (*op. cit.*, pp. 171, 172). This same distinction of two senses of 'fitting' seems at the root of Ewing's contention that "it is a synthetic proposition that it is always fitting to produce the state of affairs that is most worthy of admiration (and not, I think, a true one" (*ibid.*, p. 190), where 'worthy of admiration' is used as equivalent to 'fitting object of admiration.' Ewing, I think means to assert in this passage that it is a synthetic proposition that in all cases that state of affairs which is most fitting as an object of admiration would itself fit the situation in which it occurred were it to be produced.

which the relation of fittingness is taken to hold. Thus when it is said that pity is the appropriate emotion towards those who suffer it may be meant that appropriateness holds between an occurrent emotion (pity) and certain actual people, *viz.*, the people picked out as the objects of that emotion, when it so happens that those people suffer. Or again, it may be meant that appropriateness holds between a certain occurrent emotion, *viz.*, pity toward those in suffering, and certain people, *viz.*, the objects of that emotion.

This, however, seems a rather strained interpretation. It would have a consequence that I would not suppose acceptable to the authors we are discussing. If the directedness or reference of the attitude is just a device for picking out one or both of the particulars, *viz.*, the attitude and something else between which it is asserted that the relation of appropriateness holds, then it is at least meaningful to hold that there are or may be cases of fittingness or appropriateness as holding between an attitude and something else when, though that attitude may have an object, its object is not the thing in question to which it is related as fitting or appropriate. Suppose, to take an absurdly simple case, I pity Jones, who is not suffering, and feel indifferent towards Smith, who is suffering. Then it would be significant, if the directedness of an emotion is only a device which we use to pick out the terms of the relation of appropriateness, to assert that my emotion of pity towards Jones is appropriate to Smith—not, be it noted, another pity that might occur, a pity towards Smith, but the very pity directed towards Jones. For the directedness of the emotion is only a device, and in this case I may have used a different device, say the use of a proper name, to pick out the terms between which appropriateness holds. Even if it be claimed that this is the only device available to us for picking out the terms between which appropriateness or inappropriateness holds (and on what grounds could this be based?) the unacceptable consequence would still obtain, that though we would be unable to make such a statement as 'my pity towards Jones is appropriate to Smith' still what cannot be said here might actually obtain. No, I would suppose that the directedness of an attitude toward an object is more integral to the fittingness here under discussion than simply to be the device whereby we can refer to the particulars or facts between which the fittingness obtains. What is this more intimate connection, if it is not the radical one of being some sort of thing asserted by a semantical predicate, a feature of the reference or directedness itself or a certain sort of reference?

It may be that I have over-simplified matters. We must not forget, even when considering an attitude as an event, that it is directed towards an object. Let us state this more carefully. An attitude, as an event, is more concrete than its directedness toward an object, and includes the latter.[1] Thus an attitude taken as an event, may exemplify an appropriateness which is integral to its directedness. This, *e.g.*, may be a matter of the relation between the sort of attitude it is (say pity) and its directedness (say towards someone who is suffering). Thus what is appropriate is that an attitude of such and such a sort be directed in such and such a direction and conversely.

Let us note first that this interpretation restricts us to what may be called a wholly subjective appropriateness or suitability. That is, the suitability is not a relation between the (total) attitude and something quite extra-attitudinal (*e.g.*, between pity and certain suffering people), but is a relation between elements in or features of (in the sense of facts about) the attitude itself (*e.g.*, between the attitude's being a pitying and its being directed toward suffering people). This would not necessarily conflict with value-objectivism, for it could be held that some attitudes really do exemplify, as a relation between aspects of themselves, this sort of suitability and that this sort of suitability is uniquely a value-feature. Yet it would commit one to the view that only attitudes (emotions, acts) exemplify this sort of value—not in relation to something else (some object or effect), but simply internally, as a feature of their own structure. Moreover, even in this realm it would become impossible to assert meaningfully that any attitude ought to occur that does not. 'Ought' (or whatever value-term we use to express this sort of suitability) would be a property of an attitude with a certain structure only if and when that attitude existed. One could say that attitude *a* (that does exist) ought (or ought not) to exist by virtue of its structure; but one could not say that an attitude with

[1] Although it will serve in the present context, I cannot ultimately accept this formulation. The event, which is the occurrence of an attitude, is a complex particular of which may be asserted some fact or facts which are the psychological or existential correlates of the reference or directedness (in a semantical sense) of the attitude. The reference, as such, is not an event or part of an event nor is it a fact.

some specified structure which does not exist nevertheless ought to. One could even say that were an attitude with a certain structure to exist it would be one that ought to exist, but this of course is not equivalent to saying that although such an attitude does not exist it nevertheless ought to. And it seems to me that common sense requires that we be able meaningfully to say the latter. Hence this, like all views making value a property, runs afoul of the principle of value's independence of fact.

Although arising from a somewhat different problem, the distinction made by W. D. Ross between objective and subjective suitability is not perhaps wholly irrelevant here.[1] Ross derives his distinction from H. A. Prichard's distinction between objective and subjective rightness, as found in the latter's lecture, *Duty and Ignorance of Fact*. Prichard is mainly concerned with the problem: Is moral obligation determined by the relation of an act to the total objective situation (including its effects) or by its relation to what the agent believes about the latter? This question is primarily oriented towards the problem of what has value—even more specifically, what has a certain sort of value, *viz.*, moral obligatoriness—rather than to the problem of what is value. Yet it has implications for the latter, particularly when these two forms of rightness (objective and subjective) are interpreted as two forms of suitability.

This relevance is seen particularly in an argument characteristic of Prichard. It is to the effect that rightness, taken as equivalent to oughtness or ought-to-be-done-ness, cannot possibly be a property of an act serving as the ground of our obligation to perform that act, since we are obliged before the act occurs and independently of whether the act occurs, yet this property could only be exemplified if and at the time the act actually occurred.[2] This, it seems to me, is a perfectly sound argument and is, in fact, simply an application of the general principle of value's independence of existence. But Prichard's conclusion from it seems to me wholly unwarranted. He concludes that obligatoriness (or some

[1] *Foundations of Ethics*, ch. vii.

[2] "But, as we recognize when we reflect, there are no such characteristics of an action as ought-to-be-doneness and ought-not-to-be-doneness. This is obvious; for, since the existence of an obligation to do some action cannot possibly depend on actual performance of the action, the obligation cannot itself be a property which the action would have, if it were done" (quoted by Ross, *op. cit.*, p. 155; this lecture is now available in *Moral Obligation*, the passage quoted being on p. 37). See also the passage quoted above, note [1], p. 54.

ought-character upon which it depends) is a property of some fact about the agent (specifically, it is a character of his setting himself to perform an act) and depends upon the agent's beliefs. Thus Prichard thinks he has established subjective rightness as the true nature of moral obligation.[1]

Prichard's conclusion is apparently derived by means of the assumption that if obligatoriness (or some character serving as its foundation) is not a property of acts it must be a property of agents or of certain facts about agents. Now even within the framework of an objectivism that admits there is moral obligatoriness, in the strong sense, a further alternative remains, *viz.*, that such obligatoriness is not a property at all, that it has a different ontological status. If it were a property, it could be present only when actually exemplified by something, only when that something existed. Now Prichard shows that acts can be obligatory when they do not exist. But is his 'setting oneself to act" in any better position? Surely setting oneself to act in a certain way may be morally obligatory at times (*e.g.*, when one has the appropriate beliefs about the nature and effects of the completed act)[2] when one is not actually setting oneself to act in this way. Prichard could reply that even so the agent must exist in order that there be obligation; he could even add (and here we have pure stipulation, all semblance of proof collapsing) that the agent must have certain beliefs if there is to be obligation. But this is of no avail, for it is not the agent or his thoughts that ought to be. Granted that the latter form a *conditio sine qua non* for there being an ought, in the form of moral obligation, we still ask, *What* ought to be or to be done? Clearly something which, in many instances, does

[1] The passage, quoted in the preceding footnote, continues: "What does exist is the fact that you, or that I, ought, or ought not, to do a certain action, or rather to set ourselves to do a certain action. And when we make an assertion containing the term 'ought' or 'ought not', that to which we are attributing a certain character is not a certain activity but a certain man." Since this character—of "being bound to set ourselves to do some action"—"is a character of ourselves, there is nothing to prevent its existence depending on our having certain thoughts about the situation and, therefore, about the nature of the activity in respect of the effects." Thus the truth is expressed in the form: "I ought to set myself to do so-and-so, because *I* think that it would have a certain effect."

[2] A lesser but still relevant objection of the same general type is that we want to be able to say that sometimes people ought to have, when they do not have, certain beliefs about the nature and outcome of certain completed acts, and that, moreover, this is quite independent of their having beliefs about these beliefs.

not exist or is not being done. Moreover, even if moral obligation were to be treated as a property of the agent, our difficulty would not be avoided. For it would clearly not be a quality of the agent; it would rather be a relation in which he stood to the act he was obligated to perform. But no two-term relation can be said to be exemplified unless both its terms exist. Thus it is improper to say I am characterized by sitting (on the chair) unless the chair exists. Similarly it should be improper to say I am obligated to fulfil my promise unless the fulfilment exists (or will exist). Turning from objective to subjective fact does not help in the least here.[1] I think the reason why it may be felt to be of significance for our problem lies in the semantical dimension involved in subjective fact.

This can, perhaps, be more clearly seen in Ross's translation of Prichard's views by means of Broad's analysis of oughtness as a certain fitness or suitability. Ross writes: "Now we may distinguish several different self-exertions [Prichard's 'setting oneself to do a certain action'] which might have some claim to be considered right, or what the agent ought to do: (A) The self-exertion which is morally most suitable to the objective circumstances. . . . (B) The self-exertion which is morally most suitable to the agent's state of mind about the circumstances. . . . (C) The self-exertion which he *thinks* to be morally most suitable in the circumstances as he takes them to be."[2] Although these are all legitimate senses of right, it is the doubly subjective (C) which, according to Ross, defines what the agent ought to do.

Our concern is not with what an agent ought to do or ought to set himself to do, but with the status of moral suitability, taken as a basic value-concept. Certainly one plausible, and no doubt the most plausible, interpretation of Ross's discussion is that he takes suitability to be a first-order relation holding between particular events: on the one hand the event of a self-exertion, on the other, a set of objective occurrences, or a set of beliefs about these, or finally a belief about suitability to a set of beliefs about objective circumstances. Read in this fashion, Ross's views are to be subsumed under the general view that value is

[1] I would not dispute that the *differentiae* of moral values, and specifically moral obligatoriness, must include some sort of reference to moral agency. What this is is not relevant to the present analysis of the generic status of value.

[2] *Op. cit.*, p. 161.

a property, and must meet the difficulties involved in such a view.[1] But it should be noted that the events here (particularly in (B) and (C) between which suitability obtains) are subjective; they involve a cognitive, thus a referential, aspect. This is clear in the phrases 'state of mind about' and 'thinks to be.' It is not so clear in the term 'self-exertion.' Prichard's phrase is more illuminating: 'setting oneself to do a certain action.' Such an occurrence involves an intention to act in a certain way. Thus it might not be completely arbitrary to suggest that (B) be interpreted so that the suitability holds between the intention or reference to an act and the reference to certain (believed) circumstances, and (C) so that suitability holds between the intention of an act and reference to a suitability of the sort specified in (B). But to make this fit the way in which Ross writes, it is necessary to avoid an extreme semantical interpretation. It would seem highly inappropriate to ascribe to him the view that moral suitability is a relation between two references *qua* references. It would seem the farthest we can go in this direction, with any historical conscience, is to take moral suitability as obtaining between acts or events of referring. However, this would not only reopen all the old issues, but even add a new one. For are mere acts of referring ever related morally, do they exemplify obligatoriness? Does, *e.g.*, the occurrence of a reference to an act of benevolence stand in any specifically moral relation of obligatoriness to the occurrence of a reference to needy people? And even if sometimes it does, can this be all there is to our duty to be benevolent to the needy (as our present interpretation of Ross's (C) would require)? To say so seems absurd, and would no doubt be even shocking to the moralistic sensibilities of Sir David.

However, I think we have some slight justification in giving a semantical interpretation to some of the statements made by Ross about fittingness or suitability, as also some of those made by Broad, and quite a bit of justification in reading certain statements of Ewing in this way. In this interpretation the theory before us says that value is the being referred to (whether this means being designated or being asserted must still be determined)

[1] Particularly, it must answer: How can there be rightness (moral suitability) when the terms between which it is said to hold do not exist? Surely it may be right, suitable, our duty to exert ourselves in a certain way when we do not do so, and thus when our self-exertion stands in no relation of suitability to anything else at all.

by a fitting, suitable, or appropriate value-expression.[1] Our problem now becomes, Just what do such terms as 'fitting,' 'suitable,' 'appropriate' mean when given this semantical interpretation?

If we look to our authors we find ourselves apparently estopped. Broad tells us that the concept in question is unanalysable.[2] Ewing accepts it as undefined,[3] and indeed suggests that a non-naturalist ethical theory based upon it as the only undefined ethical concept has the advantage, in the controversy between naturalists and non-naturalists, of providing the minimum non-naturalist theory.[4]

Yet we are not left completely helpless. Ewing in particular, no doubt more inadvertently than intentionally, lets fall several suggestions that may be of aid. It would seem that there is some analogy between the fittingness of a fitting attitude and the truth of a true (descriptive) proposition. This analogy is explicitly drawn at one place where Ewing is attempting to show that his view does not involve a vicious infinite regress.[5] But of far more importance than such an incidental statement is a general structural similarity adumbrated by Ewing, though never, to my knowledge, explicitly pointed out, between the fittingness and unfittingness of attitudes on the one hand, and the truth and falsity of descriptive propositions on the other.

Let us note first that, analogously with affirmative and negative propositions, Ewing classifies attitudes as "pro" and "anti," specifying that the former are positive and the latter negative

[1] To translate 'attitude' or cognate terms by 'value-expression' is misleading in that it seems to require that the symbols involved be in a conventional language. This of course is quite irrelevant. What is necessary is that 'attitude' and similar words be taken *as* symbols in this semantical interpretation.

[2] He says that "the kind of appropriateness and inappropriateness which is implied in the notions of 'right' and 'wrong' is, so far as I can see, specific and unanalysable" (*op. cit.*, p. 165).

[3] " 'Fitting' must not be itself defined in terms of another fittingness or of anything else whatever" (*op. cit.*, p. 176).

[4] *Ibid.*, p. 169.

[5] " 'It is fitting to approve,' I suppose, entails 'it is fitting to approve of approving A,' and so on *ad infinitum*; but it is no objection to the truth of a proposition that it would entail the truth of an infinite number of propositions. . . . It is no objection to our knowing the truth of the proposition that 'London is the capital of England' to say that it entails that it is true that it is true that London is the capital of England and so on *ad infinitum*" (*ibid.*, pp. 176–7).

towards their objects.[1] Again, just as there are true and false propositions of both kinds, affirmative and negative, so there are fitting and unfitting attitudes of both kinds, pro and anti. And although Ewing sometimes uses some such phrase as 'attitude we ought to take' as synonymous with 'fitting attitude,' and, again, 'attitude we ought not to take' as synonymous with 'unfitting attitude,' he makes it clear that 'ought' here is not meant to involve moral obligation to adopt the attitude, but simply the attitude's fittingness to its object.[2] Thus, following out this analogy, just as one might say that belief is the appropriate attitude to take towards a fact and that disbelief is inappropriate, so one says that a pro attitude is the fitting attitude toward an object which is good, whereas an anti attitude would be unfitting. Thus we can see emerging a common pattern, though one which Ewing does not recognize explicitly. Affirmative and negative propositions are associated with truth and falsity. If either is true the other is false; if either is false the other is true. Moreover, the statement that an affirmative proposition is true must in some fundamental way be equivalent to the proposition itself, and the statement that it is false must likewise be equivalent to the negative correlate of the proposition. Analogously, pro and anti attitudes towards the same object are associated with fittingness and unfittingness. If either is fitting the other is unfitting, and if either is unfitting the other is fitting. Moreover, the statement that a pro attitude is fitting is in some basic sense equivalent to the pro attitude itself, and the statement that it is unfitting is likewise equivalent to the correlated anti attitude.

[1] " 'Pro attitude' is intended to cover any favourable attitude to something. It covers, for instance, choice, desire, liking, pursuit, approval, admiration" (*op. cit.*, p. 149). "But we can see various attitudes I have mentioned to have something in common that is opposed to the common element in condemning, shunning, fearing, regretting, etc., which would supply the corresponding definition of 'bad.' The former may be called pro attitudes, the latter anti attitudes. The former are positive and favourable to their objects, the latter negative and hostile" (*ibid.*, p. 150).

[2] "But what is the sense of 'ought' when we say we ought to have a pro attitude to what is good and an anti attitude to what is bad?" ". . . it seems . . . obvious to me that we are thinking of 'ought' in the sense in which it signifies fittingness rather than moral obligation. For I cannot by an act of will desire, approve, or admire something" (*ibid.*, pp. 150, 151). These passages lend verisimilitude to the interpretation that would have 'fitting' and 'unfitting' semantical predicates analogous to 'true' and 'false.' It must however be pointed out that in context they do not avoid the suggestion that 'fitting' and 'unfitting' are elliptical for 'fitting to adopt' and 'unfitting to adopt.' We must here again read beyond such occurrence-features to arrive at the semantical theory we are trying to articulate.

If this analogy can be carried through—and I repeat that in doing so we have gone far beyond our author—we may then interpret Ewing as saying that 'good' may be defined as 'object of a fitting pro attitude' in a fashion analogous to the definition of 'fact' as 'object of a true, affirmative, descriptive proposition,' and similarly that 'bad' may be defined as 'object of a fitting anti attitude' in a fashion similar to a definition of 'non-fact' as 'object of a true, negative, descriptive proposition.'[1] This way of dealing with value raises many serious issues, some of which will be discussed in later contexts, others of which, I fear, will have to be left entirely without consideration in the present essay. Just now I wish to turn to one other feature of Ewing's type of analysis.

In discussing Perry's theory of value we found a serious defect. Perry would have every interest, indiscriminately, confer value on its object. In our semantical interpretation this made interest-expressions names, whereas we saw they should be sentences and thus capable of an invalidity, comparable, in some sense, to the falsity of descriptive sentences. This defect is overcome in such an analysis as Ewing's. In our semantical reading, 'attitude' becomes 'value-sentence' and value-sentences are capable of invalidity (of being unfitting or inappropriate).

On the other hand, we saw in Perry's theory an element that made it agree in an obvious sense with everyday language but which was quite incompatible with our translation of 'interest' by 'value-term'; in fact it seemed to demand, if we gave a linguistic interpretation of his theory at all, that we translate 'interest'

[1] There could still be an important way in which truth and fittingness would not be analogous. This might be indicated, somewhat cryptically and certainly misleadingly, by saying that for 'fitting' and 'unfitting' the law of excluded middle does not hold. This dissimilarity is suggested in the following passage: "Now, if 'good' is taken as unanalysable, 'bad' will also have to be so taken, for it certainly is a positive notion and not merely equivalent to 'not good.' But if we analyse good as 'fitting object of a pro attitude,' it will be easy enough to analyse bad as 'fitting object of an anti attitude' . . ." (*op. cit.*, p. 168). If 'bad' is not properly taken as the negative of 'good,' while yet it is incompatible with good, it would seem that we must accept some neutral value. This, in developing the analogy with which we are here concerned, would suggest that, unlike descriptive propositions, attitudes must be capable of a third form: besides pro and anti attitudes, there would have to be attitudes of indifference, whose fittingness would serve to define an object of neutral value. As a matter of fact, as the sequel will show, this very dissimilarity in structure between value-sentences (as I shall speak of attitudes) and descriptive sentences can be used to argue for a type of linguistic formulation of value-objectivism.

by 'value-sentence.' For interest also includes a judgment, in the form of an expectation. This corresponds to the descriptive content, that what-it-is that is valued, in our everyday value-sentences As we have urged repeatedly, we attach value (whether positive or negative) to the fact that something is or may be the case. Thus in some way every value-sentence must include its correlated descriptive sentence.

Now there seems to be something comparable to this in the view that makes fittingness the fundamental value-concept. It should be immediately pointed out that there are differences. The descriptive element is not characterized as an expectation, as with Perry. This is a distinct advantage. It allows attitudes that could not with propriety be classified as desires to confer value. In our translation, it does not restrict the content of value-sentences to those having reference to the future. On the other hand, the relation of the descriptive element to the attitude is left indefinite. Unlike Perry, who had the interest include the interest-judgment, Broad and Ewing do not specify that the fitting attitude itself include any reference to the factual characteristics of its object, although it is clear that such a reference occurs somewhere. Again translating their statements, it is clear that for value-sentences to have validity it is necessary that there be[1] certain descriptive sentences having the same objects and stating what might be called the factual basis of value, but it is not clear whether these descriptive sentences are to be included in the value-sentences. Yet if the relationship between a fitting attitude and an associated factual description of its object is not clearly stated by these philosophers, they are quite clear in their insistence that the former requires the latter if one is to analyse value in terms of fitting attitude.[2]

[1] It would seem moreover that they must be true. If they may be false, something like Ross's distinction between subjective and objective suitability would seem to be required.

[2] This is obviously implicit in Broad's statement, already quoted in another connection, "I am not sure that 'X is good' could not be defined as meaning that X is such that it would be a fitting object of desire to any mind which had an adequate idea of its non-ethical characteristics" (*Five Types of Ethical Theory*, p. 283). Here I would suppose the clause, 'which had an adequate idea of its non-ethical characteristics' might be translated in our suggested terminology by some such expression as, 'which accepted an adequate set of true descriptive propositions about X.' It would seem that Broad is requiring that, for a desire for X to be fitting, a true description of X must occur in the same mind. This does not seem to be involved in the position as stated by

This requirement, it seems to me, lends plausibility to the semantical reading we have given this view. It quite directly shows, as Ewing recognizes,[1] that 'good' is not an ordinary, descriptive predicate. It is a predicate that can properly be used only when and because certain descriptive predicates can be used. Perhaps one is not too audacious in suggesting that it is a predicate concerning the propriety of the use of certain descriptive predicates, a predicate analogous to 'true' but not to be confused with it—though certainly this is not actually said anywhere by Ewing.[2] This would no doubt require that descriptive predicates be allowed to occur in other than declarative sentences, and that it be in these other sentences that their occurrence be said to be fitting or unfitting (as contrasted with the truth or falsity of their occurrence in declaratives). These other sentences would, to carry further this speculation, be value-sentences, or, to return to Ewing's terminology, pro and anti attitudes. Good would then be the referent of 'fitting' as a semantical predicate asserted of an affirmative value-sentence, a predicate analogous to 'true' as asserted of an affirmative declarative sentence. Bad would be the referent of 'fitting' as a semantical predicate asserted of a negative

Ewing. He writes, "It will be objected against me that it is only fitting to approve, or have a pro attitude towards, what is good because we first believe it to be good and that, if we did not believe it to be good, there would be no ground for such an attitude, so that the attitude would not be fitting. The answer is that the ground lies not in some other ethical concept, goodness, but in the concrete, factual characteristics of what we pronounce good. Certain characteristics are such that the fitting response to what possesses them is a pro attitude, and that is all there is to it" (*The Definition of Good*, p. 172). "To say it is fitting to approve A is to say that A is of such a nature as to call for our approval. We can only see whether we ought to have a pro attitude towards something by seeing what the nature of that something is, and the right pro attitude is dictated by its nature. We do not first learn what attitudes towards A are fitting and then decide that A is good; on the contrary to learn that certain attitudes towards A are fitting is to learn that A is good" (*ibid.*, p. 176).

[1] "Another argument in favour of my view is that it explains the fact that goodness is on the face of it a quite different concept from that of any ordinary quality. There is obviously a sense in which one could give a complete description of something without saying whether it was good or bad, which fact shows goodness to be something different from an ordinary quality of the thing which is pronounced good." "If something is a fitting object of a pro attitude at all, it could not fail to be so without its factual nature being different from what it is. Yet fittingness is still not itself a part of its factual nature" (*ibid.*, pp. 200, 201).

[2] This would make sense of Moore's vague contention that good is a non-natural property (*cf.* above, note [2]9 p. 5) as well as of Ross's characterization of right as a "resultant attribute." (*Cf. Foundations of Ethics*, p. 168, and my remarks on this characterization, *Philosophy of Science*, vol. xiv, 1947, pp. 339–40).

value-sentence, or of 'unfitting' as a predicate asserted of an affirmative value-sentence.

It seems to me that we have here a view that is worthy of most serious consideration. Before criticizing it, however, it is well to trace it in a contribution to axiology to which much more careful attention should be given than ever actually has been.

5*c*. *Is value the being an object of a right love?*

In Franz Brentano[1] we approach most nearly an unequivocal exponent of the view that value-terms are semantical predicates and thus do not refer strictly to any property of anything. But even here it is necessary to read beyond or to abstract from Brentano's psychologism. This is not as arbitrary as might appear. In the first place, Brentano himself lays the foundation for a clear distinction between psychology and ethics.[2] Moreover, his psychology, though characterized by him as empirical or descriptive, very obviously tries to come to grips with questions we now designate semantical.

All psychical phenomena are intentional or referential, according to Brentano. But of the three fundamental classes of them, namely, ideas, judgments, and feelings, the last two bear a resemblance to each other not extending to the first, a resemblance which clearly demands that we translate them in our linguistic terminology by 'sentences' (specifically, by 'declarative sentences' and 'value-sentences' respectively) whereas the first should be translated 'names.' This resemblance between judgments and feelings is found in an opposition in their intentionality (as contrasted with their content, which indeed is furnished by the first class). With judgment this is affirmation-denial; with feeling it is love-hate. This opposition carries with it a further distinction not applicable to ideas. One of these opposite intentions is right

[1] I have in mind particularly his lecture, *The Origin of the Knowledge of Right and Wrong* (English translation by Cecil Hague, Westminister, 1902), although portions of his *Psychology from the Empirical Standpoint* (Leipzig, 1874) are also relevant. I shall refer to the former as *The Origin* and the latter as *Psychology*, vol. i, to distinguish it from the second edition, 1924 ff., which, in vol. ii, contains some important appendices by Brentano.

[2] This seems unquestionable in his elucidation of the concept of natural sanction (*The Origin*, sections 6–11), where he likens ethical law to logical law, and in his contention that the fundamental problem of ethics is, Which end is right?, a question distinguishable from, What is the origin of our knowledge of what end is right? (*ibid.*, sections 6–18).

and one wrong. "We call anything true when the recognition related to it [*i.e.* the affirmation of it] is right. We call something good when the love relating to it is right."[1] Contrariwise, we call anything false when the denial of it is right, and bad when hate of it is right.

On this view, then, feelings are intentional in a twofold way. First, they are intentional in the way all psychical phenomena are: they are directed toward something which is "inexistentially present" in them; they have objects.[2] Second, this directedness is either positive (love, enjoyment, pleasure) or negative (hate, sorrow, displeasure), and in every case one of these is right, the other wrong.[3]

The first sort of intentionality of feelings is important for us only as an understanding of it helps to reveal that the second sort, which is peculiar to feelings, is complex and includes the intentionality belonging to ideas. That is, a linguistic rendering of Brentano's position requires us to say that the kind of reference characteristic of value-expressions is complex and includes that form which is proper to names. The relation is that between the way a value-sentence (a feeling) asserts and the way a name in that sentence (an idea) designates.[4] The second sort of intentionality of feelings, on the other hand, is very much to the point in our analysis of value. Before turning to criticism of this notion, however, it is necessary, in view of the extreme brevity

[1] *Op. cit.*, sect. 23, p. 16. Brentano apparently does not note that in his account 'good' is not analogous to 'true.' 'True,' in its strict usage (its first or non-metaphorical use, *cf. ibid.*, note 25, p. 69), is a predicate taking judgments as subjects, whereas 'good' is a predicate having not feelings, but rather the objects of feelings, as subjects. The strict analogue of 'good' in judgments is 'existence.' Just as '*x* is good' is for Brentano definitionally equivalent to '*x* is the object of a right love,' so '*x* exists' is definitionally equivalent to '*x* is the object of a right affirmation or recognition.'

[2] "We say, one enjoys, one is pleased over something, one grieves or sorrows over something" (*Psychology*, vol. i, p. 117).

[3] There is the question whether feelings do not contain judgments as well as ideas and are not thus intentional in a threefold manner. *Cf.* below, p. 106 and footnote [1] thereto.

[4] The intentionality of feeling includes that of presentation but not *vice versa*. The idea is incapable of mistaken reference. "In the presentation there is *no virtue and no moral evil, no knowledge and no error*. All this is inwardly foreign to it, and above all we can speak of a representation as morally good or evil, as true or false, only in an homonymous way, as, *e.g.*, one presentation is termed evil since we sin in loving that which is presented, and another false, since we err in asserting that which is presented . . ." (*Psychology*, vol. i, p. 292).

of Brentano's exposition, to elucidate his views here somewhat further and at our own risk, especially as they turn on the concept of 'right.'

Let us begin by noting a distinction urged by G. E. Moore, namely, the distinction between a right love and the rightness of such a right love. By making this distinction, Moore is able to deny that 'right love' is the ultimate ethical concept. Rightness is more fundamental, and it is legitimate to ask whether there are not other things besides a right love that are right, and whether there may not be cases of objects of a right love that do not themselves possess the property of rightness.[1]

Moore's criticism here assumes that 'right' designates a property, a property that can be exemplified by love but also by

[1] The formulation in the text does not literally reproduce the passage, to be found in a review of the English translation of Brentano's *The Origin*, which I have in mind, but it does seem to present one aspect of the argument, and to my mind the most cogent. There are other subtle misrepresentations connected with this basic one. *E.g.*, Moore speaks of beautiful objects as possessing the quality of being worthy of love to a higher degree than they possess the quality of rightness. Brentano would say that there is no quality of worthiness of being loved which an object could possess which is anything over and above the rightness of a love directed towards that object. Just as it is only metaphorically correct to speak of a true object, meaning an object the affirmation of which is right, so it is only metaphorically legitimate to speak of a worthy, a good, a right object, meaning strictly an object the love of which is right (*cf. The Origin*, note 25, pp. 69–70). The passage from Moore's review is: "Brentano is wrong in supposing that the conception 'rightly loved' or 'worthy of love' is the fundamental ethical concept which we mean by 'good in itself.' Sidgwick was right in holding that the concept is unanalysable; and it is, in fact, the concept which Brentano denotes by the word 'right,' when he says that a thing is good in itself, if the love of it would be *right*. Brentano recognizes *two* very important concepts when he recognizes both the concept of what it is right to love and of the *rightness* which belongs to love of such things; and the question which of these is properly denoted by the words good in itself might seem to be merely a verbal question. But it is not a merely verbal question, if, as Brentano rightly does, we take what is good in itself in the highest possible degree to be that of which it is our *duty* to promote the existence. For whereas the degree in which a thing possesses the quality which he calls 'right' must be taken into account in considering what is the greatest possible good which it is our duty to effect, the degree in which things are 'worthy to be loved' is not a measure of our duty to effect their existence. It is certain that many things, *e.g.*, inanimate beautiful objects, possess the quality of being worthy to be loved, in a higher degree than they possess that of 'rightness'; it may even be doubted whether they possess the latter at all. And it is our duty to effect that which is the most 'right' possible, not that which is most worthy to be loved. Though therefore we can agree with Brentano that everything which is good in itself is worthy to be loved, we cannot agree that everything which is worthy to be loved is good" (*International Journal of Ethics*, vol. xiv, 1903–4, pp. 115–16).

other things. This assumption however would make it completely illegitimate to treat Brentano as an exponent of the semantical view we are here considering. It was admitted above that to treat him as such an exponent does involve an abstraction from his psychological characterizations. This of course may be termed a falsification.[1] Happily, we do not need to decide this issue here. Our present interest is analytic and systematic, not historical. So far then as Brentano is used as an example of the view that value is basically a semantical predicate (wherein, *e.g.*, 'good' is defined as being an object of a right love), Moore's criticism as set out above is irrelevant, since it rests upon a tacit rejection of the view itself.

Now of course even granting that 'right' is a semantical predicate, it is important that we distinguish this predicate from subjects of which it is properly asserted. Brentano would say it is predicable of judgments and feelings.[2] Thus it is legitimate to distinguish the rightness of a right love from the right love, just as it is legitimate to distinguish the truth of a true proposition from the true proposition. But does it follow that 'rightness,' not 'right love,' is the ultimate ethical concept? Clearly not in any sense that would allow 'right' to be predicable of anything

[1] In discussing our knowledge of good, Brentano speaks of our experience of higher feelings. "We therefore notice when we ourselves have such a feeling, that its object is not merely loved and lovable, its opposite hated and unlovable, but also that the one is worthy of love, the other worthy of hatred, and therefore that one is good, the other bad" (*The Origin*, sect. 27, p. 20). In a note to this passage, the English translator writes: "This phrase ['Als richtig characterisiert'], which occurs frequently, I have translated sometimes as above, sometimes by 'qualified as right.' By this phrase and its equivalents is meant that the act (*sc.* of loving, hating, or preferring), is at once perceived by us to be a right one, bears the mark or character of rightness" (*ibid*, note 31, p. 85). All this, obviously, lends weight to the interpretation of 'right' as a descriptive predicate, designating an observable property of particulars. Against this however must be placed Brentano's repeated comparison of ethics with logic, and his use of 'right' to define 'true' (as rightly affirmed) as well as 'good' (as rightly loved). If it be said that for him 'true' and 'false' are descriptive predicates, one must at least note that he is very acutely aware of their peculiarities. Compare for example the following: ". . . whether I say an affirmative judgment is true, or its object is existent; whether I say a negative judgment is true, or its object is non-existent: in both cases I am saying one and the same thing" (*The Origin*, note 25, p. 70), and "When we say 'A is,' this sentence is not, as many have believed and still believe, a predication, in which existence as predicate is united with A as subject: The object which we assert is not a union of a characteristic 'existence' with 'A' but 'A' itself" (*Psychology*, vol. i, p. 276).

[2] Dropping the psychological overtones, we might say it is predicable of sentences—declarative and valuative.

but feelings (and judgments).[1] Thus 'right' in this sense has no meaning apart from its meaning in the phrase 'right feeling' (and 'right judgment'). Feelings may be wrong, *i.e.*, not right, but to speak of the contrast between right and wrong would be elliptical for speaking of the contrast between right feeling and wrong feeling.[2] So it is legitimate to distinguish the inquiry: What things specifically are the objects of right love (or what loves of specific objects are right) from the inquiry as to the nature of right love, but this cannot be made the basis—as Moore apparently attempts to make it—for denying the legitimacy of a semantical position in value-theory which defines good as being the object of a right love.

However, in line with his general position at the time he wrote, Moore might have contended that, though Brentano claimed to be an objectivist in ethics,[3] he had really embraced a subjectivistic view. To put it crudely: the supposed goodness and badness of things are not really properties or features of those things; when we suppose this we are mistaking characteristics of our feeling towards things with properties of the things.[4]

[1] Whether there be *two* semantical rightnesses is discussed below.

[2] A semantical predicate does not refer to a positive character in the world that could exist by itself. *E.g.*, in the semantical sense of 'truth' there *could be* no truth apart from true sentences (or propositions).

[3] With the exception of Herbart, "no one, expecially among those who hold that in the foundation of [ethical] principles the feelings must find a place, has so radically and completely broken with the subjective view of ethics" (*Principia Ethica*, Preface, p. ix).

[4] There may be a hint of this line of criticism (despite the complete failure to distinguish descriptive, semantical, and syntactical predicates) in Ross's discussion of Brentano's doctrine (though he refers to a later exponent, G. Katkov). "The Brentano school holds that 'good' belongs to a class of merely apparent predicates" such as 'good,' 'bad,' 'possible,' 'impossible,' 'existent,' 'non-existent.' These "form a class of *Scheinqualitäte* consisting in relations to certain mental activities 'characterized as right.' " Consider 'possible' as asserted of a square: "the square is not possible because a right act of thought rejects the rejection of it; a right act of thought rejects the rejection of it because the square is possible. Our thought that a square is possible can be right only if and because there is a real relation of compatibility between the attributes of equal-sidedness and equal-angledness in a quadrilateral" (*Foundations of Ethics*, pp. 280, 281). By parallel reasoning, Ross might have argued that a love of something can be right only if and because that something has a real property of goodness. But Ross, probably because he himself wishes to deny that goodness is a "constituent property" of anything, does not say this, but more feebly contends, "The theory about the nature of goodness is therefore deprived of any support which it might be supposed to derive from being able to class predications of goodness with other judgments which, while they seem to be about objects, are really about activities of mind directed towards these objects"

Such a contention gains force from Brentano's psychological terminology.[1] Even if we replace that terminology by a more semantical one, however, a certain sort of subjectivism remains. Good and bad are ruled out of the world, to be replaced by features of our references to things. They are like existence and non-existence. 'Existence' is no descriptive predicate; it is just the correlate of a true affirmative judgment (declarative sentence). To say that *A* exists is just to say that the affirmation of *A* is true. Similarly 'good' is no descriptive predicate; it is just a correlate of a right love (positive valuative sentence). To say that *A* is good is just to say that a positive valuation of *A* is right.

Alfred Tarski's famous condition for any definition of 'truth'[2] (the definition must have as a consequence that '*p*' is true if and only if *p*) may have some relevance to this issue. It is ordinarily read (and apparently Tarski so meant it) so as to fit a correspondence theory of truth, such as Aristotle's. Thus, for example, it requires of a definition of truth that it have the consequence ' 'Chicago is large' is true if and only if Chicago is large.' It seems to say a declarative sentence is true only when what it asserts is a fact. But note that 'if and only if' is symmetrical. Hence this same condition can be formulated: '*p* if and only if '*p*' is true.' Thus it is compatible with a type of semantical subjectivism that reduces

(*op. cit.*, p. 281), revealing that he, like Moore, has not grasped the notion of a semantical, as contrasted with a descriptive, predicate, and thinks of Brentano as simply trying to shift 'good' from a property of things to a property of psychical acts.

[1] Thus it leads Howard O. Eaton to formulate Brentano's position in the following way: ". . . it is Brentano's purpose to show that all values come from the operation of this third faculty [feeling] itself, and do not exist as independent entities in the objective world. . . . to say that B is good is not to perceive the goodness of B as one would its colour or smell; . . . it is the assertion that if anyone accept (or reject) B, he does so rightly. In summarizing his position with regard to the phenomena of the class of love-hate, Brentano insists: 'A phenomenon of this class is not a judgment: "this is lovely," or "this is hateful" (that would be a judgment concerning goodness or badness); but it is a loving or a hating' [*Psychology*, 2nd ed., vol. ii, p. 90]. Thus, according to Brentano, values are the products of the functioning of this third faculty of love and hate, just as intended truth and falsehood are the products of the functioning of the second faculty of judgment . . ." (*The Austrian Philosophy of Values*, pp. 52, 53). This probably errs in the direction of a psychologistic reading of Brentano as much as I have erred in the direction of a semantical interpretation.

[2] *Cf.* his contribution to "Symposium on Meaning and Truth," *Philosophy and Phenomenological Research*, vol. iv, 1944, reprinted in Feigl and Sellars, *Readings in Philosophical Analysis*, pp. 52–84.

facts to true sentences, that says, for example, that the fact that Chicago is large is nothing but the being true of the sentence 'Chicago is large.'[1] Now it seems to me that so far as Brentano has a distinctive position in value-theory, which I have stated as semantical and as involving the denial that value is a property, he is holding that goodness is not in the world, that to say that *A* is good just is to say that a love of *A* (a positive valuative sentence with '*A*' as its content) is right. That is, were we to formulate a rightness-condition for Brentano it would correspond to Tarski's truth-condition but (to produce the right ontological suggestions) with the sides interchanged: '*A* is good if and only if a love of *A* is right.' Here on our semantical interpretation 'a love of *A*' must be treated not as a description of a psychological act but as an obscure way of referring to an affirmative value-sentence about *A*. So we replace it by a name of such a sentence as '*A* is good' and we have '*A* is good if and only if '*A* is good' (*i.e.*, a love of *A*) is right.' This is to be taken in the sense which reduces '*A* is good' to ' '*A* is good' is right,' not *vice versa*. *A*'s being good just *is* the being right of the sentence '*A* is good' (Brentano would say the being right of the love of *A*). Such a view takes value out of the world entirely.[2] Value becomes simply a feature of certain references to things. Obviously this is incompatible with the objectivism within which the present essay in analysis operates.[3] It should therefore be dropped from further consideration here, not as false nor as self-contradictory but as irrelevant. However, certain

[1] This "reduction upwards" as it might be called is not ordinarily envisaged because the sentence that is used (as contrasted with its name in the sentence predicating 'true') is conceived to be a sentence in an independently interpreted object-language. But the equivalence itself does not require this. It, as a whole, is in just one language, usually referred to as the meta-language. And the sentence in the object-language that corresponds to what usually constitutes the right-hand side of the equivalence need not be interpreted. Thus though we must not say that this object-language sentence means (*i.e.*, refers to or asserts) the sentence formed of its name and the predicate 'true' we may say that it means only what this latter means, that it has no independent meaning, and that therefore clarity requires that it be replaced by the latter. This would be a semantical variety of epistemological subjectivism.

[2] It does not simply take it out of the physical world and put it in the psychical, nor does it simply assert that value is "produced by" certain mental acts.

[3] It is not subjectivistic, however, in the sense of making value relative to the individual or group, *i.e.*, to the propounder of the valuative sentence (or to the person who loves or hates). This is clear from many passages in Brentano. See, *e.g.*, *The Origin*, note 28, especially pp. 79–81.

criticisms of it may throw light upon, and also serve as a transition to, a view as to the status of value which is compatible with objectivism yet does not make value a property in the ordinary sense.

In the first place such a subjectivistic view, whether of existence or of value, raises the embarrassing questions of a criterion of truth or rightness and of its relation to the nature of truth or rightness.[1] Truth and rightness are here of course ultimate concepts; existence and value are defined in terms of them and not *vice versa*. How then can we set up a criterion of them? It would seem it must be either arbitrary or a form of self-evidence. Brentano is aware of this dilemma, and chooses the latter alternative. What judgments are true is finally determined by self-evidence, just as what pleasures are right is a matter of the higher feelings.[2] And it should be emphasized that this is the only criterion of truth and rightness. We have no knowledge that is merely probable (not self-evident). How such a view can square with empiricism—and Brentano claimed to be an empiricist—it is hard to see.[3]

Let us consider it from another angle. What is meant when it is said that a judgment is self-evident?[4] It is ordinarily meant that there is insight into the necessary connection of elements affirmed to be connected by the judgment. If we drop the psychological factor of insight, this leaves us necessary connection. Though Brentano does not repudiate the view that self-evidence involves necessary connection, it might be claimed that his general position should have led him to reject it. He holds, for example, that judgment is not a combining of ideas, and that, in fact, one can have a judgment where only one idea is involved,[5] and apparently an analogous statement can be made regarding feelings.[6]

[1] I am embarrassed by my desire to avoid here the question to be discussed later: Is 'right' as asserted of judgments exactly the same predicate as 'right' when asserted of feelings? Hence I use the circumlocution, 'truth or rightness.'

[2] There are blind judgments and lower feelings. These may be true or right: we cannot tell. See *op. cit.*, sects 25, 26, 27, and notes 27, 28, 32, 33 accompanying them.

[3] Brentano refused to treat self-evidence as merely a psychological phenomenon, *e.g.*, as a feeling of compulsion. *Cf.* his acute criticism of Sigwart in *ibid.*, note 27, pp. 73–8.

[4] Brentano points out, *ibid.*, note 29, pp. 84–5, that there is no analogous term in popular speech to mark our right feelings. Hence I shall broaden the use of 'self-evident' to cover right feelings as well as true judgments.

[5] *Cf. Psychology*, vol. i, pp. 276–7.

[6] *Cf. ibid.*, pp. 291 ff.

Hence, in these cases at least, self-evidence does not involve any necessary connection between elements affirmed to be connected by the judgment.

The argument is cogent. But then what sort of thing is self-evidence on Brentano's view? It cannot be merely clearness, or clearness and distinctness, for ideas have these features, and Brentano rightly sees that on his view ideas cannot be self-evident (since not true or false, right or wrong).[1] What possibility is left? There is one which seems obvious, but nowhere, to my knowledge, does Brentano explicitly embrace it. A judgment is self-evident if there is a necessary connection between *it* and its *truth*; similarly a feeling is self-evident if there is a necessary connection between *it* and its *rightness*. Such a necessary connection must be *sui generis*, not grounded on some further connection in the real world, the world of referents of our judgments and feelings; *e.g.*, it must not involve a necessary connection between the object of our judgment and its existence or between the object of our feeling and its goodness.

I do not believe anyone has ever held such a view. It is indeed quite implausible in terms of common sense. Moreover, there seems to be good grounds for saying that Brentano himself tacitly assumed that self-evidence in the case of feelings involved an objective, not merely a semantical, necessary connection. That is, he seems to have assumed that wherever we have a higher love for something, *A*, we know our love to be right not merely in that there is a necessary connection between '*A* is good' and the rightness of '*A* is good,' but also between *A* and its goodness.[2]

[1] *Cf.* his criticism of Descartes, *The Origin*, note 27, pp. 72–3.

[2] An illustration of self-evidence in the case of feelings is our love of insight and hatred of ignorance. In some other species, these feelings might be just reversed and yet be as strong as in our case. If asked whether the feelings of such a species were not as reliable as ours, "we should here answer decisively that such love and hatred were fundamentally absurd, that such a species hated what was undeniably good, and loved what was undeniably bad in itself. Now why, where the feeling of compulsion is equally strong, do we answer differently in the one case than in the other? The answer is simple. In the former case the feeling of compulsion was an instinctive impulse; in the latter the natural feeling of pleasure is a higher love, having the character of rightness. We therefore notice when we ourselves have such a feeling, that its object is not merely loved and lovable, its opposite hated and unlovable, but also that the one is worthy of love, the other worthy of hatred, and therefore that one is good, the other bad" (*ibid.*, sect. 27, pp. 19–20). Certainly the natural interpretation of 'we therefore notice,' etc., in this passage is that there is a necessary connection (suggested by 'therefore') yet one which is not merely

A second criticism of Brentano's position as semantically interpreted is perhaps of more immediate relevance in getting us forward in our enterprise. Here again we may start with a quotation from Moore's review of Brentano's lecture. "Is the 'rightness' which Brentano attributes to belief in the true the *same* quality which he attributes to love of the good, or it is not? He speaks of 'right' love as if it were merely *analogous* to 'right' belief . . . ; and this suggests that he thinks the 'rightness' is *not* the same quality in the two cases. In that case he is calling two different unanalysable qualities by the same name; and that he should not have expressly noticed whether he is doing so or not, illustrates the insufficient attention which he has given to the question what he means by 'rightly loved' . . . ."[1]

I would differ from Moore in that it seems to me quite clear that for Brentano 'right' is exactly the same predicate, whether

definitional (suggested by 'notice') between the rightness of a higher love and the goodness of its object. Hence if the rightness of a higher love is self-evident, it seems to involve a necessary connection between the object of that love and the goodness of that object.

Again, Brentano says that Aristotle succumbed to the temptation "of believing that we can know the good as good, independent of the excitation of the emotions." This arose "from the fact that, along with the experience of an emotion qualified as right there is given at the same time the knowledge that the object itself is good" (*op. cit.*, note 28, pp. 82, 83). Here 'along with' and 'given at the same time' seem obviously to indicate that the knowledge of the object's goodness is not the same thing as the experience of the rightness of the emotion. It is true that the passage just quoted is immediately followed by the sentence, "Thus it may easily happen that the relation is then perverted and the love is thought to follow as a consequence of the knowledge, and recognized as right by reason of its agreement with this its rule." And indeed, a little farther down we read, "the distinguishing mark is [incorrectly] sought in the special character of the idea which forms the basis of the act rather than in the act itself qualified as right." But these statements simply warn us not to suppose we have an independent knowledge of the goodness of the object of a right love. They are quite compatible with the view that the self-evidence of the rightness of a higher love involves as a consequence the necessary connection between the object of that love and its goodness as something distinguishable from the necessary connection between a higher love and its rightness.

One final instance. In speaking of feelings as themselves objects of right feelings (let us call the former feelings first-level, the latter, second-level), Brentano writes: "In order that an act of feeling may be called purely good in itself it is requisite: (1) that it be right; (2) that it be an act of pleasing and not an act of displeasing. If either condition be absent, it is already, in a certain respect, bad in itself; pleasure at the misfortune of others (Schadenfreude) is bad on the first ground; pain at the sight of injustice, on the second ground" (*ibid.*, note 32, p. 85). Here we seem obviously to have to do with a necessary connection between the character of an object (a first level feeling) and its goodness; there is here even no mention of the rightness of a second-level feeling.

[1] *International Journal of Ethics*, vol. xiv, 1903–4, p. 117.

asserted of a judgment or a feeling.[1] What *are* merely analogous are the judgments and the feelings.[2] But on this interpretation a problem arises. If exactly the same semantical predicates ('right' and 'wrong' and whatever intentionality is present in the ideas embraced) are assertable of judgments and of feelings, why are the latter merely analogous? Why do they not form a single class?

Here the historical answer is plain. Brentano was thinking of two sorts of psychical phenomena: acts of judging and acts of loving and hating. These were already marked out as very dissimilar in the traditional account. He correctly felt that the novelty of his position lay in stressing what was common to them. But if we read beyond his psychological description in order to treat him as an exponent of a semantical position in value-theory, we are faced with the problem: How are judgment and feeling to be distinguished semantically? If their semantical predicates are exactly the same, they become indistinguishable. It follows that we cannot distinguish value from fact. '*A* is good' just means that love of *A* is right. '*A* exists' or '*A* is a fact' just means that assertion of *A* is right. If semantically or referentially we cannot distinguish 'Love of *A*' from 'Assertion of *A*,' it follows that we cannot distinguish '*A* is good' from '*A* exists.' This forces the abandonment of the objectivist position in value-theory.[3]

Actually Brentano does point out a distinction between feelings and judgments that is of semantical significance, but it is obviously a source of embarrassment which he wishes not to emphasize but to play down. The objects of any two right assertions equally exist, but the objects of any two right loves need not be equally good—one may be better than the other. Brentano sees that this difference is not psychological as it would be if, *e.g.*, it were a difference in the intensities of the feelings involved.[4] Brentano's solution seems obviously *ad hoc*. Feelings embrace a peculiar species of phenomenon not to be found in either ideas or judgments, namely, choice or preference. And it is in terms of right

[1] *Cf. The Origin*, sects 22, 23.

[2] I think Moore is misled by his inability to conceive 'right' as anything but a descriptive predicate, by his inability to think of it as semantical.

[3] This theory holds that there are values as distinct from facts, thus by implication that there are facts as distinct from values.

[4] Judgments, as psychological acts, likewise differ in intensity. Moreover, we all recognize that sometimes the object of a less intense love is better than the object of a more intense love. *Cf. ibid.*, sects. 29, 30.

preferences that Brentano defines 'better.'[1] My basic criticism of this is simple. Brentano does not really connect his account of comparative value with that of absolute value; he does not define 'better than' in terms of 'good' or conversely.[2]

[1] "Whatever is true is true in a like degree, but whatever is good is not good in equal degree, and by 'better' nothing else is meant than what, when compared with another good, is preferable, *i.e.*, something which for its own sake, is preferred with a right preference" (*op. cit.*, sect. 30, p. 23). Apparently this is the same predicate, 'right,' as is assertable of judgments and feelings. Hence the difference that marks our preference lies in their content, in what they rightly or wrongly intend. This is comparative. But in what respect are objects compared in an act of preference? Clearly in their value, their goodness or badness. If this were not the case, the introduction of preference would not be relevant to the problem of an analysis of better. And Brentano is aware of this. There are, he says, (*ibid.*, sect. 31), three classes of right preferences: where something good is preferred to something bad; where the existence of something good is preferred to its non-existence; and where a greater good is preferred to a lesser. But now if preference involves a comparison of objects in terms of their goodness and badness, those objects must, in the case of right preferences, it would seem, really be good and bad. But, on the semantical view, they are not: their goodness is reduced to the rightness of our love of them. Thus when we rightly prefer *A*, as a greater good, to *B*, what we really are doing, this theory should say, is preferring the right love of *A* to the right love of *B*. This is a possible but quite implausible view. Moreover Brentano writes as though we do prefer some objects, other than feelings, to other objects. Furthermore, we can rightly ask, On what grounds is one right love said to be rightly preferred to another? Brentano, in his third class of right preferences, uses a quantitative criterion. In some cases, goods are additive. This might be interpreted: the object of more right loves is rightly preferred to an object of fewer. But if Brentano had so intended, he would not have felt called upon to qualify the objects as "in every respect the same" in order that the principle of addition be applicable to goods (*ibid.*, p. 25). Also this interpretation would seem to be improper in the case of intensive goods, *e.g.*, where the objects of our preferences are themselves feelings. "If one good, *e.g.*, one joy is in every respect quite equal to another, only more intense, then the preference which is given to the more intense is qualified as right, the more intense is the better" (*ibid.*). It would appear arbitrary indeed to hold that a more intense joy is always the object of more right loves than a less intense joy.

Furthermore, a confusion must be avoided. Brentano's view, so far as we read past his psychologism, is not that to be good is to be the object of an actually occurrent love that is right, but only that it is to be such that a love of what is good would be right were it to occur. Thus 'better' as the comparative of 'good,' should be taken to mean being the object not of more actual right loves, but simply more possible ones: more loves, if they occurred, would be right if directed toward the better. But how could this ever be determined in any particular case? The class of loves toward a given object that would be right were they to occur is not sufficiently specified for the enumeration of its elements to be feasible.

[2] This criticism differs from, though perhaps is not wholly unrelated to, a criticism of Moore's. On Brentano's views, writes Moore, "if anything is to be *better* than another, that can only be because the quality which he means by 'rightness' has degrees—a point which he has entirely failed to observe, and which proves that 'true' cannot mean 'rightly believed' " (*loc. cit.*, p. 119).

The conclusion is that Brentano, in the semantical aspects of his views, has failed to distinguish feeling from judgment, value from fact. Yet there is embedded in his ideas a concept that might fruitfully have been applied to yield such a distinction. It is what I have frequently referred to above as the intentional but non-asserted inclusion of existence in the concept of value. Writes Brentano: "It is certainly not necessary that anyone who loves something should think that it exists, or even only might exist; nevertheless every love is a love that something should exist; . . . So it seems to be a matter of fact unthinkable that a being should be endowed with the faculty of love and hate, without partaking of that of judgment."[1] More subtly, this same view is presupposed in Brentano's ethical rule: "choose the best among attainable ends"[2] and his explanation thereof: "In choosing here, account must be taken of the degree of probability. If A is three times better than B, but B has ten times as many chances of being attained as A, then practical wisdom will prefer course B."[3] Here one would suppose that 'practical wisdom will prefer course B' presupposes that it is preferable to choose a course that is not as good but is more probably attainable, and thus that, in *this* form of value (*viz.*, preferability), value involves reference to possible existence. In some sense, then, the notion of value includes that of existence in a way in which the notion of existence does not include that of value. This guarantees the difference between them. The phrase, 'in some sense,' however, is an important qualification, for Brentano clearly wishes to keep the rightness of feelings of value independent of the truth of corresponding judgments of existence in such a way that the rightness of the feeling is compatible with either the truth or the falsity of the

However, Moore comes to this conclusion by an argument based on a misinterpretation of Brentano. The argument assumes that Brentano held that 'more worthy of love' (*i.e.*, 'better') means rightly loved with a greater love, whereas, Moore contends, it does not, it means being rightly loved in a higher degree. But Brentano explicitly repudiates the view here ascribed to him; indeed, his whole doctrine of right preference is a result of this repudiation.

[1] *Psychology*, vol. ii, p. 128, quoted by Eaton, *op. cit.*, p. 56. Brentano's position is sometimes described as making feeling include judgment just as judgment includes idea. Such a view is certainly not characteristic. Brentano tends rather to stress the similarity of judgment and feeling and their common contrast to idea, which both include. It is interesting to note that the passage quoted above is a comment written after the first edition appeared.

[2] *The Origin*, sect. 17, p. 12.

[3] *Ibid.*, note 17, p. 46.

judgment of existence which the feeling somehow includes.[1] So we come to the vital question: In what way do feelings include judgments?

Brentano does not himself answer our question, but we might attempt to develop his views so that an answer is forthcoming. What we love, let us have Brentano say, is not an object, not the intentional content of an idea, but the existence of such an object. We love not *A* but that *A* exist. Such a value-sentence as '*A* is good' is hence to be translated 'That *A* exist is rightly loved.' This translation shows how the value-sentence, when fully and clearly stated, includes the existential judgment corresponding to it, and thus how value includes fact. Now this hypothetical reconstruction of Brentano's answer to our question will repay further scrutiny.

Let us start with the subject of the sentence offered above as a translation of '*A* is good.' Let us so interpret it that the sentence asserts of the existence of *A* or of *A* as actually existing that it is rightly loved. This probably would be the most natural interpretation. But it will not do. On the one hand, Brentano probably could not accept it, since he denies that existence can be a predicate whereas this interpretation would apparently require that it should be. On the other, this interpretation would conflict with the common sense requirement, accepted by Brentano, that value be not confined to that which actually exists.

Again, we might interpret the sentence given as a translation of '*A* is good' so that it is equivalent to 'The affirmation of *A* is rightly loved.' We must avoid reading this, however, as though it meant that a certain psychological event (the act of affirming *A*) is rightly loved. This would take us out of the semantical framework within which we are now working. Moreover, it is inherently unacceptable. It is to be remembered that we are trying to interpret a sentence that is offered as a translation of '*A* is good' where '*A* is good' is meant to be the type of all value-sentences. We may on occasion love, and perhaps even rightly love, psychological acts of affirming. But to say that these are the only things rightly loved, and that in fact we never mean to ascribe value to anything else, is patently absurd.

[1] *I.e.*, he wants to keep the rightness or validity of '*A* is good' independent of the truth of '*A* exists.' "The great merit of this view," writes Moore, "is its recognition that all truths of the form 'This is good in itself' are logically independent of any truth about what exists" (*loc. cit.*, p. 115).

But our semantical interpretation of Brentano allows us to avoid this psychologistic reading. 'The affirmation of *A*' is to be taken not as referring to an event but to a sentence, a sentence affirming the existence of *A*. To avoid Brentano's objection to existence as a predicate while yet not falling into Brentano's own psychologistic terminology, let us invent the solecism, 'There is *A*.' The position we are putting into Brentano's mouth now becomes: '*A* is good' is to be translated ' 'There is *A*' is rightly loved.' This result, the reader will agree, does not offer too encouraging a prospect. If it was absurd to hold that in all our value-sentences we mean to ascribe value to certain psychological acts only, it must be simply preposterous to hold that we use them to ascribe value only to certain sentences. And to crown this foolishness let us note that this set of sentences—*viz.*, existential sentences—presumably includes false as well as true sentences. That is, '*A* is good' is to be rendered ' 'There is *A*' is rightly loved' quite independently of whether 'There is *A*' is true or false.

This last affront to common sense might be avoided. We might stipulate that only when 'There is *A*' is true[1] would ' 'There is *A*' is rightly loved' be a proper rendition of '*A* is good.' But besides the inherent absurdity that would still remain—in cases where 'There is *A*' is true, '*A* is good' is to be rendered as asserting value of a *sentence*—this rendition is unacceptable, for it leaves sentences like '*A* is good' wholly unclarified wherever the corresponding existential sentence, 'There is *A*,' is false.

We could shun the ridiculousness of making existential sentences the subjects of our clarified value-judgments by stipulating that it be the truth of such sentences that so function. That is, instead of replacing '*A* is good' by ' 'There is *A*' is rightly loved' we might replace it by 'The truth of 'There is *A*' is rightly loved.' This, however, would appear to presuppose that 'There is *A*' is true and will not do for sentences like '*A* is good' where 'There is *A*' is false. We might of course try 'The truth or falsity of 'There is *A*' is rightly loved' or again 'The truth-value of 'There is *A*' is rightly loved.' This possibility hardly warrants exploration, however. For if the truth of 'There is *A*' is rightly loved, it would seem that its falsity would be wrongly loved, and if its falsity is rightly loved, then its truth would be wrongly loved. Moreover,

[1] It is hoped that the reader is sufficiently tolerant to see that this expression is elliptical for the prolix statement, 'when a sentence of which 'There is *A*' is the type is true,' etc.

if it is preposterous to say we ascribe value only to sentences, how are we to characterize the view that says we make value-assertions only concerning truth-values of sentences?

The truth is that in the last few pages we have left the realm of good common sense entirely. Everyday usage demands that we treat value-sentences as being as directly about the extra-linguistic world as are existential or descriptive sentences. 'My eldest son is a good boy' is just as directly about the extra-linguistic world as is 'I have an eldest son' or 'My eldest son has blue eyes.' Thus it would seem that no clarification of '*A* is good' is permissible that would substitute for this sentence a sentence with the name of a sentence or of a truth-value of a sentence as its subject.

However, our trouble may have been, at least in part, that we tried to get clear as to the subject of 'That *A* exist is rightly loved,' taken as Brentano's translation of '*A* is good,' without consideration of the predicate. We have, as a matter of fact, treated 'rightly loved' as a value-expression. I think there is some basis for claiming that Brentano does not avoid giving this expression value-significance. That is, he sometimes seems to use 'right' and 'rightly' in 'a right love' and 'rightly loved' to refer to a love that ought to be or that would be good. In this usage, 'That *A* exist is rightly loved' is a misleading way of putting what had better be put, 'A love whose object is that *A* exist is right.' That is, 'right' designates a value-property exemplified by certain acts of loving —*viz.*, those directed toward the existence of something.[1] This view, however, takes us once more outside our semantical framework and back into a position according to which value is a property of existents.

As I have already argued, we do have some grounds for holding that Brentano uses 'rightly loved' as a semantical predicate analogous to 'rightly affirmed.' Thus, just as the latter can be taken as synonymous with 'true'[2] so the former can be taken as designating a "truth-value" of value-sentences. But it must be a "truth-value" different from truth itself. For, if it were just truth,

[1] The reader can reconstruct appropriate statements for 'wrong,' using 'hating' in place of 'loving.'

[2] This would not be quite correct. The phrase 'rightly affirmed' is partly semantical and partly syntactical. That is, '*A* is rightly affirmed' should be rendered 'An affirmative existential sentence about *A* is true,' or ' 'There is *A*' is true.' This would allow us to interpret 'rightly denied' as well as 'wrongly affirmed' and 'wrongly denied.' Similar remarks can be made for 'rightly loved' and the phrases that correlate with it.

then 'That *A* exists is rightly loved' would be indistinguishable from 'That *A* exists is rightly affirmed.' So of course it must not be called a "truth-value." Let us coin a phrase for it and call it a "legitimacy-value." Let us, then, develop our semantical reading of Brentano so that we translate 'right feeling' by 'legitimate' and 'wrong feeling' by 'not-legitimate.'[1] These words we take to be semantical predicates different from but having the same status as 'true' and 'false.' That is, the sentences in which they occur have the names of sentences as subject-terms, and in some way serve to assert a connection or lack of connection between the sentences named and the extra-linguistic world.

Our translation of '*A* is good' has now become 'That *A* exist is legitimate,' or, to make it clear that the subject-term is the name of a sentence, we may use the solecism introduced earlier to form ' 'there is *A*' is legitimate,' which is like ' 'There is *A*' is true' in its general status as a semantical sentence but is to be kept distinct from the latter. On this reading, then, it is to be admitted that the same sentence[2] can have both a truth-value and a legitimacy-value. It would translate a value-sentence into a semantical sentence asserting of a given sentence, which also has a truth-value, a certain legitimacy-value.

In many ways this analysis looks promising. It shows how a value-sentence includes an existential (or factual[3]) sentence without asserting it, for the value-sentence ascribes a legitimacy-value but not a truth-value to the sentence it names. In fact, it so well agrees with the desiderata for a satisfactory analysis of value that it is with reluctance that I point out what seems to me to be an absolutely fatal flaw from the standpoint of a value-objectivist. This can be stated in different ways. One way is to point out that on this view a value-sentence is fundamentally different from an ordinary declarative sentence (whether existential or descriptive). It is *essentially* a semantical sentence, it cannot properly occur at

[1] 'Love' and 'hate' then indicate that the sentences in which these semantical predicates occur are affirmative and negative, respectively. See the preceding footnote.

[2] At the point we have now reached and in terms of the issues to be subsequently raised, I do not see any reason for limiting these sentences to existential sentences. Indeed, the issues at stake are still perfectly significant to one who, like myself, would rule out all existential sentences—though not sentences with the "existential" quantifier—from a correct language. The issues would still be involved as regards ordinary descriptive sentences, such as '*a* exemplifies *A*.'

[3] See preceding footnote.

the zero-level. A declarative sentence *may* be translated into a semantical sentence, since there is always a semantical sentence —naming the declarative and predicating 'true' of it—with which it is equivalent. But a value-sentence *must* be semantical, it can only appear to be at the zero-level. Now as we have frequently observed, in everyday speech value-sentences are just as directly about the extra-linguistic world as are existential or descriptive sentences, and value-objectivism takes its stand with common sense on this.

Another way of putting this same objection is to point out that there are truth-conditions which the predicate 'true' must meet, but the present view sets down no legitimacy-conditions for 'legitimate' and it cannot set down any that are strictly analogous to the truth-conditions for 'true' without destroying the distinction between 'legitimate' and 'true.' Truth-conditions have the form, to use our type-case, ' 'There is *A*' is true if and only if there is *A*.' But were we to say, ' 'There is *A*' is legitimate if and only if there is *A*' we would have destroyed the distinction of 'legitimate' from 'true.' And in doing this we would have lost everything that makes the present view attractive. It is of course hypothetically possible to stipulate some different kind of legitimacy-condition. But to do so, however, would be to destroy the parallel between legitimacy-value and truth-value, and might rule out the equivalence of a value-sentence (expressed as a semantical legitimacy-sentence) with any zero-level sentence and in any case would be incompatible with value-objectivism (which requires zero-level value-sentences).

Now there is, it seems to me, a possible way out of this difficulty which promises to retain most of the attractive features of the semantical view we have read into Brentano. It is, however, so different from anything Brentano has said that the pretence of developing his position semantically must certainly now be put aside. Let us retain the idea of legitimacy-values as paralleling truth-values, but deny that there are any sentences which have both. Let us suppose that there are zero-level sentences which are neither true nor false but are legitimate or not legitimate. A semantical sentence whose predicate is 'legitimate' must name, in its subject-term, such a sentence. Let us speculate that these zero-level sentences, which are legitimate or not legitimate but never true or false, are just the value-sentences with which we have all along been concerned. We can then set up legitimacy-conditions strictly analogous to truth-conditions. Similar to ' 'There is *A*' is true if and only if there is *A*' there would be ' '*A* is good' is legitimate if and only if *A* is good.'

I am personally convinced that there is decided merit in this suggestion—certainly sufficient merit to make it worthy of our most serious consideration. But I am not unaware that it may appear empty to the weary reader. It seems that we are back at the beginning of our enterprise. For we have '*A* is good' appearing in its own right, and it was sentences such as this that we have all along been endeavouring to analyse. However, I do think some progress has been made. On the present suggestion '*A* is good' can be seen to differ radically from ordinary descriptive sentences, from sentences assertive of fact. It is not at all like '*A* is yellow' or '*A* is pleasant' because the latter are true or false, whereas it is not; it is rather legitimate or not legitimate. Thus it is misleading in form, for it seems to assert a property of a particular, thus to be a descriptive sentence. The present proposal requires us to clarify common usage in such a way that value-sentences shall be different in form from ordinary declaratives, *i.e.*, from sentences that are true or false. Such a difference of form must, to serve our purposes, be correlated with the difference of semantic-values (the difference between legitimacy-values and truth-values) of the sentences in question. Moreover, this difference of form must be a real syntactical difference, not a merely typographical or phonetic difference in the sign-vehicles adopted. That is, there must be developed a whole logic of value-sentences that is significantly different from the logic of descriptive, declarative sentences. How is this to be done without too much violence to good usage? And when it is done, may we suppose that this form (or these forms) marking out value-sentences will help us analyse value, that it, *e.g.*, will show us what value is? These questions launch us into a discussion that must be reserved for a new section.

6

WHAT IS THE PROPER SYNTAX OF VALUE-SENTENCES?

If there is any reader who has got this far, he will probably not be deterred by the oddity of the suggestion I am about to make. Our problem is to have value in the world, not merely in our language, but to have it there in some other rôle than that of a property, whether a property of particulars or of facts. Value is to be somehow co-ordinate with fact, and thus to have a status similar to fact. What can this be? How can it be described or otherwise linguistically elucidated? Is it possible to find in the syntax of value-sentences a significant clue as to the nature of value? These questions lead us into an inquiry as to the proper syntax of value-sentences, an inquiry which, I fear, will perforce be seriously defective in scope and detail. It is meant to be suggestive only. Yet it is precisely through the results of this inquiry, seriously defective as it is, that we can gain, I shall contend, further insight in our search for a solution to our puzzle, What is value?

6a. *Are value-sentences properly rendered as imperatives?*

We can get some help here from an unexpected quarter. Rudolph Carnap, in the period of *The Logical Syntax of Language* and *Philosophy and Logical Syntax*, considered that the legitimate task of philosophy was logical analysis, the analysis of the syntax of the language of science. This position does not *seem* to offer us any clue as to the solution of our present problem. In the first place, he so interpreted it that it would seem that philosophical problems are merely linguistic, have only to do with the structure of language and not at all with the structure of the world (the latter is wholly in the province of science). To make his position relevant to our problem it is necessary to revise it in the direction of the early Wittgenstein and the early John

Wisdom.[1] The revision would make the task of philosophy the analysis of the syntax of sentences in a properly constructed language with the purpose of clarifying our grasp of the structure of fact.

But even with this revision we are still left entirely without help as to value. Carnap would have philosophy analyse the syntax of the language of science, and, on his account, science contains no valuative sentences. Yet inadvertently he did indicate a possible solution of our problem. All valuative sentences, he said, are simply disguised imperatives.[2] This for him meant that they are not really sentences at all and are to be completely ignored by philosophy. But surely another alternative is available, which Carnap did not deign even to criticize; *viz.*, that imperatives have a distinctive syntax (formation and transformation rules, to use his terminology) marking them off from declarative sentences. It would follow not that there is no logic of imperatives but that such a logic is different from that of declaratives; not that imperatives are meaningless, but that the criterion of meaning for imperatives is different from that for declaratives. If to this we can add, as we did to Carnap's views on the logical analysis of declaratives, that philosophy analyses the structure of language in order that it may gain insight into the structure of the world, then we are on the way to a solution of our problem.[3]

This inclusion of imperatives in the subject-matter for syntactical analysis does carry us beyond the language of science, at least as Carnap conceived it.[4] It carries us into the much more

[1] I have in mind Wittgenstein's *Tractatus Logico-Philsophicus* and Wisdom's papers, "Ostentation," *Psyche*, vol. xii, 1933, and "Is Analysis a Useful Method in Philosophy?" *Aristotelian Society Supplementary Volume* xiii, 1934.

[2] "But actually a value statement is nothing else than a command in a misleading grammatical form. It may have effects upon the actions of men, and these effects may either be in accordance with our wishes or not; but it is neither true nor false. It does not assert anything and can neither be proved nor disproved.

"This is revealed as soon as we apply to such statements our method of logical analysis. From the statement 'Killing is evil' we cannot deduce any proposition about future experiences. Thus this statement is not verifiable and has no theoretical sense, and the same thing is true of all other value statements" (*Philosophy and Logical Syntax*, pp. 24–5).

[3] As the sequel will show, we never arrive, or, so far as we do attain a solution, it is in the realm of insight and can never be explicitly formulated in a correct language.

[4] It is certainly a significant question, but one not to be discussed here, whether scientific methodology does not include imperatives or other valuative sentences (perhaps hypothetical in form) which are irreducible to declaratives. It is of course a subterfuge to say that methodology is not a part of the content of science, just as it is a patent absurdity that methodological sentences are really only psychological stimuli to the practising scientist.

inclusive language of everyday life. And here one of the most developed systems of imperatives is to be found in the language of the law. It is remarkable that not only lawyers but even jurists seem almost wholly oblivious of the fact that the language of law (of legal imperatives) has a quite different syntax from that of the language of science (and of declarative sentences generally). Even if occasionally it is recognized that individual sentences in the law are imperatives, it is not seen that this raises the serious question of the logical relations of these sentences to one another. It is almost universally supposed that the logic of the law is the logic of Aristotle.

Yet not quite universally. There is present in the writings of at least one philosopher of law the recognition that we have in legal norms a syntactically different sort of sentence from any scientific law. I refer to the formal theory of Hans Kelsen. This is shown in his decisive refutation of the legal realists or sociologists of law (so far as they suppose that they answer the question, What is legal law?). They have, he shows, confused legal law, which is normative, with scientific law, which is declarative of fact. So far as legal law is interpreted as simply a disguised prediction of what the courts will do, or as simply a generalization as to what any legal body or bodies have done or will do as a matter of fact, legal law is reduced to scientific law. But a scientific law is shown to be false by a single observable exception; not so a legal law. A legal law is valid[1] when broken, when not enforced in the particular case. As Kelsen points out, this is not to be interpreted as meaning that a normative generalization can still be valid when there are exceptions to it, whereas a descriptive generalization cannot. Rather, it is to be understood as meaning that no *fact* can be an exception to, and thus serve to overthrow, a legal law, whereas this is not the case for descriptive laws. A descriptive law says, If *A* is, *B* is; a legal law says, If *A* is, *B* ought to be.

Kelsen thus recognizes that valuative sentences, or "norms" as he calls them, are fundamentally different from descriptive sentences[2] in their conditions of validation or verification. Though

[1] I take it that Kelsen's use of 'valid' instead of 'true' is a tacit recognition that with imperatives or "norms" we must use a different set of semantical values from those we assign to declaratives. I prefer 'legitimate' to 'valid' since the latter is frequently used to assign a value to a statement of entailment or logical derivation.

[2] His chief concern is with universally generalized sentences, but his position can be stated for singular sentences.

a descriptive sentence may be deduced from other descriptive sentences, its verification ultimately turns on observation of fact. Norms, however, are validated by higher norms, ultimately by a highest, the basic norm.[1] Kelsen makes an important distinction, however, in the basis of validation of lower by higher norms. In static systems of norms (morality), the validation is through the content of the norms. The relationship apparently is simply that of subsumption. The lower norm falls under or is included in the higher. Thus 'You ought not lie' is validated by 'No one ought to lie.'[2] In dynamic systems of norms (legal law) the validation is by means of authorization. The higher norm delegates norm-creating power to some authority. The lower norm is validated by the fact that it was created, in the prescribed manner, by the authority set up by the higher norm.[3] Thus, 'no one ought to drive more than thirty-five miles per hour on this designated stretch of highway' is validated by reference to the way it was created, to the delegation of authority to the individual or individuals issuing it. It is not difficult to see (and Kelsen himself points this out) that a dynamic or legal system of norms is a system of imperatives (emasculated and depsychologized).

I think it is correct to credit Kelsen with a tacit recognition

[1] Kelsen has serious difficulty with this basic norm. In moral (static) systems he simply says that "The binding force of the basic norm is itself self-evident, or at least presumed to be so" (*General Theory of Law and State*, p. 112). But as to the basic law of legal (dynamic) systems he seems to be in difficulty. Sometimes he makes it hypothetical in the sense that only as we presuppose it can we have any other norms in the legal system in question (he says, "it is valid because it is presupposed to be valid; and it is presupposed to be valid because without this presupposition no human act could be interpreted as legal . . ." (*ibid.*, p. 116)). Sometimes he makes it contingent upon the actual efficacy in society of the system of laws it generates (although this is a *conditio sine qua non* not a *conditio per quam* (*ibid.*, p. 119)). I think Kelsen's difficulty might have been eased had he clearly made the distinction (which, I think, he is struggling to formulate) between proof within a system and proof of a system. *Cf.* my "The 'Proof' of Utility in Bentham and Mill," *Ethics*, vol. lx, 1949, pp. 1–18.

[2] "It is essential only that the various norms of any such system [of morality] are implicated by the basic norm as the particular is implied by the general, and that, therefore, all the particular norms of such a system are obtainable by means of an intellectual operation, *viz.*, by the inference from the general to the particular" (*ibid.*, p. 112).

[3] "The norms of a dynamic system have to be created through acts of will by those individuals who have been authorized to create norms by some higher norm. This authorization is a delegation. Norm creating power is delegated from one authority to another authority; the former is the higher, the latter the lower authority" (*ibid.*, p. 113).

of the syntactical difference between norms and descriptive sentences. But I think it would be equally correct to deny that he has explicitly grasped and stated this difference. He does of course insist that norms include 'ought' or some equivalent; this requirement may be thought of as a formation-rule. But how this 'ought' is to function is not at all clear. Nor are the transformation rules for normative systems. In fact, for static normative systems the only transformation he seems to allow is that of subsumption, which of course does not distinguish a normative from a declarative system. In dynamic systems he seems to feel that the derivation of one norm from another is something unique, quite distinct from any derivation of a declarative from other declaratives. But I think he has not put his finger on the significant difference. He notes that in a dynamic system derivation is not merely subsumption. There is present a creative act of the subordinate authority. This act determines the content of the subordinate norm, which latter, consequently, is not simply an instance of the superior norm. This leads Kelsen to make the radical statement that the various norms of a dynamic system "cannot be obtained from the basic norm by any intellectual operation."[1] This is not merely a slur upon the legal profession; it is actually incorrect. Suppose we have the norm, set up by a state legislature, that the state highway commission is to designate speed zones in which motorists are not to exceed thirty-five miles per hour. Suppose the commission designates a stretch of highway, *a*, as such a speed zone. Then 'Motorists are not to exceed thirty-five miles per hour in *a*' is derivable from the act of the legislature. This derivation uses subsumption ('The designation of *a* as speed-zone by the commission is binding' is subsumed under 'Any designation of speed-zones by the commission is binding,'), but it also uses simple factual verification ('The commission has designated *a* as a speed-zone' is verified by observation). Such a combination of operations can surely be described as "intellectual." In fact, something very analogous is highly characteristic of scientific procedure. To determine the distance a freely falling body has fallen it is necessary to know both the law of freely falling bodies (under which the given instance is subsumed) and also how long *this* body has been falling (which can only be determined by observing fact). In short, the necessity of ascertaining certain facts (just *what* is willed by the appropriate authority) is

[1] *Op. cit.*, p. 113.

not peculiar to the derivation of a legal norm from a higher norm; the same thing enters the derivation of some descriptive sentences from scientific laws.

There is, of course, a difference in the two cases. In deriving certain descriptive sentences about a freely falling body from the general law as to freely falling bodies we disregard the question as to who uttered or wrote the sentences in question. We are only concerned with what the sentences assert. But in the case of norms concerning speed limits on given stretches of highway we *are* concerned with the question as to who formulated these norms. Just what the norms oblige motorists to do is only part of the matter; to derive them from superior norms it is necessary to determine their authors. The peculiarity here lies not in that their derivation requires observation of fact as well as subsumption under a more general rule or law. Rather, it lies in the fact that the derivation may fail in either of two ways: it may fail if the norm is not issued by the appropriate authority, and it may fail if the content of the norm, what it enjoins, is improper. That motorists are not to exceed thirty-five miles per hour in *a* is validated only if *two* conditions are met: (1) if this norm is issued by the appropriate authority; (2) if it falls within the permitted limits as to content (as determined by the higher norm, the legislative act, in both cases). If an ordinary citizen, say a property-owner whose property borders *a* were to issue the norm, it would not be valid. If the highway commission issued the norm but made the speed limit less than they were empowered to make it in such designated zones, the norm would likewise not be valid.

Kelsen emphasizes the first of these two ways in which a legal norm may not be valid. In fact, he is so concerned to stress this as marking off a legal norm from a moral norm that he does not adequately recognize the second.[1] But it is precisely the duality

[1] He does not deny the second, and in some places he rather backhandedly allows it. *Cf.*, "Law regulates its own creation inasmuch as one legal norm determines the way in which another norm is created, *and also, to some extent, the contents of that norm*" (*op. cit.*, p. 134, italics mine). This recognition is perhaps clearest when Kelsen is discussing conflicts of norms, as, *e.g.*, in questions of constitutionality. "If the constitution prescribes a certain procedure to be observed in the enactment of statutes and if it also lays down certain provisions with regard to their contents, it must foresee the possibility that the legislator may not follow these prescriptions. The constitution may then designate the organ that has to decide whether or not the prescriptions regulating the legislative function were observed" (*ibid.*, p. 156). It is quite possible for the Supreme Court to find that a law properly enacted by Congress is unconstitutional in content.

of the possibility of invalidity of a legal norm, thus the duality of the negative of a legal norm and the duality of its possible failure of derivation from a higher norm, that gives us our clue to the syntactical difference of imperatives from declaratives. Let us state the matter in semantical terms. A law that is not valid may be either invalid (as involving a command that in content oversteps the limits set down by some higher law in the system) or it may be non-valid (as being issued by some individual without legal authority in the system).

Here we have a lead that may prove valuable in exploring the differences of imperatives from declaratives. But before we pursue the possibility further it may be appropriate to consider briefly the contention that imperatives may be included or rather adequately represented within the class of declaratives and hence are to be granted no distinctive logic of their own.

Carnap has denied meaning to imperatives, that is, in an ideally clarified language they would not occur. Yet certain declarative sentences would occur that, in a rather vague sense, might be said to take their place. These would be pragmatical metalinguistic sentences making such statements as, '*a* issued the command '*p*!'.'[1] Such sentences would obey the ordinary rules of

It was, of course, a chief purpose of the liberal advocates of natural law in the seventeenth and eighteenth centuries to place limits on the authority of various governmental agencies in terms of the content of the norms they could properly set up. Apparently Kelsen, as an opponent of natural law, has to hold that there are no such limits binding upon the basic norm, the constitution, in any legal system. But for him there can still be limitations as to content of subordinate norms so far as these go back to the basic norm as positive source.

[1] I am using '*p*!' as an abbreviation for the imperative corresponding to the declarative '*p*.' That is, what it is that is commanded in '*p*!' is declared to be the case in '*p*.' But we must be careful here. ''*p*!'' as it appears in '*a* issued the command '*p*!'' would appear to be the name of '*p*!', that is, of an imperative in the object language, and thus we seem committed to imperatives. What we must do is to say that, if we use the formulation of the text, ''*p*!'' names not an imperative but only certain sounds or writing. But then we could hardly say that these are a command or that *a* issued them. So the illustrative statement of the text should be replaced by something like the following: '*a* uttered certain sounds with a certain inflection of voice and other accompanying behaviour.' This would allow Carnap to remain consistent (and would, I take it, be his actual choice), but it would not allow the assimilation of imperatives into the logic of declaratives suggested in the text, for the sentences replacing imperatives would not be pragmatic metalinguistic sentences at all, but simple descriptions of extra-linguistic fact, for they would say nothing about the occurrence of other sentences (imperatives being not linguistic elements at all but simply sounds).

But may not this method of elimination of imperatives be legitimate in its own right? Why not replace all legal norms by psychological descriptions which

declarative logic, being unique only in the sense that they are formed in a specific way (they contain names of imperatives and of imperators and pragmatic predicates of certain sorts). Thus the negative of '*a* issued command '*p*!' ' is '*a* did not issue command '*p*!',' and for this pair the laws of contradiction and excluded middle hold. Likewise such connectives as 'or,' 'and,' 'if-then' as used to combine such sentences with declaratives would obey the the rules of ordinary declarative logic.

But Kelsen has already given us the refutation of such a suggestion. Legal norms are not to be confused with, nor can their unique character be retained if they are replaced by, sociological or psychological statements about them. Only confusion can result from replacing a sentence (in this case an imperative) by another which includes the name of the first and asserts of it something of material significance, something, *i.e.*, that may be true or false quite independently of any truth or falsity of the original sentence.

In this situation, however, there occurs a refinement. Professor Felix E. Oppenheim has written an article[1] which in part is an attempt to carry on the sort of linguistic analysis of law suggested by Carnap while yet admitting the soundness of Kelsen's distintion between the law itself and any science of law. Specifically, Oppenheim allows imperatives, in their own right, to remain in law as basic sentences at the lowest linguistic level (in "Language A" that deals with things). Moreover, he would distinguish between what we have called the content of a legal norm, what behaviour it obligates, and its authoritativeness, its 'official quality." However, the latter is a pragmatic feature of the imperative, not something to be found in the imperative itself.[2]

do not name these norms but simply assert certain behavioural events? What events? We must have a rule here specifying which psychological descriptions are to replace the legal norms. And this rule must not mention the norms! It would be simple enough to take ordinary language and just delete the legal norms and, like the bad boy who had extracted all the raisins from the cake, not even own up to it. But we would still want to *see* what had been done even if it could not be *said*. And it seems almost as difficult to *see* what is not there as to *mention* it! However, allowing the deletion, we should note that it *is* just a deletion in the last analysis. For ordinary language contains all the psychological descriptions which are to replace the legal norms *as well as* the norms themselves.

[1] "Outline of a Logical Analysis of Law," *Philosophy of Science*, vol. xi, 1944, pp. 142–60.

[2] What I mean here can best be suggested by an analogy. A truth-condition for '*p*' is ' '*p*' is true if and only if *p*.' An analogous authority-condition for '*p*!' would, on Oppenheim's view, be ' '*p*!' has official quality if and only if '*p*!' is

Thus its denial could not be expressed as a negative of the imperative but only as the negative of a certain pragmatic sentence about the imperative. Thus it would seem that of the two ways in which, as we saw, a legal norm may fail to be valid only one can be reflected in a sign of negation attached to the norm itself, namely, that which negates the content of the norm, the what-it-is the norm enjoins, thus constituting an opposing norm. The other, having to do with the authoritativeness of the norm, can be reflected only by a negative sign that appears in a metalinguistic sentence mentioning the norm (and also the organ issuing it).

There are several features of Professor Oppenheim's outlined logical analysis of law that disturb me.[1] However, it is well to press on to the central issue. Can the two ways in which a legal norm may fail to be valid and which *prima facie* therefore distinguish it from any descriptive sentence be taken care of by

issued by a legal organ with law-creating powers' (*cf. loc. cit.* p. 152 and *passim*). The former makes ' '*p*' is true' equivalent to '*p*,' that is, to put it roughly, a declarative sentence claims its own truth. But the latter does not make ' '*p*!' is authoritative' equivalent to '*p*!,' that is, a legal law or norm does not claim its own authoritativeness. Likewise, ' '*p*!' is not authoritative' would not be equivalent to any negative of '*p*!' but only to a pragmatic sentence mentioning '*p*!'

[1] Let me mention just three. Oppenheim dodges the whole problem of the logic of imperatives (though he makes use of the concept of the derivation of imperatives) by the device of treating imperativeness as a semantical property of sentences (p. 150). Thus for each ordinary property an individual may have there is (so I interpret Oppenheim) another which is its imperative correlate. Thus the difference between 'Smith *will be* punished by imprisonment' (a prediction) and 'Smith *is to be* punished by imprisonment' (an imperative) lies simply in their predicates and can be expressed 'Smith is punished by imprisonment' as contrasted with 'Smith is punishable by imprisonment,' and is comparable to the distinction between 'Smith is tall' and 'Smith is heavy.' This will not do at all, in my estimation. It would run afoul of an empirical meaning-criterion for undefined predicates, for I take it that it is essential to Oppenheim's proposal that 'punishable' should not designate an *observable* property. It also does not square with the recognized forms of derivation, which in common usage are different in the two cases of imperatives and declaratives (see text below).

Again Oppenheim apparently has a single metalanguage ("Language B") which is at once syntactical, semantical, and pragmatical, for it contains predicates of each of these kinds (*e.g.*, 'correct' is syntactical, 'true' is semantical, and 'having official quality' is pragmatical), and even predicates that are of two or more kinds at once ('valid' is all three, *cf.* p. 153). This it seems to me easily leads to the very sorts of confusion that the distinction between these dimensions of language was meant to eliminate. Thus, if I read him correctly, Oppenheim sets down a pragmatic criterion (a necessary and sufficient condition) for a syntactical property—*viz.*, an imperative is a basic (underived) sentence in Language A if and only if it has official quality and has not been

distinguishing between the norm and pragmatical sentences about the norm? Clearly this cannot be done by simply distinguishing a norm on the one hand from a norm of opposite content and on the other from a pragmatical sentence asserting that the norm was not authoritatively issued. For as is clear, and as I think Kelsen shows, the determination of the validity of a legal norm *always* involves the question of the authority of the issuing organ. So we may put it as follows. Are the two ways in which a legal norm '*p*!' may not be valid be expressed syntactically by two ways in which a single negative sign can occur in pragmatical sentences about '*p*!'? For example, are the two negatives associated with '*p*!' (an imperative issued by *a*) to be formulated '*a* was not authorized to issue '*p*!' ' '*a* was authorized to issue 'not-*p*!' '? It seems to me not. For neither of these pragmatical sentences is the negative of '*p*!' Rather, they are formed by adding the sign of negation to a pragmatic sentence about '*p*!'[1] They are thus the negatives of *that* sentence (*viz.*, of '*a* was authorized to issue '*p*!' ') not of '*p*!' This is intuitively clear when we note that they are declaratives. We should, I suppose, want to hold that any negative of an imperative is itself an imperative.

In connection with this last point, however, it should be noted that Oppenheim (here I think expressing Kelsen's idea of delegation) does admit pragmatical imperatives into his Language B (composed of sentences of law about expressions in Language A). Thus we might have the imperatives: '*a*, do not issue '*p*!'!' and

reversed by a higher authority (*cf.* p. 158 and *passim*). Oppenheim even speaks of "general conditions under which *any* sentence of *A*, enacted in the future, should be regarded as a basic sentence in A" (p. 158).

Then there is Oppenheim's interesting suggestion that we "distinguish between DESCRIPTIVE and PURE PRAGMATICS: The *empirical* study of the relationship between signs and those who use them is the object of *descriptive* pragmatics. The *logical* study of the pragmatical conditions of the validity of sentences belongs to *pure* pragmatics and as such, together with pure semantics and pure syntax, to logical analysis—sometimes called (pure) semiotic" (p. 154). Now it seems to me that such a pure pragmatics would be nothing but the syntax of descriptive pragmatics, and thus that the logical study of pragmatics would be no different from the logical study of descriptive language—in fact it would just be the logical study of a portion of the language of social psychology. Thus, appearances to the contrary notwithstanding, the proposal of a pure pragmatics promises no help to those who are concerned with the problem of the nature of a logic of imperatives.

[1] More strictly, the first of them is. In the second, we find a name 'not-*p*!' has replaced another '*p*!' Here 'not' is not a sign of negation but an integral part of a name. This itself is sufficient to show we cannot get our two sorts of negation of legal norms in this fashion.

'*a*, issue 'not-*p*!'!' Do these give us the proper formulation of the two negatives of '*p*!' (as issued by *a*)? Again I should say not. They[1] are the negatives of the pragmatical imperative, '*a*, issue '*p*!'!' Hence they cannot also be the negatives of '*p*!' for '*p*!' is not the same imperative as '*a*, issue '*p*!'!' Moreover, they launch us on an endless task if we suppose they show us, in the two ways they include the sign of negation, the peculiar character of the imperative. For if they do so it is in imperatives, and we could therefore display their nature only by specifying the two ways they may fail to hold by two negative imperatives at a higher pragmatical level. For example, on this account, correlated with '*a*, do not issue '*p*!'!' (as issued by *b*) would be '*b*, do not issue '*a*, do not issue '*p*!'!'!' and '*b*, issue 'not-(*a*, do not issue '*p*!'!)'!'

I conclude that the supposed clarification of the validity of legal norms *via* a pragmatic metalanguage that does not include those norms in their own right but only their names ends in a *cul de sac*. In this situation I think it may prove profitable to return to Kelsen for a further hint as to the nature of legal norms.

On Kelsen's account, a legal norm is not properly expressed by a simple imperative, '*p*!', but only by a hypothetical one, 'If *a* issue '*p*!' then *p*!'[2] Here two things should be noted. The legal norm does not appear as an equivalence and certainly not as a logical equivalence. We are not to take '*a* issues '*p*!' ' as meaning the same thing as '*p*!' or as substitutable for it. Rather, '*a* issues '*p*!' ' gives a factual condition (in the system of positive law involved) under which '*p*!' obtains. The validity of '*p*!' is not the truth of '*a* issues '*p*!' ' but is contingent upon it in the sense that through the system of legal norms in which 'If *a* issues '*p*!' then

[1] Or rather, the first is. See the preceding note.

[2] I do not find that Kelsen explicitly says this, but I think it a not unwarranted elucidation of certain things he does say. He does write, "The rule of law says: If *A* is, *B* ought to be" (*op. cit.*, p. 46). However, the context seems to indicate that the antecedent here is to describe some proscribed behaviour, the consequent then obligating the imposition of a sanction. This seems also to be the case when Kelsen is speaking of secondary norms. "Thus there must be two distinct norms: one stipulating that an organ shall execute a sanction against a subject, and one stipulating that another organ shall execute a sanction against the first organ, in case the first sanction is not executed" (*ibid.*, pp. 59–60). But in distinguishing legal (dynamic) normative systems from moral ones, Kelsen writes, "Norm creating power is delegated from one authority to another authority; the former is the higher, the latter the lower authority" (*ibid.*, p. 113). It seems to me this delegation could be expressed by such a norm as: 'If *b* issues the command, 'If *a* issues '*p*!' then *p*!,' then if *a* issues '*p*!' then *p*!'

p!' occurs, the truth of '*a* issues '*p*!' ' *creates* (to use Kelsen's term) the validity of '*p*!'. Thus this whole hypothetical is clearly an imperative. It has the force, so to speak, of its consequent, save that it makes this contingent on a fact. Moreover, this consequent is '*p*!', an imperative in the object-language. Thus though the whole hypothetical must be placed in a (pragmatic) metalanguage, since its antecedent includes the name of a sentence, yet it has the (conditional) force of the object-language imperative, '*p*!'.

Now what, in ordinary usage, would be the negative of 'If *a* issues '*p*!' then '*p*!' '? Clearly it would be a sentence constructed in the same way save that the if-then connection is denied. Here we have some latitude. We may suppose that the sentential form 'if . . . then– – –!' has rules analogous to material implication in ordinary declarative logic. If so, then the negative of 'if . . . then – – –!' would be '. . . and not– – –!' For example, the negative of 'If your wife says, 'Do the dishes!' then you're to do them!' might be 'Although your wife says 'Do the dishes!' you don't have to!' or, again, it might be 'Your wife says 'Do the dishes!' but don't you do them!' (depending on how we interpret 'not– – –!'). I think for our present purposes we need not explore the possibilities further. It would seem plausible to assume that they would all require the occurrence of the negative of the original consequent. Thus the negative of 'if *a* issues '*p*!' then p!' involves the negative of '*p*!' And this seems acceptable since, as we saw, 'if *a* issues '*p*!' then p!' has the contingent force of '*p*!' But this leads us immediately back to our original problem: What are the syntactical correlates of the two ways in which an imperative may fail to be valid?

We have, however, gained some clarification through our detour. We now see that the double negative of imperatives is not to occur in pragmatical meta-sentences only. It must be an integral feature of imperatives at the lowest level, commanding extra-linguistic events, and containing no names of linguistic expressions. It follows that if, developing a suggestion from Kelsen, we were right in taking 'If *a* issues '*p*!' then *p*!' as showing us the simplest, irreducible form of legal norm, then we do not have in legal norms the basic type of imperative. Legal norms, as metalinguistic imperatives, presuppose object-imperatives and finally imperatives that do not mention linguistic expressions at all, that is, zero-level imperatives. Let us turn then directly to such thing-imperatives.

Suppose we have the imperative, 'Donald, wear your rubbers!' There is a certain declarative, namely, 'Donald is wearing his rubbers,' which bears a peculiarly intimate relationship to this imperative. We shall speak of this relationship as one of "correspondence." It can be used in the case of any given imperative to pick out a certain declarative, the declarative said to "correspond" with that imperative. The relationship may be roughly described as that which holds between a declarative and an imperative when the declarative declares as a fact what is commanded in the imperative to be a fact. It is, I think plausible to assume that for each imperative there is a corresponding declarative. We probably would not want to say of every declarative, however, that it corresponds to some imperative, since we might want to hold that an imperative must specify who is to be the agent in bringing about what it is that is commanded.[1]

But of more importance in the present context are two other considerations. On the one hand, we have seen that for every fact there are two declaratives, one asserting it and one denying it. Is it plausible to suppose that if a given declarative corresponds to an imperative, the contradictory of that declarative corresponds to an imperative? My question of course is, Are we to allow this in a clarified language that agrees with good everyday usage? *E.g.*, if 'Donald is wearing his rubbers' corresponds to 'Donald, wear your rubbers!' are we to allow, as meaningful, an imperative to which 'Donald is not wearing his rubbers' corresponds? I would answer definitely in the affirmative. In the example given it would be, 'Donald, don't wear your rubbers!' This may be expressed by saying that for every imperative there is another whose *what* is the negative of the *what* of the former. Here then we have one kind of negative imperative. It is a kind of negative which may be said to be a reflection of the declarative negative, since for any given pair of imperatives such that one is the negative of the other in this sense there is a pair of corresponding declaratives that are the contradictories of one another.

Upon consideration of this there immediately comes to mind the possibility of treating such a pair of imperatives as contradictories. But to do so would involve a disastrous break with good usage. It is not proper to treat 'Donald, don't wear your rubbers!' as the contradictory of 'Donald, wear your rubbers!' For, although the former obviously negates the latter, there is another,

[1] We shall return to this and related questions below, pp. 156 ff.

distinguishable imperative which also, but in another way, negates the latter, namely, 'Donald, you don't have to wear your rubbers!' As this example indicates, any declarative that corresponds to an imperative should be taken as really corresponding to a pair of imperatives, each having the same *what*, but one affirmatively commanding it the other negatively. We could say that, of such a pair of imperatives, the one commands something while the other countermands the first. But this would suggest what certainly seems to me to be an incorrect view. It suggests that this sort of negative imperative cannot occur at the thing-level, that it must always be one level higher than the imperative it negates. It suggests that the negative, in this sense, of 'Donald, wear your rubbers!' is 'The imperative, 'Donald, wear your rubbers!' is hereby cancelled [or is null and void]!' The trouble with such a metalinguistic negative is just that, so far as it remains irreducibly metalinguistic, it is not the negative of a thing-imperative. For example, 'The imperative, 'Donald, wear your rubbers!' is hereby cancelled!' is, properly, the negative of some such metalinguistic imperative as 'The imperative, 'Donald, wear your rubbers!' is hereby issued!' It *seems* to be the negative of 'Donald, wear your rubbers!' because we tacitly treat it as equivalent to 'Donald, you don't have to wear your rubbers!' But to make it equivalent to the latter presupposes that the latter is permitted in its own right.

So now we have found in thing-imperatives the two sorts of negatives (as contrasted with the single negative of declaratives) which were suggested in our investigation of legal norms. An imperative may negate another in what it is that is commanded or in the quality of the command itself.[1] Thus in the case of every

[1] This has been clearly recognized by Alf Ross. (It was involved, but not clearly pointed out, in a suggestion of Menger's as to a logic of optatives, discussed below.) Following Jorgensen and Dubislav, Ross distinguishes between what he calls "the factor of demand" and "the theme of demand" of an imperative. He writes, ". . . it is necessary to use linguistic expressions which distinguish between negative imperatives in two different senses, *i.e.*, (1) imperatives with a negative theme of demand [$I(\bar{x})$=you are (not to close the door)=you are to leave it open] and (2) imperatives with a negative factor of demand, expressing that a positive imperative with an identical theme of demand is not valid [$\bar{I}$ (x)=you (are not to) close the door=the imperative 'you are to close the door' is not valid]" ("Imperatives and Logic," *Philosophy of Science*, vol. xi, 1944, p. 39). *Cf.* also T. Storer, "The Logic of Value Imperatives," *Philosophy of Science*, vol. xiii, 1946, p. 33.

If I understand him correctly, however, Mr. Ross argues that these two negatives cannot occur in the same logical system (what he says is that they

pair of contradictory declaratives such that one corresponds to an imperative, there is an imperative to which the other corresponds, and these two imperatives are such that one can be properly spoken of as the negative of the other, as negating the *what* of the other but keeping its imperative quality the same. But there is also, for each of these imperatives, another which negates it by keeping the same *what* but changing the quality of the command. Hence for every pair of declaratives of the sort specified

cannot be combined, thus allowing logical inferences involving both). If however we examine his argument it seems to turn on a certain interpretation of the factor of demand (and hence of its negation). This interpretation is that the factor of demand is an assertion of a psychological state in the commander. Thus an imperative may be given two quite independent semantical interpretations: as asserting a state of mind in the imperator (the imperative attitude) or as asserting a state of fact other than this (what is imperatived). And the negations of these are likewise mutually independent. Thus, he argues, we cannot deduce from the negation of what is imperatived the negation of the state of mind of the imperator. It is possible to command a contradiction, to have the same imperative state of mind toward a certain content and toward its negation (*cf. op. cit.*, p. 40).

This argument, to my mind, shows that Ross has not grasped the radical significance of his own distinction between the two rôles of negation in imperatives. His argument really implies there is only one kind of negation—though it has two interpretations as one gives two interpretations of imperatives. It should be noted that when one interprets imperatives as asserting states of mind in their imperators, their negations are simple negations (as for any descriptive sentences). On this interpretation there is no additional negation (in any syntactical sense) that can occur in connection with the theme of demand. The theme of demand is not an assertion (or negation) of any other fact than the state of mind of the imperator; so any symbol in it that looks like a negation ('no' 'not' 'un-' etc.) is just part of the positive description (either affirmed or denied) of the state of mind (including verbal activities) of the imperator. As soon as one admits that there are syntactically two different kinds of negation in imperatives, then any interpretation of imperatives must be such as to preserve this difference. This does not disprove their independence, but it does show that one cannot prove their independence by giving different interpretations of imperatives. Rules governing their use, in relation to one another, must be set up so as to accord as nearly as possible with everyday speech. I would suppose we ought to treat as invalid or illegitimate any command whose *what* involves a contradiction, not because people cannot utter such commands, but because common sense would recognize them as improper commands, as senseless, as not properly constructed, as commanding nothing.

Menger has made it a law of optative consistency that wishes with contradictory *whats* cannot be conjoined. But he vitiates what appears to be his insight here by giving a psychologistic interpretation of the wish-element (*Reports of a Mathematical Colloquium*, second series, issue 1, 1939, p. 61).

R. M. Hare has distinguished between the "descriptor" and the "dictor" of an imperative, corresponding to my distinction between what is commanded and the command-element. But by allowing the negative to attach only to the former he destroys the possibility of allowing his distinction to aid him in the problem we are here considering. See footnote pp. 141-3 below.

there seems to be a set of four imperatives, illustrated by our example as follows:

1. Donald is wearing his rubbers.	1a. Donald, you have to wear your rubbers! 1b. Donald, you don't have to wear your rubbers!
2. Donald is not wearing his rubbers.	2a. Donald, you have to refrain from wearing your rubbers! 2b. Donald, you don't have to refrain from wearing your rubbers!

It is easily seen that 1a and 2a exclude each other in the obvious sense that if either is fulfilled the other cannot be, since they affirmatively command contradictory *whats*. But 1b and 2b do not so exclude each other. Although the *whats* are here also contradictory, the quality of the command is in this case negative, and thus *either* 1 or 2 would be considered as compatible with *either* 1b or 2b in the sense of stating conditions that would constitute a fulfilment. Thus I think it would not be too much of a reform of common usage to conjoin 1b and 2b as a single imperative. We would then have for each pair of declaratives of the sort specified a trio of imperatives. Corresponding to the law of contradiction for declaratives we could have a law of exclusiveness for imperatives, such that for any trio of the kind just indicated, not more than one (semantically stated, not more than one can obtain or hold good). Similarly, corresponding to the law of excluded middle there would be a law of exhaustiveness, such that for any trio of the kind indicated, at least one (semantically put, at least some must obtain or hold good).

This difference as to negatives is itself sufficient to show that a logic of imperatives, to square with common usage, must be different from any proper logic of declaratives. Realizing this we probably will not be surprised if we discover, in consonance with everyday usage, that the rules of "binary" connectives are also different in imperative logic from what they are in declarative.[1] This of course follows for any connectives that can be defined in terms of 'not' and some other connective. It would also seem to be the case for connectives not so defined. Suppose 'and' to be

[1] Strictly if the rules are different the connectives are. A connective just *is* the rules that govern its use; it is not a certain sequence of letters as sensible shapes or vowel and consant sounds. Moreover, I think it is highly misleading, epistemologically, to treat 'not' as a connective. But this is irrelevant in the present context.

such a connective. In declarative logic 'and' is so used that from 'The prisoner was first handcuffed and then given a private audience with the judge' there follows 'The prisoner was given a private audience with the judge.' But we would not want in imperative logic to have 'and' so used that from 'Let the prisoner first be handcuffed! and let the prisoner then be given a private audience with the judge!' there followed 'Let the prisoner be given a private audience with the judge!' We should probably want to allow the latter imperative to follow not from the former alone but only from the former plus the declarative, 'The prisoner has been handcuffed.'

The conjunctive imperative consequently should not be taken as entailing its components taken separately. Moreover, although it does seem to entail the pair of hypothetical imperatives formed by taking one of its component imperatives as the consequent and using the declarative corresponding to the other component as antecedent and then doing the same with the other component imperative, still it would not seem proper to treat it as logically equivalent to such a pair. For example, from 'Give me pen and ink!' there does seem to follow both 'If you give me a pen, then give me ink!' and 'If you give me ink then give me a pen!', yet the original conjunctive imperative does not seem to be equivalent to this pair of hypothetical imperatives. For it might be that both the antecedents of these imperative hypotheticals are false, in which case we should want, in analogy with declarative hypotheticals, to say that the imperative hypotheticals therefore held good (were legitimate) quite irrespective of whether their consequents did. That is, suppose you do not give me a pen, then we should probably wish to say that the whole hypothetical, 'If you give me a pen then give me ink!' was legitimate quite independently of whether 'give me ink!' was by itself legitimate or not. The same of course can be said for 'If you give me ink then give me a pen!' Hence both hypotheticals could be legitimate even if neither of their consequents were. This, however, would be clearly incompatible with the sense of the conjunctive categorical imperative. Also it should be noted that although 'Give me pen and ink!' does seem to entail 'If you give me a pen then give me ink!' but does not entail 'Give me ink!' yet we are not to say that it entails 'If you do not give me pen then do not give me ink!' Though the 'and' does not entail the separability of the components it unites, neither does it prohibit it.

Or suppose 'or' to be such an undefined connective. In ordinary declarative logic we use 'or' so that 'The defendant was sentenced to death or was set free' follows from 'The defendant was sentenced to death.' But we would not want to use 'or' with imperatives so that 'Hang the defendant or set him free!' followed from 'Hang the defendant!'[1]

It thus seems quite clear that a logic of imperatives must differ in its transformation rules and its rules for the formation of complex sentences (by the use of simple sentences and connectives) from declarative logic. Indeed, it seems rather obvious that the formulation of such rules for a logic of imperatives will require a rather extended analysis of common usage before any assurance of adequacy to the latter can be attained. It is not the purpose of the present writer to try to develop such a set of rules, nor is the accomplishment of such a purpose indispensable to the specific task undertaken in this essay. But what is necessary in trying to determine the status of value and its relation to fact is to gain some insight into how we are in general to construct imperative sentences so that their relation to their corresponding declaratives is clear and their relations to one another are capable of definite rules which differ, at least in some respects, from the rules for their corresponding declaratives.

It seems to me that there are three promising ways in which such a clarification might proceed. One is to construct imperatives out of their corresponding declaratives by adding a sign of imperativity, but leaving formation and transformation rules otherwise unchanged when applied to the sentences thus formed. Another is to use entirely different symbols for imperatives and their connectives from those used for declaratives. This would require a new set of formation and transformation rules for imperatives.

[1] It may be contended that the anomalies of the logic of imperatives in everyday speech are due to a failure to distinguish between a disjunctive command and commanding a disjunction, between a conjunctive command and commanding a conjunction, between a negative command and commanding a negation. It might be claimed that connectives uniting imperatives are exactly the same (obey the same rules) as connectives uniting declaratives. The reason they appear not to do so would be that what is commanded is on occasion compound, and we must not confuse the connectives that unite commands with those that unite contents commanded. We must not confuse 'Put on your parachute! and jump!' (which does imply 'Jump!') with 'Let both of these be the case: that you put on your parachute and that you jump!' (which does not imply 'Let this be the case, that you jump!'). We shall turn to this possibility shortly, in connection with a suggestion of Karl Menger.

A third is to form imperatives from the same names as declaratives but to use a different sentential form to combine these names into atomic sentences and different rules for connectives to build molecular sentences from atomic sentences. We shall find that each of these procedures has advantages but also disadvantages as judged by everyday usage, and although the writer will advocate the last as throwing the most light on our problem, he will be forced to admit that it too is misleading.

In the development and criticism of these alternatives it is desirable to consider them, as far as possible, in forms they have actually assumed or in presentations that at least suggest them.

Until quite recently the possibility of a logic of imperatives was almost completely ignored. There has of late been some attempt to rectify this situation. For the most part, however, the effort has been half-hearted, due to a failure to appreciate that such a logic must be irreducible to ordinary declarative logic. Some of these attempts would reduce imperative logic to a part of declarative logic, making imperatives a certain (disguised) sort of declarative.[1] This we can now see to be quite unacceptable,

[1] Thus Herbert G. Bohnert ("The Semiotic Status of Commands," *Philosophy of Science*, vol. xii, 1945, pp. 302–15) suggests that imperatives be regarded as ellipses for declarative disjunctions, one alternative of which is the content of the imperative, put in descriptive form, the other being a non-expressed penalty. For example, 'Cease this strike!' spoken by a Nazi to a Norwegian mining town could be treated as an elliptical form of 'Either this strike ceases or no one in this town will eat.' Karl Menger had made the same suggestion (*Reports of a Mathematical Colloquium*, Second Series, Issue 1, 1939). He wrote: "The statement 'I command p' . . . may be interpreted as 'Unless p, something unpleasant will happen (*e.g.*, I shall be angry or you will be punished)' " (p. 59).

This suggestion has certain strange consequences. One is that imperatives are true or false. Another is that from any declarative it is possible to derive the corresponding imperative; from 'The strike ceases' it is possible to derive 'Cease the strike!' For, from any declarative it is possible to derive a disjunction one of whose members is that declarative, the other a statement of a penalty. Put semantically this would entail (I take it) that if any given declarative sentence is true then the command ordering that situation to occur which the true declarative sentence describes is also true. I do not know what 'true' means when asserted of imperatives. If it entails that the imperative is legitimate in any sense involving the assertion that what is commanded by the true imperative ought to be or is good, then surely Bohnert's position is just absurd, for it implies that whatever is is right or as it ought to be.

But the fundamental objection is that, to make an imperative even appear to be rendered by a declarative disjunction, it is necessary to read one of the alternatives *as* a *threatened penalty*. It might seem plausible to render 'Cease the strike!' by 'Either you will cease the strike or you will not eat,' but it hardly seems common sense to render it by 'Either you will cease the strike or you have blue eyes,' yet logically the latter rendition has the same form as the former.

for no portion of ordinary declarative logic displays the characteristics demanded if one is to have two irreducible negatives of an atomic sentence (to emphasize just one of the peculiarities of imperatives we have noted).

There are other essays in imperative logic that would make such a logic isomorphic with the whole of declarative logic and thus trivialize its separate development. This results, for example, if one simply builds imperatives by adding to their corresponding declaratives a sign of imperativity (such as '!') but leaving the declaratives otherwise unchanged, specifically, keeping the same connectives[1]. Such trivialization is the symptom of a failure to grasp the profound differences between the logical behaviour of imperatives and declaratives in everyday usage.

However, there is an essay giving some hints as to how a logic of imperatives can be developed (actually it is formulated for the most part in terms of optatives). It builds imperatives from their corresponding declaratives by the addition of a sign of imperativity yet retains as fundamental the distinction between imperatives and declaratives. I refer to Karl Menger's "A Logic of the

If it will not do, it must be for psychological reasons. It is therefore clear that Mr. Bohnert's suggestion furnishes no syntactical criterion that can be used to mark those declaratives that can, in elliptical form, function as imperatives. Moreover, that he has chosen disjunctions (rather than other forms of compound declaratives or for that matter simple declaratives) has no logical, but only a psychological, basis—and to this writer not a convincing one. The long emphasis upon sanctions in various voluntaristic theories of law gives specious reasonability to the view that commands inherently include, at least tacitly, reference to reward or punishment for their fulfilment or non-fulfilment. But the nature of a command, as such, includes no such reference. To suppose it does is to confuse linguistic analysis with causal explanation.

[1] This is the case with the outline of a satisfactional logic of imperatives of Hofstadter and McKinsey in their paper, "On the Logic of Imperatives" (*Philosophy of Science*, vol. vi, 1939, pp. 446–57). They also recognize the possibility of a logic of correctness of imperatives, but do not develop it.

These authors think of imperatives as having satisfaction-values analogous to the truth-values of declaratives. Indeed they suggest that we "understand an imperative to be satisfied if what is commanded is the case" (p. 447), that is, if the corresponding declarative is true. In such a logic of imperatives "all imperative-connectives can always be eliminated from a sentence, and . . . all imperative-connectives except for one '!' symbol [which transforms a declarative into its corresponding imperative] can always be eliminated . . ." (p. 452). The fact that in this system "every sentence involving the mark '!' [is] equipollent to a sentence not involving this mark, shows that the introduction of the '!' is superfluous" (p. 453). The authors admit that this system is "in a sense trivial" but urge that "it is nevertheless useful to recognize triviality for what it is and where it appears" (p. 453), a sentiment with which the present writer concurs.

Doubtful. On Optative and Imperative Logic."[1] I shall use these hints to state a position which goes beyond what Menger actually says. I really think something approximating it must have been vaguely present in his mind, although his main interest was quite different from ours. Put in its simplest terms, this position avoids trivializing the logic of imperatives by allowing imperatives to be built from molecular as well as from atomic declaratives, but refusing in general to allow the connectives of these "root-declaratives," as I shall call them, to travel out, to apply to the whole imperative in which they occur. If we put the root-declarative within parentheses in the imperative,[2] this position allows connectives within parentheses in imperatives, but in general it requires that they stay there, that they not be confused with nor permitted to affect the connectives of the imperatives within which they occur.

As I have said, we have at least some hints of this view in Menger's paper. First, it is clear that he would build an imperative from its corresponding declarative and a sign of imperativity.[3] Second, it is clear that he allows imperatives to be built from root-declaratives that are molecular,[4] and he clearly distinguishes the connectives in these root-declaratives from the connectives of the imperatives in which they occur.

These features are clearly present in his treatment of negative connectives. He distinguishes an imperative with a negative sign from an imperative without such a sign but whose root-declarative is that of the former but with a negative sign.[5] Thus from a given declarative four imperatives may be built by the use of negative connectives.[6] And it must be emphasized that these are four distinct imperatives; the law of double negation and the travelling

[1] *Reports of a Mathematical Colloquium* (*Publications of the University of Notre Dame*), 1939, second series, issue 1, pp. 53–64.

[2] Suppose, for example, we write '$(p)!$' for the imperative built by using 'p' as the root declarative, '$(p.q)!$' for that built from '$p.q$' and so on.

[3] He uses the expression 'Cp,' which he interprets, 'I command p,' and similarly, 'Dp,' which is to be read, 'I desire p.' The use of the personal pronoun indicates, I fear, that Menger has not rid himself of the supposition that imperatives and optatives are psychological descriptions, that is, are really declaratives. We shall read beyond this.

[4] He allows, for example, 'Cp′,' which is built from 'p′,' that is, from 'not-p,' and 'C(p&q),' which is built from 'p&q,' that is from 'p and q.'

[5] In his terminology, he distinguishes, 'I don't command p' from 'I command not-p' ('C′p' from 'Cp′').

[6] From 'p' can be built 'Cp,' 'Cp′,' 'C′p,' 'C′p′.' In our notation these are '$(p)!$', '$(\sim p)!$', '$\sim(p)!$', '$\sim(\sim p)!$'.

of the negative sign from root-declarative to whole imperative[1] or *vice versa* are not permitted.

These features also seem to be present in Menger's thoughts as to other connectives. The one definite case he gives is the conjunctive connective, and even here we must make the qualification that his position, as stated above, holds for optatives but not for imperatives.[2] He gives no argument for his distinction in this respect between imperatives and optatives, and the distinction does not seem intuitively correct so far as common usage is concerned. Hence for the theoretical exploration of this alternative we shall drop it. Moreover, we need to generalize for all connectives, and to say that any declarative connective may occur in a root-declarative in an imperative,[3] but as so occurring we are not to suppose that the connective can be removed from the root-declarative and engender a molecular imperative, equivalent to the former imperative, whose components are the imperatives formed from the components of the root-declaratives of the former.[4]

In the two features mentioned, the present view as to a logic of imperatives and its relation to a logic of declaratives seems to have been more or less clearly in Menger's thought. But there is a third feature that Menger's essay at least vaguely suggests and which is sufficiently interesting to warrant mention. It is to the effect that

[1] To make his treatment of the negative square with that of other connectives it would have been better if, instead of 'C′p,' etc., Menger had used '(Cp)′.' On the other hand, Menger's actual notation here is not without bearing on the issues we shall raise.

[2] He writes, "If I command (p&q) then, in particular, I command p and I command q. But if I wish (p&q), then, at least according to one of the ways in which the word 'wish' is used, it does not necessarily follow that I wish p. If p and q are what in economics is called complementary goods (like a cigarette and a match), then it is quite possible that I wish (p&q) without wishing either one of the goods by itself" (*loc. cit.*, p. 59). Thus, although 'C(p&q)' is logically equivalent to '(Cp&Cq),' 'D(p&q)' is not logically equivalent to '(Dp&Dq).'

[3] We might be hesitant to allow this. For example, we might not want to allow that 'if-then' could occur in a root-declarative in an imperative (we must remember that this would be a declarative not an imperative connective). But even this has possibilities. One can imagine Jehovah commanding: 'Let it be such that if rain falls then the fields will be green!' And this imperative would not, incidentally, be equivalent to 'If rain, do you fall! then fields be ye green!' But this is not essential. Suppose only some declarative connectives are allowed ever to appear in root-declaratives of imperatives. Then for *these* connectives we are not, on the alternative now being explored, to allow in general that they can leave the root-declarative and combine imperatives formed from the components of the original root-declarative.

[4] That is, we are not to allow in general or without qualification that where 'c' is any connective $(pcq)! \equiv (p)!\ c\ (q)!$ (using the notation we suggested above).

the connectives uniting simple imperatives into compound imperatives behave just like the corresponding connectives for declaratives.

Consider, for example, Menger's treatment of pairs of optatives united by the conjunctive connective, where the conjoined optatives are formed from the same root-declarative by means of the use of negative connectives. As we saw, with each root-declarative we can construct four optatives in this manner. Now, the total number of combinations of these, two at a time, is sixteen. Eliminating redundancies and pairs that differ only in the order of their members, this leaves six combinations.[1] But Menger, in stating the possibilities, mentions only four.[2] And of these four he rules out one (in which the quality of both component optatives is affirmative, but one has a root-declarative which is the negative of the root-declarative of the other) as excluded by a law of optative consistency. Why did he simply omit two combinations? My guess is that he was here guided by the desire to conform with common usage. This is borne out by the fact that the three combinations he retains are to be read 'I wish p,' 'I wish not-p,' and 'I am indifferent to p.' Moreover, the two combinations he simply omits would be read, still following his own language, 'I wish p but I also don't wish p' and 'I wish not-p but I also don't wish not-p.' Now these two seem to sin not against some special law of optative consistency but against the ordinary law of contradiction.[3] They are formed of two optatives having exactly

[1] They are:

(1) $(p)! \cdot \sim(\sim p)!$
(2) $\sim(p)! \cdot (\sim p)!$
(3) $\sim(p)! \cdot \sim(\sim p)!$
(4) $(p)! \cdot (\sim p)!$
(5) $(p)! \cdot \sim(p)!$
(6) $(\sim p)! \cdot \sim(\sim p)!$

[2] These are, in his language:
"(1) Dp&D′p′ or briefly Dp (I wish p).
"(2) D′p&Dp′ or briefly Dp′ . . . (I wish p′).
"(3) D′p&D′p′ . . . (p is indifferent to me).
"The fourth possibility Dp&Dp′ is excluded by the law of optative consistency" (*op. cit.*, p. 61).

In the preceding note I have numbered the first four possible combinations to correspond with Menger's numbering.

[3] It may be that Menger meant to rule them out by his assumption II. "II. Dp does not belong to M_0. (There shall be no doubt as to whether or not I wish p.)" (*ibid.*, p. 61). If this is formally adequate to eliminate combinations (5) and (6) of our list, then our question simply becomes, Why did Menger put down assumption II and what does it involve as to negative connectives of optatives?

the same root-declarative but differing in the quality of the whole —one being affirmative and one negative. It may not be too far-fetched to suppose that Menger thought of the imperative negative as behaving in imperative logic in the same way as the declarative negative in declarative logic.[1]

When we come to deal with other connectives of imperatives our case for claiming that Menger treated them as having exactly the same rules as the corresponding connectives of declaratives is even more tenuous, though I do not find he says anything that would conflict with this. Let us, therefore, consider it as a possibility just in its own right. This view could still avoid the trivialization of imperative logic by insisting that (a) the formation rules for imperative sentences differ from the formation rules for declarative sentences (the former requiring root-declaratives and a sign of imperativity) and that (b) there be transformation rules for imperatives that have no counterpart in declarative logic. In explanation of (b) I have in mind that although in general we are not to allow connectives in root-declaratives to become or to affect connectives of total imperatives, yet under certain conditions they might do so. Let us use Menger's case of complementary goods, such as a cigarette and a match. Here 'Give me a cigarette! and give me a match!' does entail 'Give me a match!' (the connective joins two imperatives and so acts as the corresponding connective in declarative logic), but 'Give me a cigarette and a match!' does not entail 'Give me a match!' (the connective joins declarative elements in the root-declarative).[2] On the other hand, if goods are not complementary but independent a new sort of transformation is allowed. Suppose that a pencil and a match are thus independent goods. Then we might wish to allow that 'Give me a pencil and a match!' does entail 'Give me a match!'[3]

We can envisage a comparable situation with 'or.' As combining total imperatives it behaves just as its counterpart in

[1] It might be supposed that (3) is incompatible with the law of excluded middle. To this it could be replied that on Menger's own treatment of declarative logic (as 3-valued) this would not constitute a difference. But this would be irrelevant to our present purpose. The correct reply is that, on the view now being investigated, (3) does not conflict with the law of excluded middle for imperatives (or optatives). For both members of the combination are negative (and the negative sign attached to the root-declarative is, as we have seen, to be kept insulated, without effect upon the negative sign attaching to the whole).

[2] '$(p)! \cdot (q)!$' entails '$(q)!$' but '$(p \cdot q)!$' does not entail '$(q)!$'

[3] '$(r \cdot q)!$' in this case does entail '$(q)!$'

declarative logic. Thus 'Hang the prisoner!' entails (but of course is not equivalent to) 'Hang the prisoner! or set the prisoner free!' But when the goods are incompatible, as in this case, an 'or' in the root-declarative stays there, without bearing upon possible transformations of total imperatives. Thus 'Hang the prisoner!' would not entail 'Hang the prisoner or set him free!'[1] On the other hand, where the goods are compatible we might want to allow a new kind of transformation. Supposing hanging the prisoner and handcuffing him are compatible. Then we might want 'Hang the prisoner!' to entail (but not be equivalent to) 'Hang the prisoner or handcuff him!' (where 'or' has the force of 'at least one').[2]

Without having made a careful study of it I should say offhand that a logic of imperatives might be built along these lines that would preserve the anomalies of the connectives of imperatives (including negatives) as found in good everyday usage. Let us suppose, then, for the sake of the argument, that this can be done. Has it anything to offer us in our job of trying to gain insight through syntax into the status of value and its relation to fact? I think it has a great deal to offer. It will be noted that on this programme the *what* that is commanded[3] is literally presented in the imperative, as the root-declarative of the latter. And when the *what* is negative or a conjunction or disjunction of possible facts (and this is frequently the case in ordinary thought), this character is literally preserved in the form of the root-declarative, and preserved, be it noted, as a character of the *what* of the imperative. Moreover, the value-element does not appear in the form of a predicate. This reflects our contention that value is not a property; specifically, though value somehow attaches to facts it is not a property of fact. Syntactically, the linguistic expression of value is *via* a sentence-form (not the mere sign of imperativity but the whole form of the imperative). This raises serious problems for our objectivism which may be pointed up by the question, 'Can a sentential form reveal anything about the non-linguistic world?', a consideration of which, however, must be postponed.[4] But the present programme for a logic of imperatives

[1] Thus '$(p)!$' entails '$(p)! \vee (q)!$' but '$(p)!$' does not entail '$(p \vee q)!$'

[2] '(p)!' would in this case entail '(p$\vee$r)!'

[3] More generally, what it is, that is valued, is present as a constituent of the value-sentence. For a discussion of the relation of imperatives to other value-sentences, see below, pp. 155 ff.

[4] See below, Section 7a.

would seem to suggest linguistically how value might involve or be about fact without being a property of fact and yet be extra-linguistic, *i.e.*, expressible in sentences at the zero-level, not in sentences that mention others (the declaratives stating the *what*).

But along with all these advantages, the present proposal carries a serious disadvantage as well. What it is that is commanded appears as a root-declarative from which the imperative is built. It thus seems to occur *literally*, as a declarative sentence in its own right, within the imperative. Thus, for example, 'Donald, wear your rubbers!' would be translated into something like '(Donald is wearing his rubbers) do it!' It is to be remembered that it is the corresponding declarative itself, not its name, that is to function as the root-declarative of an imperative.[1] So also we must here avoid the dodge of indirect discourse, of, for example, translating the above imperative by 'Let it be the case that Donald is wearing his rubbers!', for indirect discourse if properly clarified requires the mentioning of a sentence or what, for our present problem, amounts to the same thing, the mentioning of the sense of a sentence (perhaps not as the sense of a specified sentence but as the sense of some sentence).[2]

Let us suppose, then, that the root-declarative in an imperative just is a declarative in its own right, *viz.*, the declarative that corresponds to that imperative. This would require that every imperative assert, state as a fact, its corresponding declarative. This certainly does *not* square with good usage. 'Donald, wear your rubbers!' does not include the statement that Donald is wearing his rubbers, nor does it require that it be a fact that Donald is (or will be) wearing his rubbers if the imperative is to hold good or be legitimate as an imperative.[3]

There might seem to be a way out of this difficulty, a way suggested by Menger himself in the paper to which reference has already been made. May we not say that the root-declarative, though literally included in an imperative, is not an asserted

[1] Otherwise, on this programme, imperatives could never occur at the zero-level, which would be disastrous, as we have seen.

[2] This is a pretty cavalier way of disposing of a host of problems connected with the analysis of indirect discourse, but I can't see anything else to be done in the present context.

[3] It might be taken to imply that Donald is not wearing his rubbers. I would rather doubt that it does, but if so, then imperatives cannot be taken as representative of all value-sentences, for certainly 'It was a good thing that Donald wore his rubbers' does not imply that Donald did not wear his rubbers.

proposition (nor a negated one), but is doubtful?[1] As a psychological suggestion this is irrelevant and, moreover, false. But Menger means it as a logical proposal. As such, it involves us in a three-valued system of declarative logic. This is too high a price to pay. That is, it is too high if it means that such a three-valued system is to replace the ordinary two-valued logic of truth and falsity.[2] The latter certainly cannot be dispensed with if we want a logic that squares with the behaviour of declarative sentences in ordinary speech. Moreover, to require that all sentences that can appear as root-declaratives in imperatives shall be doubtful (neither asserted nor negated) does not itself in any way meet the difficulty we now face. That difficulty can be met only on the additional assumption that doubtful sentences may be either true or false. For what we want is that the imperative can hold good independently of whether or not what it is that is commanded is [was or will be] a fact. To say this, however, requires the traditional two-valued classification of declaratives. Now of course if the three-valued logic is merely to be added, as an independent calculus in no way intended to replace the two-valued calculus which is still to remain indispensable to any adequate formalization of ordinary language, then there is no objection to Menger's proposal, so far as the present issue is concerned, save that it is beside the point.

If we are thoroughly aware that the behaviour and the sense of imperatives in everyday speech is not adequately reflected in the "clarification" that builds imperatives from their corresponding declaratives by adding a sign of imperativity, then we are in a position to see that another feature of Menger's notation is misleading. His proposal would distinguish two imperative

[1] Menger writes: "In building up a logic of wishes and commands we shall deal merely with propositions that, in the sense of the logic of the doubtful, are neither asserted nor negated, *i.e.*, with doubtful propositions" (*loc. cit.*, p. 59). To this we might add the remark that although in support of the above statement Menger says, "The objects of our wishes and commands are neither impossibilities nor necessities" (*ibid.*, p. 59), he has previously told us that besides tautologies the class of asserted propositions "may contain other propositions expressing *e.g.*, observations, psychical laws, etc." (*ibid.*, p. 54), and that if a given proposition is an asserted proposition then the negative of it belongs to the class of negated propositions. Thus the class of doubtful propositions does not include all propositions other than the necessary or impossible (the three classes, asserted, negated, doubtful, are mutually exclusive).

[2] This seems to be what Menger proposes. *Cf.* the first two paragraphs of his essay and his statement, "One of the reasons for the failure of Molly's interesting attempt [to develop a logic of normative propositions] is that it was founded on the 2-valued calculus of propositions" (*ibid.*, p. 59).

negatives by having the negative connective attach in the one instance to the root-declarative and in the other to the sign of imperativity itself.[1] This seems at first quite unobjectionable, and does, in fact, throw some light on imperative negativity, since, as has been emphasized, we do negate a given imperative sometimes by commanding the negative of its *what* and sometimes by negating the quality of its command-element. But now we can see that Menger's proposal, though enlightening, is yet objectionable. Neither the root-declarative nor the sign of imperativity is properly to be taken as a component sentence in the imperative. There are simple or atomic imperatives, and in the case of any such the *only* sentence is the *whole* imperative. Any negative connective must attach to it. If it be retorted that this throws too much weight upon an historical accident, the accident that it has become the tradition to treat the sign of negation as a sentential connective, two replies could be made. The first is somewhat *ad hominem*. It is to the effect that Menger is within that tradition and has not, in the proposal under discussion, disavowed it. The second is really substantial and germane to our inquiry. At least in one respect the tradition is no mere accident. Whether the negative is properly considered to be a connective, it certainly is sentential, as is clear from the consideration that it is the syntactical correlate of the semantical predicate 'false,' which can only be ascribed to sentences. There is no such thing as a negative name. A "negative term," so called, is an abbreviated negative description which, by using Russell's analysis of descriptions, can always be eliminated. This feature of a clarified language—that the negative sign only attaches properly to sentences, never to parts of sentences that are not themselves sentences—is all we need for our present point.

What we are saying, then, is that if, as we have found to be the case, there are two mutually irreducible negatives for every affirmative imperative, these should properly be represented by two different signs, each attaching to the total imperative. Once this is seen for negatives, however, we note that the whole proposal as to connectives collapses. We were going to distinguish connectives within root-declaratives from connectives of total imperatives. The latter were to behave just as their name-sakes in declarative logic. The former, save under specified conditions, were to remain insulated within the root-declarative. But now

[1] Thus the two sorts of negative of 'Cp' are 'Cp′' and 'C′p.'

we find ourselves forced to admit two different negatives for total imperatives. Thus imperative connectives cannot be the same as declarative. Moreover, our basic recognition that we cannot admit that a simple imperative contains a declarative as a component leads immediately to the denial that there are any connectives within such an imperative.

Now all of this might be admitted by an advocate of the proposal for a logic of imperatives now under consideration if a radically different interpretation of that proposal were given. It might simply be denied that the root-declarative is a sentence. We may be said to build an imperative by taking a declarative and adding a sign of imperativity. But *in* the context of root-declarative-in-an-imperative the symbol that looks like a sentence is not to be taken as a sentence (and of course it is not the name of a sentence). So likewise if we start with a compound declarative and build an imperative, the root-declarative contains no connectives, it only appears to do so.

However, if this manages to avoid the difficulties which arise from supposing the root-declarative really is a sentence within the imperative built upon it, it also manages to avoid all the advantages of that suggestion. That imperatives have a *what* that is commanded, that this *what* may itself be negative or compound, and that as such it is to be distinguished from a negative or compound total imperative, and that this *what* can always be stated in a declarative that corresponds to the imperative—all these features are simply absent from the logical form of imperatives on the present interpretation. However much the root-declarative and certain signs that it includes may look like declarative sentences and their connectives, this appearance is logically irrelevant And if, moreover, the connectives of imperatives simply behave as connectives of declaratives, we have just another trivialization of the logic of imperatives.[1]

If, on the other hand, it be held that the rules for connectives

[1] Another trivialization of imperative logic is to be found in a suggestion of R. M. Hare's ("Imperative Sentences," *Mind*, vol. lviii, 1949, pp. 21–39). He draws a distinction similar to that in the proposal just considered between the root-declarative and the sign of imperativity, though this way of putting it is misleading since he makes a similar distinction within declaratives. In both imperatives and declaratives there is the "descriptor," which describes what it is that is being said, and there is the "dictor," which does the saying (the commanding or stating). It is his contention that the various logical connectives, including the negative, serve only to bind together descriptor elements to which what he calls the "dictor" is then externally added. He con-

of imperatives must take into consideration what is present in the root-declarative and thus do not simply duplicate the rules for declarative connectives, then it must be admitted that such rules are not merely formal, that they are determined by something that could not be known through any knowledge of the structure of the imperatives. It would be as though in declarative logic we had special rules for 'not,' 'and,' 'or,' and so on in the case of sentences with colour-predicates as contrasted with sentences with odour-predicates. Indeed, it would make imperative logic just such a peculiar, non-formal and non-formalizable portion of ordinary declarative logic. As contrasted with such a specious distinction between the *what* and the command-element in an imperative it would be much less misleading to write imperatives as whole sentences that are just different from declaratives and

cludes that since all logical operations are performed on descriptors and these are common to declaratives and imperatives, the logic of imperatives is identical with the logic of declaratives.

This has some strange consequences. One, which I am not sure Mr. Hare fully grasps, is that logic would have nothing to do with sentences (a sentence must have a dictor but the addition of a dictor to any given descriptor is obviously an extra-logical matter). He does say, in speaking of the relation between premises and conclusion in a valid inference, that "we could ignore the dictors" and that "there is a factor, the descriptor, which is contained in both indicatives and imperatives, and that it is this descriptor that we operate with in most, if not all, logical inferences" (p. 30). "In fact, it is the descriptive part of sentences with which formal logicians are almost exclusively concerned; and this means that what they say applies as much to imperatives as to indicatives; for to any descriptor we can add either kind of dictor and get a sentence" (*ibid.*). This however fails to see that it takes a full sentence to describe a state of affairs, and it is only in a psychological sense that one can be said not to assert when one describes. This, it seems to me, is clear in itself, and is implied in what I said about our reference to facts (they cannot be named but only asserted).

But if Mr. Hare is not too clear on this consequence of his position he is fully aware of another. He sees that on his proposal connectives are to behave in imperative logic just as they do in declarative. He points out that on his view 'Put on your parachute and jump out' entails 'Jump out' and 'Post the letter' entails 'Post or burn the letter.' Mr. Hare apparently attempts to mitigate this paradox by distinguishing between command and obedience. He writes, "When I said above that to command C is to command c_1 I did not mean that to obey c_1 was to obey C" (p. 33). Again, he says, "We cannot indeed, when given a command, infer other commands from it, and think that by fulfilling them we have fulfilled the original command, and done all that we were told to do; but we can infer that unless we fulfil at least the deduced commands we have *not* done all that we were told to do" (p. 33). Now this mitigation of the paradox operates, so it seems to me, only by confusing imperatives and declaratives. To say, ' 'John, jump out' has been obeyed' is equivalent to saying, 'John has jumped out,' and to add that therefore ' 'John, put on your parachute and jump out' has been partially obeyed' is to say that what is asserted in 'John has jumped out' is part of what is asserted

have different connectives. Such a procedure would moreover meet the difficulties we have seen to be attendant upon a literal inclusion of the corresponding declarative in any imperative.

This turns our attention to the second alternative mentioned above as to the construction of imperative sentences that will serve to clarify everyday usage while yet remaining essentially true to it. Why not simply use different sentential variables for imperatives from those used for declaratives and use different signs, with different rules, for their connectives? Here the task of exposition can be very materially curtailed, since, fortunately, we have, in outline, the proposal of just such a logic. I refer to Professor Thomas Storer's paper, "The Logic of Value Imperatives."[1] Professor Storer proposes a sentential calculus whose basic

in 'John has put on his parachute and jumped out.' No one doubts that 'John has put on his parachute and jumped out' entails 'John has jumped out.' The point at issue is precisely whether 'John, put on your parachute and jump out!' entails 'John, jump out!' To say that obeying the latter is part of what would be involved in obeying the former only serves to confuse the two entailments.

In conclusion let me say that while I agree with Mr. A. F. Peters that "while I agree with Mr. Hare that it would be wrong of logicians to confine their attention to indicative sentences, . . . Mr. Hare's attack is in important respects confused . . . and his method of bringing to logicians' attention the need to study imperative sentences cannot be recommended" (*Mind*, vol. lviii, 1949, p. 535), Mr. Peter's attack is in important respects confused and his method of bringing to logicians' attention the need to study imperative sentences cannot be recommended. For if Mr. Hare trivializes imperative logic by reducing it to the same logic as that found in indicatives, Mr. Peters trivializes it by reducing it to psychology. ["To command both that the floor be scrubbed and that the floor not be scrubbed is not to contradict oneself, although of course it is to make whoever is being commanded bewildered and wonder which command is to be obeyed" (*loc. cit.*, p. 538; for a longer but more obvious instance of psychologism see his treatment of 'Polish the floor or wipe the dishes' on p. 540).] Let me hasten to add that I do not confuse Mr. Hare's confusions with his trivialization: the latter can be accomplished without confusions. But Mr. Hare's article is full of confusions (*e.g.*, that a logical formula can state that something is the case—*i.e.*, be an empirical sentence (p. 35), that since a logician doesn't concern himself with the actual truth or falsity of individual sentences, he can eliminate the concepts of truth and falsity entirely (pp. 36–7), besides the above-mentioned confusion of entailments holding between commands and entailments holding between sentences stating that commands have been obeyed).

[1] *Philosophy of Science*, vol. xiii, 1946, pp. 25–40. Although Mr. Storer did intend to propose a logic that would help to clarify axiological issues, he wished to avoid taking sides in the controversy between objectivist and naturalist; he wished, that is, to develop a tool that could help sharpen the statement of *any* axiological position. Moreover, he seems not to have had in mind the specific set of problems with which the present essay tries to come to grips, namely, problems concerning the categorial status of value, its relation to fact, and so on. Thus it must not be supposed that Mr. Storer's proposal was oriented in a direction specifically favourable to the point of view of the present essay.

symbols are sentential variables divided into two mutually exclusive classes, *viz.*, indicative sentential variables and imperative sentential variables. The logical constants serving as connectives by which compounds of these elements are formed likewise fall into two classes which we may respectively designate "indicative connectives" and "imperative connectives" as the compounds formed by their use are indicative or imperative. These connectives are defined by means of matrices; for indicative connectives the ordinary two-valued truth-tables are used, for imperative connectives Mr. Storer uses three-valued matrices. As an alternative method he uses an axiom set giving rules of derivation. It is divided into three subsets, *viz.*, postulates whose sentential variables are indicative only, are imperative only, and are of both kinds.[1]

A particularly valuable feature of Mr. Storer's proposal is that it allows imperatives to be built by combining indicative and imperative components. I think this is an important desideratum for a logic that is adequate to common usage. We have already seen instances of such imperatives in dealing with legal norms. A few other examples are: 'If he strikes you, turn the other cheek,' 'The water is hot and you are to wash the dishes,' 'Either you have already repaired the damage or you are to do so immediately' each of which is an imperative as a whole but contains a declarative component. In fact, although Mr. Storer thinks some to be unintuitive, our author shows, by the matrix method, how all possible compound sentences both indicative and imperative could be built from component sentences, whether indicative or imperative or both, taken two at a time. Although I am not competent to judge the matter technically, this procedure of uniting two-valued and three- (or multi-) valued calculi in one system seems to me to offer a great deal in the way of a logical clarification of the transformation rules of ordinary language.

[1] This axiom-set formulation raises the interesting question, which we must leave entirely aside, whether there might be a logic of imperatives whose formulae are tautological not in the ordinary sense but in the sense that, represented by matrices, there is some value other than truth such that it appears at every place in such matrices. Mr. Storer, on the basis of a "profound conviction" rejects such a possibility. It follows that all formulae in his logic are indicative in character, though they may unite imperative elements. Thus he finds it plausible to have certain indicative connectives that will unite two or more imperative sentential variables into compound indicative ones.

However, from the standpoint of one trying to determine the status of value and its relation to fact, there is a very serious deficiency in Mr. Storer's proposal. The relationship between an imperative and the corresponding declarative which states as a fact what the imperative commands is left unrepresented. The form of the imperative does not indicate what declarative, if true, would state the fact which is the fulfilment of the imperative. Thus it is not indicated how an imperative somehow includes a declarative without asserting it.

Perhaps this statement should be qualified, for in a curious way Mr. Storer's system would allow a reflection of this relationship I have called " correspondence" in the case where the corresponding declarative is compound. He of course has nothing to mark out a simple imperative with a compound *what, i.e.*, whose corresponding declarative is compound; perhaps he would reduce this to a compound imperative with simple *whats*. But he does have an interesting reflection of the structure of compound declaratives in the (more complex) structure of compound imperatives, so that if there were a way of picking out the simple declaratives that correspond to simple imperatives it would become possible to pick out the compound declaratives that correspond to compound imperatives.

By way of illustration take negation. Mr. Storer has two imperative connectives which may be thought of as negative, one of which ('—') he speaks of as "the operation of negation" the other ('σ') as "the operation of cancellation." These are defined by matrices as follows (supposing that for imperatives there are three possible values): The operation of negation transforms an imperative with either extreme value into an imperative with a value of the opposite extreme, and an imperative with mean value into one with mean value. Thus it is the same structurally as the negative connective for declaratives—which of course transforms a true declarative into a false and a false into a true—save for the addition of the case of imperatives with mean value.[1] The operation of cancellation transforms an imperative of any value into one with mean value. There is of course no comparable connective in the traditional two-valued system of declaratives.[2]

1

c	—c
2	0
1	1
0	2

p	~p
T	F
F	T

2

c	σc
2	1
1	1
0	1

p	?p
T	F
F	F

Thus we may say that Mr. Storer's imperative sign of negation reflects the ordinary declarative negative connective in such a way that where we happen to know what declarative corresponds to a given imperative then we can know what declarative corresponds to the negative of that imperative, namely, the negative of the corresponding declarative. But in the case of cancellation we are left without such a means; even if we know what declarative corresponds to a given imperative we have no method of picking out the declarative corresponding to the cancellation of the latter. Since however cancellation is a "unary" connective we may suppose that we are left with either the original declarative or its negative, between which we have no means of choosing.[1] This, I think, curiously indicates the relationship between the two negatives of imperatives and the single negative of declaratives. Suppose that 'Richard is coming' corresponds to 'Richard, come here!' Then 'Richard is not coming' corresponds to the negation of 'Richard, come here!' but we are left without a means of choosing between 'Richard is coming' and 'Richard is not coming' for the declarative corresponding to the cancellation of 'Richard, come here!'

This curious device of a certain matrix-isomorphism is also available for 'if-then,' 'or,' and 'and' as indicative and again as imperative connectives.[2] It is not, of course, essential to Mr. Storer's system considered simply as a logical calculus. It is the result, I feel sure, of his having an eye for a possible interpretation that would fit common-sense usage. But on this very score it seems

[1] If, that is, we may suppose there are just two unary connectives of declaratives: that of negation and that of identity, the latter building a sentence with the same truth-value from any given sentence, that is, transforming a sentence into itself.

[2] Here an inspection of the matrices themselves must suffice. I use Mr. Storer's method, such that rows give values for the compound with the value of the first element given on the left, and columns give values for the compound with the value of the second element given at the top.

if-then:

i	2	1	0
2	2	1	0
1	2	2	1
0	2	2	2

⊃	T	F
T	T	F
F	T	T

or:

+	2	1	0
2	2	2	2
1	2	1	1
0	2	1	0

v	T	F
T	T	T
F	T	F

and:

x	2	1	0
2	2	1	0
1	1	1	0
0	0	0	0

·	T	F
T	T	F
F	F	F

to me open to criticism. Though one desideratum for a logic of imperatives that shall square with everyday language is that it have some neutral semantical value, and thus that imperatives be at least three-valued, there are other desiderata as well. One we have stressed is that imperative connectives behave in certain cases differently from their indicative counterparts. In terms of the interpretations Mr. Storer seems to have in mind, 'Put on your parachute and jump!' would entail 'Jump!' and 'Go to bed!' would entail 'Go to bed or keep on playing!' In any case, the curious help we get, from the way he defines certain imperative connectives, in picking out compound declaratives that correspond to compound imperatives, seems to involve a similarity in behaviour of the imperative connectives with their declarative counterparts that does not square with common speech.

The chief objection to this second alternative, however, remains that it does not structurally reflect the relationship between the members of pairs of sentences such that one is a (simple) imperative and the other a declarative stating as a fact what the imperative commands to be a fact. Thus we are led to our third alternative which requires that the logic of imperatives be at least in part developed as a functional calculus, that is, that the structure of simple imperatives be articulated. This is not of course incompatible with the second alternative, but may be considered as an extension of it, necessary to make the logic of imperatives adequately reflect the sense and behaviour of declaratives in everyday speech.[1]

So far as I am aware, no one has as yet seriously undertaken the exploration of this possibility.[2] Hence the proposal I am about to make will be extremely vague, tentative, and undeveloped. Moreover, I am keenly aware that since I am not a logician the

[1] Mr. Storer would agree with the desirability, but perhaps not with the necessity, of this extension. He writes: "while the symbols and definitions presented here are all one needs in order to deal with a large portion, if not all, of axiology, certain desirable extensions are apparent. Certainly one would want to consider the question of quantification and closure. The gap that is here to be bridged is commonly overlooked by philosopher and non-philosopher alike, and derivations are made from imperative premises with machinery of the functional calculus developed for indicative sentences" (*op. cit.*, p. 38).

[2] I have myself put out the barest suggestion of such an approach in "A Categorial Analysis of Value," *Philosophy of Science*, vol. xiv, 1947, especially pp. 340–3.

proposal may embrace the most egregious errors in the form of logical impossibilities or absurdities, and of course I do not want to be a part to such a mistaken undertaking even though my purpose is not the construction of a logical calculus but rather the philosophical analysis of value.

The suggestion, reduced to its simplest terms, is that an imperative be composed of the same names as its corresponding declarative, but that it have a different sentential form from the latter. In trying to make this at all plausible I find I am handicapped by having started with the imperative as representative of value-sentences. Our proposal would seem to fit other forms of value-sentence much more naturally. However, I shall have something further to say as to other forms of value-sentence presently, and in any case imperatives, along with other value-sentences, require analysis.

Let us take a case. 'Run!' may be considered an elliptical form of 'You are to run!' It is the sense of the present suggestion that this imperative and the declarative corresponding to it, which we shall take to be, 'You will run,' are composed of the same names, *viz.*, 'you' and 'run.'[1] But they are put together, in the two cases, in sentences having different structures, as shown by the structural or syncategorematic words 'are to' and 'will.' In the declarative sentence the names are usually spoken of as performing the functions of subject ('you') and predicate ('run'), respectively. We shall probably be tempted to say the same thing concerning the functions these terms perform in the imperative. Is it permissible to say that 'you' is the subject and 'run' the predicate in 'You are to run!'? In one sense, yes and in another, no. Clearly there is an analogy. This can be put most forcibly by saying that in both the declarative and the imperative 'you' names a particular and 'run' a universal. This, as we have already remarked, must be gathered from the places of these names in the sentence-structures. As names they just designate their designata: that these designata are a particular and a universal must be

[1] I use 'name' both in a broader and in a narrower fashion than is sometimes the case. A name is any expression that designates in its own right (without benefit of its place in a linguistic context) and whose designation requires the existence of its designatum (as contrasted with a sentence which can refer even when false). *Cf.* above, footnote [1], p. 22. To say that a name is a proper name or a common noun or a pronoun or a predicate or a relation is, in each case, to say something about it not *as* a name but as occurring in a certain context in a sentence or set of sentences.

gathered from the way the names occur in the sentence-structures. Thus there is something common to the place of 'you' in the sentences, 'You are to run!' and 'You will run,' such that that place shows that 'you' names a particular. Call this, if you will, the being a subject of the sentence in each case. Likewise there is something common to the place of 'run' in the two sentences, such that that place shows that 'run' names a universal. Call this, then, the being a predicate of the sentence in each case. But this similarity must not blind us to the fact that there is a difference. Consider, again, the place of 'you.' In the imperative this place indicates that 'you' names a subject of command, a particular that is to be the agent bringing a fact into being. It also indicates, in the simple case under consideration, the particular whose exemplification of a certain property would be the the fact the agent is to bring into being. In the declarative the place 'you' occupies indicates simply that 'you' names a particular as exemplifying the universal named in the predicate-place. Likewise we must admit a difference, though it is perhaps less striking, in what is shown through the place of 'run' in our two sentences. In the one case it indicates a universal whose exemplification is to be brought about; in the other a universal that is exemplified.

Having stated these differences, however, we are brought back to another similarity. The place for names in each of these sentence-structures, unlike the names themselves, share with the whole structure the peculiarity that any instance of them may be mistaken. Carrying over our results from the preceding section we shall say that just as 'You will run' may not be true so 'You are to run!' may not be legitimate. Moreover, if 'you' happens to name a universal, its occurrence in the subject-place in either sentence is improper. I think the best way to handle this impropriety is by ruling it out of a perfectly clarified language. But such dictatorial acts do not change the nature of the situation, which reasserts itself in the problem, Is a given sentence to be allowed to occur in an ideally clarified language? For names just name; they do not, *as names*, show that their designata are particulars or are universals. This is done through their location in sentences. Thus they can be put in the wrong location; a name that actually names a universal may be put in the subject-place of the sort of sentences with which we are here dealing. And such sentences, though not false or illegitimate in the ordinary sense, are somehow wrong and illbegotten even though, or rather because, they have the structure of sentences.[1] Now this sort of wrongness or illbegottenness in a sentence is different from the sentence's not being true or not being legitimate. A declarative's not being true requires that the names for the right sorts of entities, entities of appropriate categorial status, have been entered in the proper locations. Similarly for an imperative that is not legitimate. Still there is an analogy between the wrongnesses. Not only does a name that has been entered at the wrong place in a sentence (since it names the wrong sort of entity) still name; if its very location did not function referentially we couldn't claim that that was the wrong place for that name. However, *this* is not the analogy I wish to stress here. What is here important is that declaratives and imperatives are similar not only as wholes (they are still meaningful when not true or not legitimate, as the case may be); they are also similar in that in each place for names in their respective structures wrong names may be entered, in the sense of names of entities of the wrong categorial sort.

It should be noted that a certain complication may be required if we press our analogy between the structures of imperatives and their corresponding declaratives beyond the case, represented by 'Run!' and 'You will run,' where the predicate is of the first type. Laying aside any doubts as to the acceptability of undefined descriptive predicates of types higher than the first, that is, of there being properties of properties, we could restate what was said above by adopting a suitable type-rule. We would only need

[1] I am aware that this may be urged as a serious defect not specifically in my proposals as to imperatives but generically in my treatment of names. It will be said, and quite correctly, that my suggestion requires a knowledge of the world (though not an empirical knowledge in the ordinary sense), *viz.*, a knowledge of whether something named is a particular or is a universal, before we can answer the syntactical question whether specific sentences are well-formed. I plead guilty to the fault, if it is one; and if it is, I claim all philosophically proper languages are heir to it, in one form or another. It reduces to the question whether we shall admit distinctions that after all we *can*, and therefore *should*, make. We can distinguish between the hue, sky-blue, and the categorial status of being a universal, of being exemplifiable by various particulars, even though, as I would admit, sky-blue is to be found in our actual world only as a property of particulars. If this be the case, then it must be a synthetic proposition, in some sense, that sky-blue is a universal. And a clarified language will have a name for sky-blue that is neutral on the issue as to whether sky-blue is a universal: such a name will not, *in itself*, show that it is not to appear as the subject of ordinary sentences (with first-order predicates).

to note that such a type-rule is not a rule as to names *per se*, but as to name-places in sentences. In itself there would seem to be no difficulty in supposing that there be a type-rule for imperatives analogous to that for declaratives. Thus just as 'Red is sweet' or 'John exemplifies George' are illbegotten, so would 'red, be ye sweet!' and 'John, exemplify George!' But there might in addition be a sort of illbegottenness for imperatives not shared by declaratives. Suppose we allow, in our clarified language, such a declarative as 'Aboveness is transitive.' I should suppose, in harmony with common usage, we would want to treat 'Aboveness, be ye transitive!' not as being not legitimate but as being illbegotten. We should probably wish to prohibit all imperatives save those whose subject-place or places indicated that names of particulars only could properly occur in them. The reason for this may be that in ordinary usage the subject of an imperative is taken to name the agent that is to bring about the state of affairs; or again, it may be that only states of affairs of the lowest order (the exemplifications of first-type properties by particulars) are felt to be appropriate matters of command, or of any valuation. In any case, I think that common sense tends to reject as absurd the idea of anyone's commanding universals to have certain properties. Thus there may be a sort of illbegottenness in the case of imperatives for which there is no parallel in the case of declaratives. My hesitancy in this matter arises, I think, from my feeling that perhaps such a sentence as 'Aboveness is transitive' is itself illbegotten. It might be that it should be replaced by a syntactical sentence, or possibly its misleadingly empirical appearance cancelled by a device showing its categorial character. This last suggestion brings up the provocative question as to whether we should not allow categorial imperatives, imperatives whose corresponding declaratives are not factual statements but categorial assertions. The present context, however, is not the place in which to explore this possibility.

With these similarities and differences in mind, I suggest that there be carried out a functional analysis of imperatives whereby these will contain the same names as declaratives but have a structure different from, and yet analogous to, theirs. In this way we shall be able to speak of the subject and predicate or again, in the relational form, of the function and its arguments in the case of imperatives just as in the case of declaratives, though it remains clear that there is an important difference.[1] The latter case, that of a relational imperative, is illustrated by the sentence, 'You are to mow the lawn,' to which the declarative prediction, 'You will mow the lawn,' corresponds.

We can now see how in the forms of simple declaratives and imperatives the relationship I have called correspondence is reflected. Take any given simple imperative. We can see, on the proposal I am offering, which declarative it is that states as fact what the imperative commands. It is the declarative that has the same names as are to be found in the imperative in the positions analogous to those they occupy in the imperative. Whenever this is the case we shall speak of the declarative and the imperative as "having the same content." Thus we can see by their forms that 'You will run' corresponds to 'You are to run!' (or simply 'Run!'), and 'You will mow the lawn' to 'You are to mow the lawn!' (or simply 'Mow the lawn!').

But now what about transformation rules that will reflect everyday usage? It seems to me entirely feasible that a functional calculus for imperatives be developed, though of course my inexpertness here may blind me to some insuperable difficulty. I would suppose, however, that its rules would differ in some important respects from the traditional functional calculus for declaratives. To borrow an example from Professor Storer, we should not want 'Someone, hang the prisoner!' to be derivable from 'Executioner, hang the prisoner!' although in declarative logic 'The executioner has hanged the prisoner' does entail 'Someone has hanged the prisoner.' Again, in declarative logic from 'Every item in the cargo has been jettisoned to try to float

[1] The following notation may suggest what I have in mind: Let '$A_{(a)}$' represent an ordinary subject-predicate declarative. Then '$A_{\{a\}}$' could be used for the imperative to which '$A_{(a)}$' corresponds. Again, '$R_{(a,\, b)}$' can be representative of the ordinary relational declarative. Then '$R_{\{a,\, b\}}$' could be used for the imperative to which '$R_{(a,\, b)}$' corresponds. I have here so far acceded to the tradition as to represent predicate-names by upper-case letters, subject-names by lower-case. This is misleading. The location to the left of or within the parentheses or braces is sufficient to show the place in the sentence; the names should occur in these places but with no such differentiation in their own forms. Thus a clearer notation would be: '$a(b)$,' '$a\{b\}$,' '$c(d, e)$,' '$c\{d, e\}$.' This, however, would involve too great a break with established conventions to be seriously proposed. It would also be inadequate if one wished to allow sentences with predicate terms (*i.e.*, names that in other sentences occur in the predicate-place) as subjects.

the ship' and 'Crate *a* is an item in the cargo' we can properly infer 'Crate *a* has been jettisoned.' But we might not want to allow an analogous inference in imperative logic. If, *e.g.*, there is no chance of floating the ship unless all the cargo is jettisoned we might wish to say that 'Jettison crate *a*!' followed not from 'Jettison all the cargo!' and 'Crate *a* is an item in the cargo' alone, but only from these *plus* the declarative 'All items of cargo other than crate *a* have been or will be jettisoned.'

As already indicated, such a functional calculus of imperatives, analogous to but differing in some important respects from the traditional functional calculus of declaratives, could be united with a sentential calculus of imperatives and declaratives like that proposed by Professor Storer and considered an extension of the latter.[1] With the achievement of such a logic of imperatives, or, rather, of a combined logic of declaratives and imperatives, we seem well on the way toward a syntactical clarification of everyday language that will properly reveal the status of value and its relation to fact. But there are still two serious deficiencies in our programme. On the one hand, imperative sentences are too specific in their form, too restricted in their rules of formation, to stand as representative of all value-sentences. We should do a grave injustice to everyday usage were we to require that every value-sentence be, in a clarified language, translated into an imperative. We shall consider this problem immediately. On the other hand, even within the area of imperatives proper our proposal is seriously defective. It does allow us to pick out the declarative corresponding to any given imperative. And it allows us to see that we are concerned with the same ultimate entities in each case—in the simplest instance, a particular and a universal. Even more. It shows, through the analogous forms of the sentences, that in commanding something to be a fact we are

[1] This would, with the double negative for imperatives, require some new rules as to equivalences of imperatives with universal and existential operators. For example, 'Not (all cars actually turn right)' would ordinarily be treated as equivalent to 'Some cars actually do not turn right.' But 'Cancel (all cars are to turn right!)' is not equivalent to 'For some cars cancel (turn right!)'—or, put perhaps somewhat more readably, 'It is not the case that all cars are to turn right!' is not equivalent to 'In some cases cars do not have to turn right!' This is seen when we note that 'All cars are to turn right!' is as effectively cancelled by 'In some cases cars are to not turn right!' as by 'In some cases cars do not have to turn right!' Perhaps the proper equivalent of 'It is not the case that all cars are to turn right!' is 'In at least one case a car either is to not turn right or does not have to turn right!' This may indicate the sort of problem involved if the present proposal is to be carried out.

doing something like, though different from, stating that it is a fact. Yet all this is not quite enough. What is commanded, in imperatives occurring in everyday usage, is that a fact be brought about, namely, the very fact that the corresponding declarative asserts. But if we may suppose that the form of a fact is somehow revealed in the declarative asserting that fact, or merely that the only proper reference to a fact is *via* a (declarative) sentence asserting that fact, then the imperative should somehow in its own structure include the very structure of the declarative corresponding to it. This is not the case in our proposal. In fact, I cannot at present see how to make it the case without literally including the declarative in the imperative to which it corresponds, and this can be allowed only upon pain of requiring the imperative to assert the fact it commands. So I am in the unpleasant position of having to face the possibility that in no clarified language can something vital to the status of value be said or even shown. I hope that I am wrong and that this defect may be overcome, but for the present I cannot see how. It may be mitigated, however, by a proposal I shall make in Section 7.

6*b*. *Are value-sentences properly rendered as normatives?*

It is now time to take stock. We started this section by assuming that if we could discover in everyday usage a set of sentences whose logical syntax was different from that of declaratives we might see in this difference a reflection, in language, of the difference of value from fact. Moreover, such a difference would allow us to develop a suggestion coming from Brentano to the effect that the relation of value to fact is somehow found or at least represented in the relation of a certain semantical predicate, call it "legitimacy," to another, usually spoken of as "truth." I think we have found in imperatives a set of sentences of the desired kind. But, if this be granted, may we not suddenly find ourselves embarrassed with riches? It would seem that the same admission should be made for many other sorts of non-declarative sentences, for optatives, hortatives, interrogatives, normatives (*i.e.*, sentences containing 'ought' as an auxiliary verb) and so on. Possibly we must wait for the development of special logics for each of these sorts of sentences before we can really see what value is and how it is related to fact. This would be somewhat discouraging. Strictly, it would be no argument against the position I am taking, but sociologically it would reduce it to absurdity. And I must admit that I am sufficiently human to desire not to be reduced, even sociologically, to absurdity. So, for practical purposes I am required to do something about the wealth of non-declarative sentences in ordinary discourse. And I believe I can make out something of a case, even theoretically, for economy.

In the first place, there is the possibility of reducing the number of forms of non-declarative sentences by claiming that some are just disguised cases of others. For example, it is possible to hold that social etiquette requires that we dissemble as to the sort of sentence we are using in certain situations. Thus questions may be treated as polite commands, either obligating large scale action or the giving of information.[1] My wife invariably commands me to wipe the dishes by the question, 'Everett, wouldn't you like to wipe the dishes for me?' And I disguise my imperatives to students at examination time by using the gentler form of the interrogative. I can even conceive it to be not too implausible to treat optatives as the hesitating enunciation of fiats by those sensible of the limitations of their powers. We leave it to Jehovah to proclaim, 'Let there be light!' We lesser imperators must be satisfied with the mild optative, 'Would it were light!'

But the case of normative sentences is different; I do not believe they are in all cases simply weak or polite imperatives. By a 'normative sentence' I mean such sentences as 'I ought to go,' 'It would be a good thing if Iowa lost this game,' 'The right thing to do is to keep your promise.' They can perhaps be described as sentences which state that some fact ought to be (or to have been). Usually, but not necessarily, this fact is a fact of human behaviour. I would wish to call 'There ought to be no earthquakes or other natural disasters' a normative sentence. On the other hand, I would like to exclude merely causal sentences. I do not wish to call such a sentence as 'You ought to install new points' (where this is elliptical for, 'To get more regular firing of your engine, you ought to install new points') a normative sentence. Of course it might be said that such a sentence is not merely causal, that it obligates a means because it tacitly obligates an end as well (*e.g.*, 'You ought to get more regular firing of your engine'). But if so, it is possible to translate such a sentence into two, one of which is normative

[1] There have been several recent suggestions to this effect. *Cf.* R. M. Hare, *loc. cit.*, particularly p. 24.

the other causal (stating a necessary condition for the occurrence of that state of affairs which the normative sentence says ought to be).

That not all normatives can be treated as disguised imperatives seems clear on the following considerations. There is properly no imperative in the past tense, but there are normatives in this tense. It is good usage to say, 'Chamberlain ought not to have yielded to Hitler at Munich,' but I cannot in good usage now order Chamberlain not to have yielded to Hitler at Munich. It might be said that, from a logical standpoint, tense is just a confusion, since it involves relativity to the time of utterance, which is something outside what is said. This confusion can be eliminated, so it might be thought, by putting the date in the sentence itself and then using a tenseless verb.[1] Thus we could have, 'Chamberlain, do you not yield to Hitler at Munich in 1938.' But this will not do either. We see immediately that such an imperative is permissible if uttered before but not if uttered after the event commanded, which fact indicates an ineradicable relativity of the imperative to the occasion of its utterance.

And this relativity embraces more than the time element. Most imperatives are in the second person. One does occasionally command oneself, usually, it would seem, when one is fairly confident the command will not be obeyed. But a case could be made for saying that in doing so one treats oneself as someone else. Now the second person (whether singular or plural) is relative; its reference depends upon the circumstances of its occurrence. There are of course imperatives in the third person, as, for example, 'Donald is to rake the lawn!' But these are comparatively rare. Moreover, when they do occur they are usually addressed to a third party who is tacitly commanded to carry the explicit command to the person indicated. Thus, on a given occasion, the imperative, 'Donald is to rake the lawn!' may well be an elliptical form of 'Command Donald to rake the lawn!' which is in the second person. Similarly, sentences that may seem to be imperatives in the third person, since addressed to someone by means of a proper name, may perhaps be plausibly interpreted as imperatives in the second person with a label indicating the occasion of reading which will make them imperatives. Thus my wife leaves a note on the kitchen table, 'Everett, light the oven at 12!'

[1] I take it Mr. Hare's proposal, *op. cit.*, p. 26, amounts to this.

Here 'Everett' is strictly not a part of the imperative. Now, I am not sure that I wish to press this line of analysis to its extreme, to say that it would be correct and clarifying to translate all imperatives into the second person where not already in the second person. But surely the vast majority of them either are in, or are properly translated into, the second person, and thus are relative to the occasion of their use.[1]

I need hardly point out that normative sentences are different in this regard from imperatives. They occur quite indifferently in all persons. Moreover, no harm to their intention would be done if they were all translated into the appropriate third person, though their elegance might suffer somewhat in the process. Thus 'I ought to go' easily becomes 'Everett ought to go,' and 'You ought to read this book to the end' is easily restated '——— ought to read this book to the end,' where you, gentle reader, insert your own name in the blank.

There is even a third way in which imperatives may be relative to the occasion of their utterance. Like all sentences they can occur only as someone enunciates or writes them. But in the case of other sentences, including normatives, the question who is the speaker is logically irrelevant. Not so for at least some imperatives. As Kelsen has shown, the validity of a legal imperative is relative to the organ creating that imperative. It is true that we saw that this could, in some cases and in a certain sense, be put into a higher imperative by using some such form as that present in 'If *a* command '*p*!' then *p*!' But this either leads to an objectionable infinite hierarchy such that no imperative in it can be shown, by its content, to be valid, or it takes us to a basic norm, whose validity is not thus formulated in a higher norm. And in adopting the latter alternative Kelsen is unable to avoid appeal to the conditions of occurrence in order to determine

[1] Fiats seem to offer a special difficulty. In many cases, however, this is only apparent. 'Let the prisoner be brought to the courtroom!' would probably be elliptical for 'You [referring to the appropriate law-officer] are to bring the prisoner to the courtroom!' Even the potentate's magisterial 'Let there be a day of feasting!' is probably shorthand for an ordinary imperative in the second person, as would be revealed to the appropriate subordinates did they not hasten to make the fiat effective. But with the Lord God the matter is different. I am not quite sure how to handle His fiats. When He says "Let there be light!" no one apparently is addressed; no person, no thing is obligated to carry out the command. Unless it be the world, already in existence but in darkness (yet this would be blasphemy, for then not God but the world of darkness would be the creator of light). Perhaps I had better not explore this matter further.

the validity of the basic norm (and thus essentially of the whole hierarchy).[1]

Thus in certain ways (in respect to time, to commanded and to commander) imperatives are, at least for the most part, unavoidably relative to the conditions of their occurrence. In this they are analogous to declaratives having demonstrative pronouns as subjects, *e.g.*, 'This is green.' I think this is one of the reasons why they are so frequently mistranslated into meta-linguistic psychological descriptions, why, *e.g.*, it is tempting to translate 'Wipe the dishes!', uttered on a certain occasion, by 'Mrs. Hall said 'Wipe the dishes!' to her husband.' But as we have seen any such translation into a meta-sentence will not do. It follows that we cannot avoid the prescription of good usage: imperatives are by nature relative to the conditions of their occurrence.

This is a severe restriction upon imperatives and shows that normatives, as a class, cannot be treated as weak or disguised imperatives,[2] for normatives do not fall under it. For example, we cannot properly translate 'Chamberlain ought not to have yielded to Hitler at Munich in 1938' into an imperative because we cannot reproduce the situation to which the appropriate imperative would be relative.

Must I then admit that imperatives and normatives form two irreducible classes of non-declarative sentences? I think not. For although normatives cannot be absorbed in the class of imperatives, the converse offers hope. In the first place, if we want a direct translation, we can preserve the relativity to the occasion of the imperative. Normatives can be put in the second person, and can retain, in their tense, a reference to their own occurrence. Thus 'Give me that book!' can be replaced by 'You ought to give me that book.' But since normatives do not have to be relative

[1] As we have seen, Kelsen might be able to mitigate this outcome by distinguishing between proof (as the establishment of validity) within a system and proof of a system.

[2] That questions and optatives seem to share this restriction is perhaps indirect evidence of the legitimacy of treating them as polite or feeble imperatives. Real questions, as contrasted with rhetorical ones, are always addressed to some actual or possible hearer or reader. Thus they are relative to the occasion of their use. I think most optatives are so likewise (at least in the imaginations of their producers), although I must admit the case is not so clear. On the other hand, the few suggestions toward an optative axiology that have actually been made (*e.g.*, Menger, *loc. cit.*, and Russell, *What I Believe* and *The Philosophy of Bertrand Russell*, pp. 719 ff.) make clear the relativity of optatives by putting them in the first person singular.

to their occurrence, we are not restricted to such direct translations. Thus the imperative just instanced, occurring in a certain set of circumstances, could be replaced by 'Mrs. Hall ought to give [have given] Everett that book at t_n.' Moreover, if we wish to bring in the authority of the commander, this too is possible. If we have a delegating command, such as, 'If the judge commands the executioner 'Hang the prisoner!' then, executioner, hang the prisoner!' we can replace it by the normative, 'If the judge commands the executioner, 'Hang the prisoner!' then the executioner (legally) ought to hang the prisoner.'[1] If we were actually to carry out this replacement of imperatives by normatives, the effect on the whole, no doubt, would a softening of the practical effectiveness of our language.[2] But this is a psychological matter which may here be disregarded because it does not enter the sentences involved themselves. It is like the difference in tone of voice in which one and the same imperative may be uttered. It is not like the way in which the occasion of utterance of an imperative enters the imperative in the tense or the reference of the second person pronoun or verb-form of the imperative.

To treat imperatives as a subset of normatives requires that we treat imperatives as having, in some more complicated form peculiar to themselves, the generic structure of normatives. This I think would be correct. Compare 'You ought to run' with the imperative 'Run!' taken as elliptical for 'You are to run!' In each, the location of 'you' indicates that 'you' names a particular; that of 'run' that 'run' names a universal. Moreover, the whole structure in each shows that the sentence enunciates an ought:

[1] It will be noted that I have carried over the antecedent of the imperative unchanged in the normative replacing it. This calls for two remarks. If 'Hang the prisoner!' be taken as the name of an imperative, then it would seem that we still have unabsorbed imperatives (in the object-language). This could be avoided either by saying that 'Hang the prisoner!' is just a name of a set of sounds (for in suggesting that imperatives be absorbed in the class of normatives I am not proposing that the law profession nor even that philosophers change their linguistic habits) or by changing the antecedent to read, 'If the judge says that the executioner ought to hang the prisoner.' The latter alternative, however, seems to weaken the antecedent by referring to mere talk as contrasted with commanding. Here it might be helpful to distinguish between the act of commanding, which, of course, can never enter any sentence, not even an imperative, and an imperative taken as a sentence. We are concerned only with the latter: the former is a matter of social psychology.

[2] This is perhaps a rash statement. All I ought to say and all I need to say is that such a change in our actual use of language would probably be associated with other behavioural changes.

the particular ought to exemplify the universal named. But in the imperative there is an added factor: the agent to bring about this fact is indicated by the subject. The subject-place not only indicates what particular ought to exemplify some property; it also shows the agency by which this is to occur. There is then a double ought involved in the imperative: the fact that ought to occur and the agency that ought to bring it about. This can be more clearly seen in a slightly more complex example. The imperative, 'Donald is to wear his rubbers!' as uttered to Donald's father is not properly translated by the normative, 'Donald ought to wear his rubbers!' For, although the sense of the latter is included in the imperative, the imperative also involves 'You [Donald's father] are to bring it to pass that Donald does wear his rubbers!' Now, if our proposal is correct, this further imperative element (just expressed in quotes) must itself be properly translatable into normative form. I think it can be. However, simply to put it 'You ought to bring it to pass that Donald wears his rubbers' seems inadequate. Part of this inadequacy, as already noted, is the softening of the psychological effectiveness, which may here be disregarded. But this is only part. I think Kelsen has correctly spoken of the *creation* of a norm, and of this as not something peculiar to legal imperatives. Every imperative, by its structure, indicates that the ought attaching to the agency that is to bring into being the fact that ought to be is an ought created, at least to some extent, by the conditions of occurrence of the imperative. Thus we see why the imperative form is ineradicably relative. This however does not prohibit its translation into the normative form, but makes the imperative a peculiarly complex species of the latter. Thus our example, 'Donald is to wear his rubbers!' is replaceable by some such involved normative as, 'Donald ought to wear his rubbers and you ought, because I say so, to see to it that he does.' Here it is the 'say so' in the clause 'because I say so' that is suspect, (the 'because' is innocent enough, being elliptical for a conditional of which the antecedent is asserted). This would seem to involve a mentioning of the total sentence in which it occurs (or the imperative of which that total sentence is a translation) and thus the possibility of semantical paradoxes. I do not at the moment see how this sort of self-reference can be avoided. However it does seem clear that it is not due to our attempt to treat imperatives as a kind of normative, but to the assumption that imperatives tacitly involve a reference to the conditions of their own occurrence—an assumption which certainly seems sound, but which, if not made, would serve to lighten our present task.

I am proposing, then, that imperatives be treated as a complicated sort of normative. Thus in trying to analyse the status of value and its relation to fact it behoves us to turn to the simpler, generic form that all normatives possess. Here again we may speak of a declarative as corresponding to a normative. The relationship is that between a sentence stating something to be a fact and a sentence asserting that it ought to be a fact. This, of course, cannot be correctly said as I have just said it. Not only is it improper to refer to facts by common nouns (such as 'fact'), but to say that a normative sentence asserts that a fact ought to be involves the further error of talking as though oughting-to-be were a property a fact might or might not have. This is all wrong. It might help simply to pair 'fact' and 'value' and say a declarative sentence asserts a fact, whereas a normative asserts a value. But this in no way shows that a value, though it is not a fact, either in whole or in part, is in some peculiar way, which we are trying to grasp, intimately related to a certain fact—the fact, as we have wrongly stated it, asserted by that declarative sentence which corresponds to the normative sentence asserting the given value. But we have advanced somewhat by turning from imperatives to normatives. The generic structure of a normative is more obviously analogous than is that of an imperative to the generic structure of a declarative. In 'You ought to run' the place of 'you' is not indicative of agency in bringing about a fact, but only of the particular that ought to exemplify the property designated in the predicate place. Thus when we, on our present proposal, require that the declarative corresponding to a given normative have the same content, that is, have the same names occurring in the analogous locations, we gain more insight into the relationship between value and fact just because the sentence-structures involved are more analogous. 'Exemplifies' and 'ought to exemplify' in such sentences as 'John exemplifies tact' and 'John ought to exemplify tact' indicate *prima facie* very analogous sentence-structures.

Now, the very obviousness of this analogy as to form may cause a difficulty, though I think it is only terminological. The reader may be asking, "Are not normatives just a form of declarative? After all, 'Donald ought to rake the leaves' does declare something, *viz.*, it declares that Donald ought to rake the leaves—it doesn't command it or ask it or wish it." In answer I must remind the reader that I am not trying to change people's everyday use of language but rather to understand it and particularly to separate superficial similarities and differences in sentential structures, due to demands of social etiquette or pleasing style, from fundamental ones, necessary to saying the sorts of things everyday language does manage to say. Now it seems to me that such sentences as 'Donald, will you rake the leaves?', 'Donald, rake the leaves!', and 'Donald, you ought to rake the leaves' are in everyday usage alike, in what they manage to say, in an obvious way in which they all differ from 'Donald is raking the leaves.' If the superficial similarity of the latter with one of the former is to be marked out by calling them both declaratives, then we need some other term to mark out the latter as fundamentally different from *all* the former. 'Descriptive' might do, save that it is frequently used to mark off certain sentences from logical formulae or from *a priori* sentences. 'Indicative' might be used except that exactly the same objection would apply to it as to 'declarative.' Moreover, we sometimes wish to speak of subjunctive sentences as a form of declarative, *i.e.*, as contrasted with normatives, whereas 'subjunctive' is usually contrasted with 'indicative.' There are no doubt objections, from the standpoint of common conventions, to any consistent nomenclature, and I have not thought it necessary to be rigorous. I hope the reader will grant me his indulgence.

However I must now turn to an issue which is not merely terminological. Is there not a kind of value-sentence which is not normative in form, indeed, which is obviously declarative? And thus does not the programme of getting at the status of value through the structure of value-sentences collapse? The kind of sentence I have in mind is indicated by the following examples: 'John may not be intelligent but he certainly is good,' 'The study of philosophy is worth while,' 'The outlook here is beautiful,' 'Most pleasures are innocent and, indeed, good.' This kind of sentence may be roughly characterized as one in which a value-term occurs as predicate. I propose to call them "value-predicating sentences." It is surely undeniable that such sentences, or at least an appreciable number of them, are value-sentences, that they really do assert not fact but value. Yet as they stand they are not normative in form, and it is not at once clear how we could replace them with normative sentences without doing violence to ordinary language. They seem to be genuine declaratives marked out only by the fact that they have value-predicates.

Moreover, our difficulty in any attempt to assimilate value-predicating sentences to normatives is not confined to the matter of keeping to good usage. We seem to be plunged by any such attempt into the centre of a long and furious controversy between two objectivistic schools of ethics—nay, worse, to be guilty of destroying by fiat the very possibility of their opposition or at least the means of its statement. I refer to the conflict between "intuitionism" and the two forms of "hedonism", to use Sidgwick's terminology, or between the "deontological" and the "teleological"[1] standpoints, to use words that have acquired some general currency more recently. One may mention Kant's ethics of duty as against Bentham's ethics of pleasant consequences, Prichard's and Ross's neo-Kantian ethics of right as against Moore's ideal utilitarianism. It would not be wholly unfair to say that for Bentham[2] and Moore all sentences that are irreducibly value-sentences can be properly stated in the value-predicating form. Kant and his followers would deny this and require that certain normative sentences be not reducible to value-predicating sentences. These latter philosophers, however, would not go to the other extreme: they would not say that all value-sentences nor even that all moralistic value-sentences were properly reducible to a certain sort of normative sentence, *viz.*, a sentence asserting a duty or obligation. They thus hold that there are at least two ultimate value-concepts, indicated by such words as 'good,' on the one hand, and 'duty,' 'right,' 'obligation,' 'moral ought,' on the other.

I am going to try to make plausible a view that in certain respects may be considered a compromise on this issue but which (and this is of more importance in my estimation) allows the issue nevertheless to be stated and perhaps even with some clarification. The view will side with Bentham and Moore in allowing only one ultimate value-"concept." It will agree with Kant, Prichard, and Ross, however, in contending that the element of ought, as found

[1] Prichard (*Moral Obligation*, p. 116) ascribes this terminology to J. H. Muirhead, *Rule and End in Morals*, pp. 6–8. Bentham, I believe, coined the term, 'deontology,' but used it for any investigation of duty or obligation.

[2] It is, I think, correct, as against a general tradition of interpretation to which Moore himself added impetus, to treat Bentham as an objectivist in ethics. *Cf.* my "The 'Proof' of Utility in Bentham and Mill," *Ethics*, vol. lx, 1949, pp. 1–18.

in duty, rightness, and similar concepts, is not reducible to goodness, in the sense of a value-quality, combined with some descriptive property or properties. It will have an affinity with a suggestion of Broad and Ewing to which allusion has already been made, that we treat ought-to-be, in a certain form, as the only ultimate ethical concept, and good as a form thereof. Yet the discussions of these men bring in so many issues that are irrelevant to our purpose—that of simply discovering and stating, so far as it is in our power, the categorial nature of value or, if you prefer, its ontological status—that it is advisable to devote some space to disentanglement. Not that these other issues are not themselves interesting and important: but they are not our present concern.

A very provocative article by H. A. Prichard is devoted to the task of showing that we should answer in the affirmative the question, "Does moral philosophy rest on a mistake?"[1] In it, Prichard supposes that the purpose of moral philosophy is to supply the thoughtful inquirer with an answer to the question, "Is there really a reason why I should act in the ways in which hitherto I have thought I ought to act?" So far as this may be taken to mean that moral philosophy is to furnish motivation to people to do what they conceive they ought to do—and there is perhaps some slight basis for supposing this consideration to be present in Prichard's thought,[2] it is wholly irrelevant to our present undertaking. What motivational effects the pursuit of moral philosophy ought to have is a practical—a moral and educational—not a philosophical question.

But even a more theoretical interpretation of Prichard's view of moral philosophy (one for which there is more justification than for the practical interpretation just given) leads into irrelevancies, as far as we are concerned. This more theoretical interpretation would have Prichard suppose that moral philosophy seeks a certain knowledge about motivation, *viz.*, the knowledge whether there are any motives directed either toward a good of the agent or toward some other good which, in general, could induce the agent to do what he thinks he ought to do.[3] Indeed,

[1] *Mind*, vol. xxi, 1912, pp. 21–37, reprinted in *Moral Obligation*, pp. 1–17. My references will be to the former.

[2] A very clear-cut example of its presence is to be found in chapters xi and xii, "Why Should I Be Moral?" of W. T. Stace's *The Concept of Morals*.

[3] For example, Prichard is concerned with the question whether a certain motivation (the desire for some good) can in general give rise to the sense of duty as a derivative motivation. *Cf. op. cit.*, p. 26.

this same interpretation can be given to Prichard's account in his lecture, "Duty and Interest,"[1] of several historically important moral philosophers, with the addition that a certain possible ambiguity, expressed by the phrases 'the agent's advantage' and 'the agent's good' now becomes more apparent. This ambiguity can be brought out, I think, by the question, 'Does moral philosophy seek the knowledge whether there is a completely non-moral motivation (a desire for something, such as pleasure, which is, if it occurs, just a fact, not a value) which leads us to do as we think we ought; or the knowledge whether there is a moral motivation other than our sense of duty or obligation (say a desire for some good taken as a value) which leads us to do as we think we ought?' But whatever the refinements, this interpretation requires that moral philosophy be devoted to essentially psychological questions. There can be no doubt that historically ethicists have been to a very great extent concerned with just such questions of motivation, questions, that is to say, of fact, questions as to what kind or kinds of motives actually lead us to perform acts we conceive to be right or good. And the controversy between the deontologists and the teleologists is one of the most striking cases in point.

I propose to leave such questions entirely aside. This resolution carries with it important consequences for an associated group of questions, those concerning means and ends and their relations. Most of these are disguised forms of the factual questions as to motivation we have just agreed are not relevant to our undertaking. 'Is anything but pleasure sought as an end?' 'Does one ever do one's duty for its own sake?' 'Is anything ever desired simply as an end-in-itself?'—these are examples of the sort of question we are to ignore as being merely factual.

Now there is a kind of question about means and ends which *is* relevant to our inquiry. It has sometimes been expressed by using the terms 'intrinsic' and 'extrinsic.' I have in mind such a question as 'Are there two irreducibly different kinds of value, *viz.*, intrinsic values and extrinsic values?' or again, 'Do means-values have a different status from end-values?' I think myself that this sort of question can be suitably answered by distinguishing between two kinds of value-sentence. An extrinsic-value-sentence can be properly stated only as a certain sort of compound sentence, one part of which states an empirical law, another the value of a

[1] Delivered before the University of Oxford on 29 October, 1928, and published by Oxford University Press.

component in the law other than that which is said to be extrinsically valuable. Thus 'Money is extrinsically valuable' is to be taken as asserting that there is something of value to which money is related by an empirical law. I state this very loosely[1] because my present purpose is simply to indicate that the recognition that there are genuine axiological questions relating to means and ends does not commit one either way on our immediate problem as to whether value-predicating sentences can properly be rendered as normatives. It will be noted that in my "solution" I wrote "there is something of value . . .," and I was careful to avoid using quotation marks. Thus the issue as to the correct form of this component of the compound which gives the sense of the extrinsic-value-sentence is left open. Certainly the distinction between means and end does not commit one to the view that there are value-predicative sentences that cannot properly be rendered as normatives. Even were it held that means and ends were irreducibly different kinds of value one could still claim that they were properly rendered by normative sentences, though it would then be necessary to distinguish between two forms of ought, which might be designated by the expressions 'means-ought' and 'end-ought.' Thus the 'ought' in 'You ought to take the higher offer' might be taken as short for 'means-ought' and the 'ought' in 'You ought to respect the feelings of others' for 'end-ought.'

There is another issue involving the concepts of means and ends which, although it is not merely psychological but is a genuine value-problem, is simply a moral problem and so not relevant to the question of the general status of value. I think it is present—along with much else—in Dewey's[2] frequent contention that means and ends are inseparable, and that the value of the end is something that cannot be determined apart from the means which as a matter of fact must be used for its attainment. The issue I have in mind is not, at least in its obvious sense, the old one whether the end justifies the means. It is rather the

[1] A more careful formulation is given in *Philosophy of Science*, vol. xiv, 1947, p. 341.

[2] Neglect of any discussion of Dewey's position in the present essay is not an indication that I consider him to be a non-objectivist but rather that I have never been able to make up my mind as to how he should be classified on this most basic issue in axiology. I think it is clear that if he were to be classified as a value-objectivist it would be more appropriate to group him with the teleologists than with the deontologists.

question whether the attainability of the end has any bearing upon its value. As thus stated, my own answer is already obviously determined. The principle of value's independence of fact involves the rejection of a view requiring that the valuableness of a value is determined to any degree by its attainability, *i.e.*, by the probability of the occurrence of the corresponding fact. Any supposition to the contrary is due, I think, to the confusion of a given value with a related moral value, the value of devoting one's time and energy to the achievement of the former. I think I should be willing to accept the principle that one ought to devote one's energies to the task of trying to realize only those values concerning which there is some reasonable hope not only that they can be realized but that one's efforts will help to realize them. But it should be noted that this principle not only is itself a value-sentence (I have formulated it as a normative) but presupposes the occurrences of value-sentences—sentences concerning the valuableness of the values (call them "end-values" if you please) to be realized—that say nothing about realizability. It is thus clear that the issue such a principle raises is not the general issue of the status of value.

So generally in this controversy between teleologists and deontologists, I propose to leave aside all questions about moral values as specifically moral. I think it may be fairly assumed that moral values are restricted to situations involving acts and therefore agents, and in some sense, their motivation. Indubitably there are genuine value-questions (as contrasted with merely psychological questions) concerning motives. 'Ought one do one's duty from the sense of duty, or is it sufficient just to do the duty, say from a desire for good, whether one's own or another's?' 'Is it ever one's duty to act from a certain sort of motive?' 'Is not the type of personality that is constantly analysing his motives to see whether they are sufficiently disinterested, as contrasted with one that is objectively oriented towards the values to be achieved, morally bad?' These, I admit, are genuine value-questions, but they are questions as to moral values *qua* moral, and so I leave them aside. Thus I omit to examine the quaintly archaic discussion of Ross concerning whether it is ever one's duty to promote one's own happiness,[1] as similarly the whole issue, Do we ever have duties to ourselves or are all our duties to others? Indeed, I omit the whole discussion to be found in certain of the deontologists on

[1] *Foundations of Ethics*, p. 272.

whether what ought in the moral sense to be, that is, what is a duty, on the one hand, and what is morally good, on the other, are not entirely different classes of values.[1] This discussion might seem to be relevant for it apparently concerns the question, Are there two irreducible kinds of value-sentence, *viz.*, normative sentences and value-predicate sentences? I think, however, that this is a false appearance. I think the issue is not ultimately whether there are two kinds of value in the sense of two different ontological statuses of value, but whether there are two kinds of thing that are valuable and even more specifically (and to continue to use the improper predicative form) whether there are two kinds of thing of which moral value may be predicated. As I understand it, these deontologists, when they say an act either is or is not as it ought to be whereas the motive giving rise to it is or is not good, are trying to distinguish two sorts of entity in the total moral situation concerning which a value-assertion can be made. Moreover, they are saying that the moral value of each of these is independent of that of the other. And this could be said in either the normative or the value-predicative form, but for another reason (to be specified) the normative form seems more appropriate. Let us then put the matter thus. In a given actual or hypothetical moral situation whether the motive is as it ought to be and whether the act is as it ought to be are independent questions.

To this formulation there seems to be an objection explicitly stated by both Prichard and Ross. Consider Ross's statement:

[1] It is one of Prichard's chief contentions, and Ross follows him in this, that the moral ought, moral obligation, attaches to the act itself, not to the motivation, whereas moral goodness is a character of the motivation and, possibly, the agent, (in virtue of his motivation) but not of the act. I quote a characteristic passage from Prichard's "Duty and Interest." "The fact that I have given *A* credit in order to spite his rival *B*, or again, in order to secure future favours from *A*, has, as we see when we reflect, no bearing whatever on the question whether I ought to have given *A* credit. The real paradox in the conviction [that we act only out of self-interest] lies in its implication that there is no such thing as moral goodness. If I gave *A* credit solely to obtain future favours, and even if I gave him credit either thinking or knowing that I ought to do so, but in no way directly or indirectly influenced by my either so thinking or knowing, then even though it has to be allowed that I did something which I was morally bound to do, it has to be admitted that there was no moral goodness whatever about my action" (p. 25). And in similar vein Ross writes, ". . . the doing of a right act may be a morally bad action, and . . . the doing of a wrong act may be a morally good action; for 'right' and 'wrong' refer entirely to the thing done, 'morally good' and 'morally bad' entirely to the motive from which it is done" (*The Right and the Good*, p. 7).

"That action from a good motive is never morally obligatory follows . . . from the Kantian principle, which is generally admitted, that 'I ought' implies 'I can.' It is not the case that I can by choice produce a certain motive. . . ."[1] I shall not attempt to meet this apparent objection by plunging into a discussion of free will. I shall simply by-pass it by pointing out that it is not really an objection to the suggestion I have just made. Ross is obviously using 'ought' in a distinctively moralistic sense that can only apply to moral agents. I, on the other hand, used 'ought' in a generic sense, a sense in which the question, 'Can all values be expressed in ought-sentences?', however it be answered, is at least sensible.[2]

Beside many psychological and moralistic questions, the controversy between the deontologists and the teleologists has involved certain distinctively epistemological questions, questions as to how we know value in the sense of being able to verify or otherwise establish value-sentences. One of the bones of contention in this struggle seems to have been the issue, Do we ever have a direct knowledge of duty, or must duty be known through a

[1] *The Right and the Good*, pp. 4–5. Ross also uses another argument which, although it is relevant only to a certain deontological position, *viz.*, that which states that we ought to act from a sense of duty, is nevertheless interesting by virtue of its unsoundness. He writes, "Now if the sense of duty is to be my motive for doing a certain act, it must be the sense that it is my duty to do that act. If, therefore, we say 'it is my duty to do act *A* from the sense of duty', this means, 'it is my duty to do act *A* from the sense that it is my duty to do act *A*' " (*ibid.*, p. 5). This, says Ross, involves the contradiction of saying both that it is my duty "to-do-act-*A*-from-the-sense-that-it-is-my-duty-to-do-act-*A*" and that it is my duty "to-do-act-*A* simply." But wherein is there any contradiction here? Ross fails to observe that I may have *two* duties—the duty to perform a certain act and the duty to have a certain motivation, *e.g.*, to act from a sense of duty. And these duties may be independent. On his own account my motive may be morally bad when I do what is my duty, and my motive may be morally good when I do what is incompatible with my duty. If this involves no contradiction—and of course it does not—then neither does the position that if I do act *B*, which it is my duty to refrain from doing, from the sense that it is my duty to do *B*, then I have discharged my duty, *i.e.* *one* of my *two* duties in the situation, in acting with such a motivation. Similarly, if I do act *A*, which it is my duty to do, but not from the sense of its being my duty, then I have only performed *one* of my two duties. It is plain that Ross reads 'my duty' so that I can have only a single duty in a given situation, which begs the whole question.

[2] I am using 'ought' in the wider of Broad's two senses. "In its narrower sense it applies only to actions which an agent could do if he willed. But there is a wider sense in which there is no such implication. We can say that sorrow ought to have been felt by a certain man at the death of a certain relation, though it was not in his power to feel sorrow at will. And we can say that virtue ought to be rewarded" (*Five Types of Ethical Theory*, p. 161).

process of deduction from some value-predicative sentence (plus factual sentences)? Here of course we must distinguish genuinely epistemological questions from such psychological questions as the genesis of our moral beliefs. Mill, rightly I think, held that many of our moral convictions are acquired as a matter of fact without our thinking of any connection between them and the principle of utility. Yet he also held, and quite consistently, that they are justifiable only so far as they can be derived from that principle.[1] Prichard and Ross, correctly, I think, held that we frequently have the experience which may be described as a direct apprehension of something as our duty or as morally obligatory. They frequently write, however, as though this experience were itself sufficient to show that there is something illogical about trying to establish statements about duty by deducing them from statements about effects and statements about what is good or advantageous.[2] But, as I have indicated, we shall leave aside the epistemological question how value-sentences are established or overthrown. Thus we are not concerned whether there are self-evident sentences asserting moral obligation, whether duty can be known intuitively, whether all value-sentences are derivable from a sentence stating a highest good, and similar questions. These are surely questions of great philosophical importance and, in some generalized form, are not restricted to ethics but concern the very bases of axiology. However, we have chosen, somewhat arbitrarily perhaps, to confine ourselves to the problem, What is value? and, more immediately, we are concerned with the question, What is the proper syntactical form of value-sentences? So even these extremely significant epistemological questions must be left to one side.

Having put aside all these entanglements in other issues I think we can still find something of significance for our special problem in the controversy between the deontologists and the teleologists.

[1] *Cf.*, *e.g.*, *Utilitarianism*, Everyman's ed., p. 22.

[2] I think the following passage from Prichard is a case in point: ". . . we do not come to appreciate an obligation by an *argument*, *i.e.*, by a process of non-moral thinking, and . . . , in particular, we do not do so by an argument of which a premise is the ethical but not moral activity of appreciating the goodness either of the act or of a consequence of the act ; *i.e.*, . . . our sense of the rightness of an act is not a conclusion from our appreciation of the goodness either of it or of anything else" (*Mind*, vol. xxi, 1912, p. 29). Prichard clearly supposes this passage to be relevant to his position that obligations are self-evident (footnote, *ibid.*, pp. 29–30) and that what is right cannot be derived from what is good (*ibid.*, p. 30).

Indeed, in a certain sense I think we can with some propriety claim that the central issue between these two schools can be stated as an issue concerning the correct form of value-sentences. The deontologist claims, as against the teleologist, that there are normative sentences irreducible to value-predicative and factual sentences. Has he any argument for this? I think, in a sense, that he has. It is, however, deeply embedded in his answers to other questions, and particularly to those of the kind I have just called "epistemological." It will be necessary to try to abstract it from this context.

Let me start with a quotation from Prichard. He is speaking of utilitarianism in a generic sense. "It takes its stand," he writes, "upon the distinction between something which is not itself an action but which can be produced by an action and the action which will produce it, and contends that if something which is not an action is good, then we *ought* to undertake the action which will, directly or indirectly, originate it. But this argument, if it is to restore the sense of obligation to act, must presuppose an intermediate link, *viz.*, the further thesis that what is good ought to be. The necessity of this link is obvious. An 'ought,' if it is to be derived at all, can only be derived from another 'ought'."[1] Leaving aside the psychological, moralistic, and "epistemological" issues here raised, I think that it is not improper to interpret this passage as asserting, or perhaps I had better say, as implying, that normative sentences cannot be reduced to value-predicating and causal sentences because some of them at least say something that no set composed wholly of sentences of the latter sorts can say. They say that something (we need no longer restrict this, moralistically, to acts) is obligatory. To use a less moralistic term, normative sentences assert a "value-requiredness" not asserted in the ordinary value-predicative sentence. They say—how else can I put it than in their own most distinctive form?—that something ought to be.

I think that a variant of this contention can be found in a valuable essay by Professor William Frankena.[2] I would like here again to quote a very characteristic passage. Mr. Frankena writes, ". . . Moore regards intrinsic value as a quality which is really

[1] *Op. cit.*, p. 24. Prichard goes on to say that the argument also presupposes that the apprehension of the something good will give rise to the apprehension of the obligatoriness of the act that will produce it.

[2] "Obligation and Value in the Ethics of G. E. Moore," in *The Philosophy of G. E. Moore*, ed. by P. A. Schilpp, pp. 91–110.

intrinsic, and which is also simple and non-natural. Now my contention is that if this conception of its nature is correct, then intrinsic value cannot be possessed of any essential normativeness or obligatoriness. It cannot be part of its very meaning that it enjoins us or any other agents to take up a certain attitude toward it. I should even say that if this conception of intrinsic value is correct, then Moore is wrong in saying that 'A is intrinsically good' is synonymous with 'A ought to exist for its own sake,' since the notion of what ought to exist for its own sake has a complexity which the notion of intrinsic value is not supposed to have. It involves the notions of obligation and of existence and of a kind of relation of the things in question to existence, and can hardly represent a simple quality."[1] We are not concerned with this passage as a criticism of Moore[2] but rather as stating an objection to the reduction of normative sentences to value-predicative sentences. The objection is quite clear. No value-predicative sentence whose predicate is simple and undefined can say the sort of thing a normative sentence says, for a normative sentence, precisely in its value-aspect, is complex, it combines obligation and existence. And this can be easily generalized if we are willing to say that all value-predicative sentences can be reduced to ones with simple, undefined predicates.

The reader is, of course, aware that the author of the present essay cannot accept Professor Frankena's statement of the case. A normative sentence is not complex in the way he says: its normativity is no more complex than the declarativity of a declarative sentence. A normative sentence asserts neither existence nor that something is in some relation (say obligatoriness) to existence. Or, to state it in terms of the other supposed element in the complex, obligatoriness or oughtness is not an independent element. It could not be united with some element other than existence[3]

[1] *Op. cit.*, pp. 98–9.

[2] Moore wrote a long and somewhat rambling reply to Frankena the upshot of which, from our standpoint, can be roughly formulated by saying that though value-predicative sentences are not identical with any normative sentences they are logically equivalent to (*i.e.*, entail and are entailed by) certain normatives (*cf. ibid.*, pp. 608–11). Apparently Moore has at least partially capitulated to the deontologists. The whole discussion is unnecessarily complicated by a moralistic formulation, in terms of a God with duties as to what sort of world He shall create.

[3] 'Obligation to do,' in specifically moralistic normatives, is no exception, for it is just elliptical for 'ought to bring an act into existence,' *i.e.*, it is a statement that such and such an act (or the initiation thereof) ought to be.

to form a different complex. However, I think Frankena is quite right in saying that obligation to exist, or as we put it earlier, value-requiredness, is not simple *in the way* a simple quality is simple. It is rather simple in the way exemplification is simple. But, as an earlier perplexity of ours to which we shall return indicates, this is not quite right either. Ought or obligation are properly expressed as 'ought to exemplify' and thus seem to be more complex than 'exemplifies.' I shall not reopen the issue here how value includes fact, but I would like to remark upon an analogy. The use of such a term as 'requiredness' suggests the analogy of a normative sentence to a declarative in the apodictic modality. 'Business men ought to be honest' seems analogous to 'Coloured patches must be extended.' As a matter of fact, I think there is an analogy, but we must be careful to see just where it lies. It does not lie in the element of necessity. I do not personally believe in objective or factual necessity. I could express this by refusing to permit synthetic *a priori* sentences, by ruling out of my language, as ill-formed, any synthetic sentence that contained any such term as 'must,' 'necessary,' or so forth. But I think it is more revealing and categorially more significant to allow that synthetic *a priori* sentences may be properly formed, but to consider them all false. This shows we might have had a world in which there were factual, necessary connections. In such a world, however, there would not be two things united in such connections, namely, actual exemplification and the necessity thereof. 'Must be' is not properly analysed, categorially, as a complex of 'must' and 'exemplifies.' It is just in this sense that 'ought to be' is analogous to 'must be.' The requiredness in a normative sentence is different from that asserted in an apodictic, factual sentence, but something like the same peculiar union with exemplification while still preserving simplicity of form is present.[1]

Just what is this value-requiredness that normatives possess but value-predicative sentences lack? I think it is to be found in the form of the normative. As we have seen, a normative has a structure sufficiently analogous to that of a declarative so that it is not improper to speak, in both cases, of the predicate-place and the subject-place or subject-places in them in which names are to occur. The difference may then be said to lie in the "relation"

[1] One difference is obvious. '*a* must be *A*' entails '*a* is *A*,' but '*a* ought to be *A*' does not entail '*a* is *A*.' I am simply saying that all of these sentences are equally elementary in form.

(in a misleading use of that term) between the predicate-place and the subject-place. In the declarative the predicate designates a property asserted to be exemplified by that which is named by the subject. In the normative the predicate designates a property which it is asserted ought to be exemplified by that which is named by the subject. It is in this way that the value-requiredness is expressed. And this, I fear, cannot be said much more clearly. Certainly we cannot properly *name* (as of course I have improperly been naming) the value-element. It is just this "relation" that a value-predicative sentence lacks. If value is a property, however unnatural, its requiredness-to-be-exemplified is necessarily omitted from it; it is the sort of thing that is or is not exemplified, and that is the end of the matter.

It seems to me that it is something similar to this sort of view, when the question of the categorial status of value is disentangled from other issues, toward which the deontologists have been groping in their controversy with the teleologists. Let me point out just one, albeit a very significant, straw in the wind. It is the contention, on the part of the deontologists, that duty or rightness attaches to acts by virtue of the fact that they are of a certain kind, that is, that they have certain other properties: it is not a question of mere regularity, such that any act possessing some certain property, *A*, also (as a matter of fact) exemplifies rightness. It would seem rather that the rightness is not just another property of the act, but attaches to, or is indeed constituted by, the act's possession of *A*. Thus Prichard writes: "For wherever in ordinary life we think of some particular action as a duty, we are not simply thinking of it as right, but also thinking of its rightness *as constituted by* the possession of some definite characteristic . . . we do not think of the action as right *blindly*, *i.e.*, irrespectively of the special character which we think the act to possess; rather we think of it as being right *in virtue of* possessing a particular characteristic of the kind indicated by the phrase by which we refer to it. Thus in thinking of our keeping our promise to *X* as a duty, we are thinking of the action as rendered a duty by its being the keeping of our promise."[1] It is true that in this passage Prichard is not directly grappling with our problem. He is opposing the teleologists. He is saying that an action which is right is so not by virtue of the consequences (say advantages to the agent) with which it is regularly connected, but by

[1] "Duty and Interest," pp. 15–16. First and last italics mine.

virtue of its being the kind of act it is. But whether Prichard was aware of it or not, this comes close to saying that rightness is not a property at all, or that if it is it doesn't behave in the way ordinary properties behave. Keeping one's promise is right not in the sense in which it may also be, say, a difficult act to perform, nor even, supposing this were an empirical law, in the sense that it is always the source of a favourable response on the part of the promisee. That is, it is not just the exemplification of another empirical or descriptive property. Being the keeping of a promise requires, "constitutes," the rightness of the act. Yet 'right' is not just another name for the property of keeping a promise, nor is it a class-name for all those properties the possession of which constitutes the rightness of a right act. For these other properties are descriptive: their possession by an act is just a fact. 'Right', by contrast, is a value-term: it is a significant question to ask whether a given act which is admitted to be a case of promise-keeping really is right—as Ross's discussion of *prima facie* duties makes clear.

Ross has indicated the peculiarity of rightness, on the deontological view, by speaking of it as a "resultant attribute" and by clearly distinguishing its dependence upon the exemplification of another property, the "right-making attribute," from the dependence of an effect upon a cause. I quote a rather significant passage. "Now it is clear that it is in virtue of my thinking the act to have some other character that I think I ought to do it. Rightness is always a resultant attribute, an attribute that an act has because it has another attribute. It is not an attribute that its subject is just directly perceived in experience to have, as I perceive a particular extended patch to be yellow, or a particular noise to be loud. No doubt there are causes which cause this patch to be yellow, or that noise to be loud; but I can perceive the one to be yellow, or the other to be loud, without knowing anything of the causes that account for this. I see the attributes in question to attach to the subjects merely as these subjects, not as subjects of such and such a character. On the other hand, it is only by knowing or thinking my act to have a particular character, out of the many that it in fact has, that I know or think it to be right."[1]

All this, as I put it above, may be treated as a groping on the part of the deontologists toward the view that rightness is not a

[1] *Foundations of Ethics*, p. 168.

property at all, that the element of obligation, of value-requiredness, is properly reflected not in any predicate-term but in a sentential form, the form of the normative sentence. 'My keeping my promise to *X* is right' would then be a misleading way of saying what is much more properly said by 'I ought to keep my promise to *X*' (which is seen to differ from 'I do keep my promise to *X*' not by possessing a new predicate but by putting the same subjects and predicate in a new sentential "relation"). The value-requiredness is a requiredness to exemplify.[1]

[1] Since writing the above there has come to my attention a passage in Prichard's recently published essay, "Moral Obligation," which must be put over against the interpretation of the deontological position I am proposing. In it he opposes what he takes to be a suggestion of Hume to the effect that 'ought' and 'ought not' express some new relation between a subject and an attribute, different from that expressed by 'is' and 'is not.' Of this he says, "there can neither be nor be thought to be any such relationship. For as we recognize when we reflect, the only relations in which a given subject of attributes can possibly stand to a given attribute are those of possessing and not possessing it, no third alternative being possible. And consequently, when we assert that *X* ought to be educating *Y*, we cannot possibly be asserting that *X* stands to the act of educating *Y* in a relation indicated by the word 'ought' which is neither that of possessing it nor that of not possessing it" (*op. cit.*, p. 92).

I think that Prichard committed a serious mistake in this passage. He confused, it seems to me, a "different relation" with an "alternative relation." He rightly saw that the law of excluded middle is valid, that there is no third *alternative* to a subject's possession or non-possession of an attribute whereby if the subject stood in this "relation" to the attribute it would neither possess it nor not possess it. Alternatives are necessarily mutually incompatible. "Relations" that are merely different are not. So 'ought' and 'ought not' could express different relations between a subject and attribute from those expressed by 'is' and 'is not' without abrogation of the law of excluded middle. Thus it is quite possible to assert that *X* stands to the act of educating *Y* in a relation indicated by the word 'ought' which is *different from* but not *incompatible with* the relation of possessing it or not possessing it and thus is *in addition to* the latter.

Nevertheless, though this passage may, as I think it does, reveal a serious mistake in Prichard's thought, it also unmistakably shows that he did in one place consciously reject the view toward which I have suggested that both he and Ross were generally, though perhaps unconsciously, groping. I still wish to urge this suggestion, however, on grounds already presented. These amount to the queerness of rightness, as a property of acts, and of obligation to do some act, as a property of agents. These, as we have seen, are "resultant" properties. Moreover, they are strange in not demanding existence in the way ordinary properties do. An act that does not exist can be right, though a man who did not exist could not be tall. An agent can be obligated to do an act that never has existed and never will exist, though a man can not be a father to a child that never has existed and never will exist. Most basically, these properties differ from ordinary properties in their intentional inclusion of existence, to put the matter in my phraseology. All these queernesses are recognized by the deontologists; hence I cannot avoid feeling that they are not too far from an admission of the irreducibility of normative to value-predicative sentences.

Thus in a certain abstract sense and on a certain interpretation of their views I am siding with the deontologists as against the teleologists. Normative sentences cannot properly be rendered as value-predicative sentences, for the former assert the value-requiredness of the exemplification of some ordinary, empirical property not asserted by the latter. But now I propose to go a step further. I shall try to make plausible the position that value-predicative sentences can properly be rendered as normatives. This, obviously, is a hazardous undertaking. Our own analysis has shown us how different the two sorts of sentence are, and there is no need to emphasize the frequency of occurrence of value-predicative sentences in ordinary speech. But perhaps some encouragement may be gained from our recognition, through the discussion in Sections 2, 3, and 4 of the present essay, of the serious difficulties involved, from the standpoint of common sense itself, in treating value as a predicate. We are, then, already aware of the advisibility of some sort of reformulation of everyday value-predicative sentences. Thus the possibility that they may be considered a kind of normative sentence may not seem just absurd.

The suggestion I am about to make is, indeed, a rather natural one to make in our present situation. It is that value-predicative sentences are all elliptical; they are abbreviated or, better, incomplete normatives. For some reason, be it commendable social discretion or reprehensible personal laziness, we do not in such cases want to formulate the whole normative sentence. We omit, as the case may be, the subject or the predicate. To make it appear that we have a full sentence we throw the whole into an apparently declarative form with a value-term as predicate. On this suggestion there are two major classes of value-predicative sentences; those that have omitted the normative predicate and those that have omitted the normative subject or subjects.

An example of the first is 'John is good.' That such a sentence in incomplete, as it stands, is indicated by our sense of the relevance of such a question as 'Why do you say so?' meaning to elicit not a statement of the speaker's motivation in uttering 'John is good' but a specification of the respect or respects in which John is said to be good. Suppose the utterer of 'John is good,' when so accosted, to reply by the words, 'I say 'John is good' because he is always kindly.' It then would not seem too inappropriate to claim that 'John is good' in this situation was elliptical for 'That John is always kindly is good' or 'It is good that John is always kindly.' This last sentence apparently asserts besides a value a fact, namely that John is always kindly. I do not wish to dispute this. It may well be that every value-predicative sentence similar to 'John is good' (in hiating or suppressing its real predicate) is in part an elliptical factual assertion. But if so, we may set this factual element aside, for clearly it is not all. The value-predicative sentence is also a value-sentence and it is this which for the moment we are trying to analyse. Let us put this component in the subjunctive form, not meaning thereby to indicate any contrary-to-factness but just value-assertiveness as *different* from factual assertiveness. In the situation considered above, 'John is good' is, in respect of its value-component, elliptical for 'It were good that John be always kindly.' To generalize, value-predicative sentences in ordinary speech having the form '*a* is good,' where '*a*' is the name of a particular,[1] are incomplete in their value-component in a way which can be expressed by the use of a variable, '*a* is good' thus being properly rendered 'There is a property, *X*, such that it were good that *a* exemplify *X*.' Now this last sentence, it seems to me, is as it stands a perfectly good normative. It would probably seem more acceptable, as giving the full sense of '*a* is good,' than, for instance, 'There is a property, *X*, such that *a* ought to exemplify *X*'; but this I think is mainly because the value-requiredness in it is less harsh ('it were good that' is a softer expression than 'ought to'). I shall return to this presently. We may then preserve and even I think clarify the meaning of such everyday expressions as '*a* is good' (where '*a*' names a particular) by replacing them by a conjunction similar to 'There is a property, *X*, such that *a* ought to exemplify *X* and *a* does exemplify *X*.'

Value-predicative sentences in everyday speech of the second sort I mentioned, *viz.*, those omitting their normative subject or subjects, represented by the instance, 'Pleasure is good,' could be handled in an analogous way. We could say, *e.g.*, that 'Pleasure is good' is an incomplete and misleading way of saying 'There is a

[1] The alert reader may accuse me here, and in what follows, of inconsistency. Have I not said that a name is just a name; that whether it name for example a particular depends on the place it occupies in a sentence? My reply is that I was speaking of a properly constructed language. Value-predicative sentences are not only incomplete, they are also ambiguous in form. We must guess whether what occurs in their subject-place or places should properly, in the complete normative they incompletely and ambiguously express, occur in the subject-place or the predicate place. We base this guess on the usual place of the occurrence of the name in question in declarative sentences.

particular, *x*, such that it were good that *x* exemplify pleasantness' or 'There is a particular, *x*, such that *x* ought to be pleasant.'[1] But I do not feel that this would present the sense of such sentences as 'Pleasure is good' as ordinarily used. Suppose someone has just uttered the sentence, 'Pleasure is good.' We say to him, "What do you mean?" There is a fair chance that he will reply in some such vein as: "Surely you wouldn't deny that anything that is pleasant is good—at least in so far as it is pleasant, disregarding, that is, that it may also be unpleasant or may produce unpleasant consequences." If this sort of reply is commonsensical, and I believe it is, then we have at least some grounds for the following generalization. Value-predicative sentences of the type '*A* is good,' where '*A*' names a universal, are incomplete and misleading normatives of the form 'For any particular, *x*, if *x* exemplifies *A* then it were good that *x* exemplify *A*' or (more harshly) 'For any *x*, if *x* exemplifies *A* then *x* ought to exemplify *A*.'

A certain complication again enters our analysis owing to the tacit factual assertion, along with the value-assertion, that seems to be present in such expressions as '*A* is good.' In the illustration given above, this appeared in the italicized portion of "anything *that is pleasant* is good." This is perhaps too narrow a formulation of it. We would probably want to interpret 'Pleasure is good' so that it included the assertion that it were good that some things exemplify pleasantness which in fact do not. On the other hand some factual restriction does seem required to render the sense of 'Pleasure is good.' 'Pleasure is good' is not properly rendered 'Everything ought to be pleasant' nor even 'It were good that everything be pleasant.' This I think is obvious common sense. But just what is wrong with such a rendition is not so obvious. On the one hand, it may be that some doubt as to the attainability of value is operative. We are aware that it is impossible (empirically speaking) that everything (*i.e.*, every particular) be pleasant.[2] I have alluded to this very briefly above. It may be that we feel that pleasure is good up to some point but not beyond it. Perhaps as things now are, every actual pleasure is good, but were every particular to be pleasant it would not be good. This

[1] Since this analysis is not going to be adopted it is immaterial whether we add 'and *x* is pleasant.'

[2] Of course it is categorially impossible that everything be pleasant if 'everything' include in its range every entity, for example, universals.

is a perfectly possible view and could be stated in our normative terminology (with the addition of certain declarative clauses). This is at least indicated by the following: 'For any particular, *x*, if *x* is pleasant does not imply that more than *n* things are pleasant, then it were good that *x* be pleasant.' There may be other possible bases of our reluctance to render 'Pleasure is good' by 'It were good that every particular be pleasant.' However, as I have indicated, the difficulties seem to turn on the tacit factual assertion involved, not on the propriety of translating the value-assertion into the normative form.

In assessing the feasibility of the programme I am suggesting, *viz.*, that of treating all value-predicative sentences of ordinary speech as disguised and incomplete normative sentences, I would ask the reader to be indulgent as to specific formulations. Usually when we utter a value-predicative sentence we are saying something very complex in what appears to be a simple sentence, something whose analysis requires a careful consideration of the total context and an expansion of the analysed sentence into a number of sentences. Essentially what I am suggesting is that value-predicative sentences in ordinary speech be treated in their valuative aspect (*i.e.*, abstracting from tacit or associated declarative assertions) as incomplete normatives saying either that some particular or particulars ought to exemplify some unspecified property or that some property ought to be exemplified by some unspecified particular or particulars or perhaps by all particulars or all particulars actually exemplifying some other property. But I am not unaware that even in this very broad formulation my proposal must face objections. I shall deal briefly with three.

The first of these can be disposed of quickly since already considered in an anticipatory fashion. It is this. To say that something is good implies that it exists, whereas to say that something ought to be implies that it does not exist. Hence, so the objection runs, value-predicative sentences cannot be treated as disguised normatives. This objection could be met head-on. It could be pointed out that ordinary value-predicative sentences do not always imply existence (as in the case of 'The proposed system of roads is excellent'), nor do ordinary normatives always imply non-existence (as in the case of 'Under the circumstances you did all that you ought to have done'). But I propose to meet the objection obliquely. Grant the supposition as to ordinary speech. Let us clarify ordinary speech by separating off any existential components in declarative sentences. This device will leave value-assertions pure, and will meet the present objection against saying that the proper form of value-assertion is the normative.

The second objection is in part what I had in mind in speaking of 'ought to exemplify' as frequently too harsh an expression to render a value-predicative, and in suggesting that we use 'it were good that – – – exemplify' instead. Now so far as we have here just a psychological issue, representing an urbane temperament reacting against puritanicalism, this meets the situation. It is not the specific words used, the "overtones" of the notation, but whether value can always properly be rendered through the sentential form that is the real problem. There is, however, a distinction frequently marked by the difference between 'ought' and 'good' which is not merely psychological. Often when we say something ought to be we wish to imply that anything incompatible therewith ought not to be, whereas we do not always mean when we say that something is good that anything incompatible therewith is not good.[1] Suppose these two situations to be incompatible, that my house be painted white and that it be painted green. 'Ought' is frequently so used that 'My house ought to be painted white' entails 'My house ought not to be painted green.' On the other hand, 'good' is frequently used so that 'It were good that my house be painted white' does not entail 'It were not good that my house be painted green.'

I think there is some significant distinction frequently embodied in our use of 'ought' and 'good' (and cognate pairs of terms). But that it is something over and above any difference between normative and value-predicative sentences and has no bearing upon the question whether the latter can be treated as incomplete forms of the former seems to be borne out by our very illustration. In it, 'good' did not occur as a predicate-term but as a part of the normative form of two normative sentences. Let me put this more directly. In its generic form the normative sentence is no more "intolerant" than the ordinary value-predicative sentence.

[1] It is characteristic that Ross, in *The Right and the Good*, speaks of *prima facie* rightness and *prima facie* duty but never of *prima facie* goodness. It will be remembered that '*prima facie*' as applied to rightness and duty is not used to indicate mere appearance but to deal with that serious problem for all deontologists: what to do with conflicts of duties. Ross's solution is to say that various conflicting *prima facie* duties are "parti-resultant attributes," each belonging to an act by virtue of some one component of the act, whereas "*being* one's duty is a toti-resultant attribute, one which belongs to an act in virtue of its whole nature and of nothing less than this" (p. 28.)

It does not exclude alternatives. That is, two elementary normative sentences with incompatible content are not contradictory. By 'incompatible content' I mean sets of subjects and predicates which, if used in declaratives, would make them contradictory by virtue, or on the assumption, of some empirical law.

In the light of this consideration and of the "intolerance" of 'ought,' which I have just admitted, I am compelled to grant that '*a* ought to exemplify *A*' does not properly represent the generic form of normative.[1] I dislike doing so because '*a* ought to exemplify *A*,' by its structural analogy to '*a* does exemplify *A*,' suggests the simplicity of the normative form of sentence while retaining the difference of the normative from the declarative form. On the other hand, such a formulation as 'It were good that *a* exemplify *A*' while it avoids the "intolerance" of '*a* ought to exemplify *A*'

[1] I am assuming that if there is a law such that *a* cannot exemplify both *A* and *B*, then '*a* ought to exemplify *A*' entails '*a* ought not to exemplify *B*.' I assume this simply on the basis that this is the way we ordinarily use 'ought.' It might at first glance be supposed that if we were to extend to all normatives, as I propose to do, the analogue to the law of contradiction stated above (p. 128) for imperatives, this would entail the intolerance of all normatives (those I have expressed with 'good that' as well as those formulated with 'ought'). A moment's reflection will dispel this assumption, however. It *seems* as though we assert *p*, in what I have called the "softer" normative, 'It were good that *p*' and thus, if *q* implies $\sim p$, we seem required to exclude the possible combination 'It were good that *p* and it were good that *q*.' But this rests on the failure to take seriously our repeated contention that a normative does not contain its corresponding declarative, and that the normative negative loosely expressed as formed by negating the what-it-is that is valued is a negative of the whole normative not of some component of it. Here is another example of the misleading character of the form, 'It were good that *a* exemplify *A*.'

The whole matter of intolerance, as well as certain problems involved in comparative value-statements, might be more expeditiously handled if our basic normative form were comparative rather than positive. We would then use 'It were better that *a* exemplify *A* than that it exemplify *B*' to represent the generic form of normative. Then the harshness or intolerance of '*a* ought to exemplify *A*' would be seen in the proper formulation of this normative: 'For every *Y*, it were better that *a* exemplify *A* than that it exemplify *Y*.' Likewise the softness of 'It were good that *a* exemplify *A*' would be revealed in the appropriate translation 'There is a *Y* such that it were better that *a* exemplify *A* than that it exemplify *Y*.'

I do not propose to develop this suggestion further. It may have some perfectly absurd consequences; I am not competent to judge. Moreover, it is misleading in a way we have objected to in the case of other proposals. For example, it would require that we translate '*a* is good' as follows: 'For some *X* and some *Y*, it were better that *a* exemplify *X* than that it exemplify *Y* and *a* does exemplify *X*.' Now even if we omit the factual component here, it looks as though we were denying that '*a* is good' is properly treated as elementary, and such an appearance is to be deplored.

is a poor way of indicating the generic type of normative for it looks like a metasentence, a sentence about '*a* exemplifies *A*,' which, of course, we cannot have as the basic form of normative. In this situation the best we can do, it seems to me, is sometimes to use '*a* ought to exemplify *A*' and sometimes 'It were good that *a* exemplify *A*,' depending on our purpose.[1]

We are now in a position to deal, rather peremptorily perhaps, with a difficulty that may have long bothered the reader. How, it may be asked, can aesthetic statements be plausibly rendered as normatives? I want to say immediately that I am concerned only with this difficulty so far as it may be treated as a form of our second objection. It may well be that any adequate analysis of such a sentence as '*a* is beautiful' is extremely complex. The apparent predicate here may perform several functions at once. There may be an empirical property, perhaps even a quality, of beauty that some particulars exemplify. It may be that '*a* is beautiful' in part is elliptical for '*a* exemplifies *A* and when *b* notes that *a* exemplifies *A*, *b* experiences a state having the property *B*.' There are certainly many possibilities of analysis of aesthetic statements. But even were the present author capable of pursuing this investigation (his only encouragement to do so being that almost no one has tried it!) it would be out of place in the present essay. But so far as sentences such as '*a* is beautiful' are value-sentences, so far as 'beautiful' functions to some degree as an apparent value-predicate, the analysis of aesthetic statements is relevant here. Let us make clear that we are concerned only with this aspect of '*a* is beautiful' by substituting for it '*a* is aesthetically good.' Now it does seem violent to treat this sentence as a disguised form of 'There is a property *X* such that *a* ought to exemplify *X*.' But the violence I think is due to the intolerance of 'ought.' So we can use our softer form of normative. We then suggest that '*a* is aesthetically good' be treated as an incomplete and disguised form of the normative, 'There is a property *X* such

[1] Here an arbitrary notation is valuable. The notation suggested above, *viz.*, '$A_{\{a\}}$' for the normative for which the corresponding declarative is '$A_{(a)}$' can be so interpreted as to preserve the simplicity and zero-level character of the basic normative form while yet avoiding "intolerance" in what we have called its value-requiredness. This would likewise be true were we to accept the comparative form as basic. We could, *e.g.*, write '$AB_{\{a\}}$' for the normative improperly formulated 'It were better that *a* exemplify *A* than that it exemplify *B*.' '$AB_{\{a\}}$' seems to show itself as not compound and not a metasentence.

that it were aesthetically good (or fitting) that *a* exemplify *X*' (together perhaps with 'and *a* does exemplify *X*').[1]

The third objection I wish briefly to consider is that my proposal, by treating value-predicative sentences as incomplete normatives, automatically and arbitrarily settles the issue between deontologist and teleologist against the latter, indeed, it destroys the possibility of the latter's stating his position at all. This I simply deny. The issues between the two can be stated in the sort of language I propose and are, it seems to me, even clarified thereby with one exception. So far as the teleologist means to say that value is reducible to one basic sort of thing and this sort of thing is just a unique property, say a quality, then I would agree with what I think I have found in the deontologists. I would say that there is a form of value which is not itself properly spoken of as a property: I have indeed generalized this and proposed that we deny that value is ever to be thought of as a property. However, there are good grounds for questioning whether this basic categorial issue was ever very clearly present in the minds of teleologists (even, for that matter, in the dogged worryings of G. E. Moore). The issues that were explicitly present in their struggle with the deontologists can, I think be stated without the use of value-predicative sentences.

These issues (leaving aside purely factual questions as to motivation and related psychological matters) can be conveniently grouped under two heads. The first group may be epitomized

[1] My formulation here raises another issue which I should like to dodge were it not that anyone who has read thus far must be sufficiently motivated to find me out. If I admit different kinds of goodness—aesthetic, moral, etc.,—must I not, on my account, grant a separate form of value-sentence to express each? For the present I must be satisfied to answer briefly and thus apparently dogmatically (I cherish the hope that I may explore at some future date the problem, What kinds of value are there?). First, I would say that even were it necessary to admit structurally different kinds of value-sentences to express different kinds of value, it seems plausible to suppose that they may all be forms of normative sentence. Second, it may be that the structural differences required relate solely to the sorts of things which are to be named in the subject and predicate places, and that these differences (plus ever-present tacit or associated factual assertions) may be stated in declarative sentences. Thus, '*a* is morally good' may be elliptical for 'There is an *X* such that it were good that *a* exemplify *X*, *a* does exemplify *X*, *a* is a person, *X* is a motivational trait.' I do not mean that this sketch of a type of possible analysis of '*a* is morally good' is at all satisfying, nor shall I venture even such a sketch of '*a* is aesthetically good.' But it may serve as a hint of a line of analysis that might be explored and that would save me from the embarrassment of having to admit a plurality of fundamentally different structures of value-sentences.

by the question, Is there a unique kind of value (represented by duty and right) exhibited only by acts of moral agents, and to be contrasted with one or more other sorts of value exhibited by other sorts of things? The teleologist opposes the deontologist's affirmative answer to this question.

Although actually the controversy over this sort of issue has been carried on through a mixture of value-sentences, some being value-predicative, some normative, it could, it seems to me, be stated wholly in terms of value-predicatives. The problem then is whether all sentences similar in form to '*a* is right' or '*a* is a duty' can be properly replaced by sentences of the form '*b* is good and *a* stands in relation *R* to *b*' (not excluding the possibility that *a* is identical with *b*). But if the problem can be stated by means of value-predicatives (as though *all* kinds of value were properly expressed as predicates), it can also be stated by means of normatives (as though *all* kinds of value were properly expressed by the normative sentential form).[1] Indeed, there would be a clarification in this latter way of stating it. The deontological position, that duty, *e.g.*, is a unique form of value as contrasted with good, though stressing the difference between duty and good, yet holds that both are forms of value, and hence that both are to be contrasted with ordinary empirical properties. But if duty and good are expressed by predicate-terms, how is their common contrast with ordinary empirical properties to be indicated? Apparently we simply have to know which predicate-terms are value-terms and which not. But this likeness of duty and good (*i.e.*, both being values) would be brought out by our proposal. We then simply ask, Is there a unique form of normative dealing with acts of moral agents and irreducible to the normative form (however combined in actual instances with declarative sentences dealing with other sorts of thing)? And the teleologist's position (on this first sort of issue) is quite adequately indicated by a negative answer to this question.

The second group of issues can be dealt with under the heading, Can all legitimate value-sentences be derived from one or a few having the character of standards of value (plus certain declarative premises)? The teleologist would answer this with an affirmative, the deontologist with a decided negative. To show that this issue can be stated without the use of value-predicatives

[1] To state the issue it would then be necessary to admit in some sense different varieties of the normative sentential form. See the preceding footnote.

it is necessary to show that standards of value need not have the value-predicative form. A "standard of value," in the sense in which I am using this phrase, is a generalized value-sentence. This, however, is not a sufficient characterization. 'Every instance of promise-keeping is an instance of duty' is a generalized value-sentence but is not a standard of value in my sense; similarly with 'Every instance of pleasure is an instance of good.' The additional feature necessary is that a standard of value include a factual law. Moreover, the factual law must be included in a certain way. This might be roughly formulated as follows. A standard of value is a generalized value-sentence asserting the value of everything related by a factual law to some specified kind of fact so that whenever the thing (which is asserted to have value) occurs something of the specified kind also occurs. An instance is the following: 'Everything whose occurrence is regularly related, by a law, with an occurrence of pleasure is good.' It might be necessary in order to be true to the thought and spirit of the teleologist—but at the risk of cutting down the generalized scope of his position so as to take certain questions of motivation into account—to add a further requirement to the effect that the law must be of the causal form and must state that the fact of the kind specified must always succeed in time the occurrence of that which, on the standard, is asserted to have value. We then would state our instance as follows: 'Everything whose occurrence is regularly related, by a law, with a subsequent occurrence of pleasure is good.'[1]

The example just given is in the value-predicative form. Can it be put in the normative form I have proposed? I believe it can, and with a clarification that agrees, so it seems to me, with everyday usage. We would then have: 'For any *X*, if any exemplification

[1] It may be noted that my formulation does not specify any kind of value. That issue is separated under questions of the first sort. Thus the following would be a standard of value: 'Every initiation of an action which is regularly related by a law with a subsequent occurrence of an act which is a keeping of a promise given by the agent is a duty.' Now even when 'standard of value' refers to generalized value-sentences of this sort, as well as of the sort involving value in the form of good, as in the example about pleasure; I think the deontologist should answer in the negative the question, Can all legitimate value-sentences be derived from one or a few standards of value (plus certain declarative sentences)? I say this because it seems to me to distinguish the position of the deontologist that the legitimacy of duty-sentences is determined wholly by reference to the character of the act of which duty is asserted, and not at all by the character of *anything* else with which its occurrence may be regularly associated.

of X is related by a law to a subsequent exemplification of pleasure, then it were good that X be exemplified.'[1] Here, then, we have a normative formulation of the hedonic standard of value.[2] It can readily be seen how, by substituting a variable (taking names of properties for its values) for 'pleasure)' this can be generalized to cover all standards of value. Thus I think we can feel assured that issues of our second group, turning on the teleologist's contention that all legitimate value-sentences can be derived from one or a few standards of value plus certain declarative sentences and the deontologist's denial of this, specifically in cases of duty-sentences and right-sentences, can be formulated in normative (plus declarative) sentences.

This concludes my attempt to make plausible the very radical suggestion that we treat all genuine[3] value-sentences of everyday speech as properly expressible in the normative form. Where they are not already in that form, we are justified in treating them as disguised or incomplete normatives. This is not of course a proposal that anyone—not even the philosopher—reform his speech habits. Good speech etiquette, economy of time, stylistic variety, and many other considerations would argue against actually casting all value-sentences into the normative form. Only for the philosophic purpose of trying to see just what sort of thing we are saying when we utter a value-sentence and of thereby gaining some insight into the status of value is such a grammatical simplification proposed. Moreover, even for this purpose the proposal may be simply absurd. There may be things (and

[1] One might be tempted to write this, in accordance with the notation suggested earlier, '$(X)\ (x)\ (\exists y)\ \left[(X_{(x)} \supset P_{(y)}) \supset X_{\{x\}}\right]$' where '$P$' is an abbreviation for 'pleasant.' But when one notices that the first horseshoe is a declarative connective and the second normative and remembers that normative operators like those in the formula, which of course is as a whole normative, in general have somewhat different rules from those governing their declarative correlates, one doubts whether, in the present condition of normative logic, such symbolization is at all clarificatory.

[2] It should be noted that though it makes pleasure the standard of value it does not make it a value; it does not, *e.g.*, say that for every x (with or without some factual restriction) it were good that x exemplify pleasantness. This was intentional. There has been much too much confusion of 'X is a standard of good' with 'X is good.'

[3] There are, it seems to me, many pseudo-value-sentences in current usage which might appear genuine on the surface but on a moment's reflection are seen to be declarative in intent. Here are a few random examples. 'We ought to get a shift of wind with that cold front.' 'That is a good illustration of the sort of cheating objective examinations permit.' 'He is the best scorer on our team.' 'At the rate he usually drives, John should be here now.'

value-things, not factual things) we mean to say in some common value-sentences that just cannot be said by means of normative sentences. I am not at present aware of any, but my extremely cursory review of value-sentences in everyday speech is no guarantee that there are none. Let us hope that philosophers will devote more serious attention to this sort of question in the near future.

However, even if the present section should turn out to be mistaken in suggesting that all genuine value-sentences can be properly reduced to normatives there would remain the contention that normatives (and imperatives if imperatives cannot be treated as a kind of normative) are syntactically different from declaratives. This I think, for all its defectiveness, the present section has established. Specifically, I claim that by showing how imperatives may be treated as a special kind of normative I have furnished grounds for supposing that certain characteristic differences of imperatives from declaratives generically distinguish normatives from declaratives. I am supposing, for example, that normative connectives behave differently from their declarative namesakes. Let me use the negative for illustration. It will be recalled that imperatives have two irreducible negatives, as contrasted with the single negative of declaratives. It seems reasonable to believe that this holds generally of normatives. Put conveniently but misleadingly, it is possible to negate a normative either by changing its normative quality (from 'ought' to 'not-ought' or from 'it were good that' to 'it were not good that') or by negating that about which a normative claim is made. Put more correctly, for every contradictory pair of descriptive declaratives there is a set of four normatives having the same content, two being normatively affirmative, two normatively negative. We may use the normative form of the illustration we offered earlier for imperatives.

1. Donald is wearing his rubbers	1a. Donald ought to wear his rubbers. 1b. There is no ought[1] about Donald's wearing his rubbers.
2. Donald is not wearing his rubbers	2a. Donald ought to refrain from wearing his rubbers. 2b. There is no ought about Donald's refraining from wearing his rubbers.

[1] There is no single unambiguous way of expressing this normative negative in everyday speech. 'Not-ought' would be excellent but unfortunately is not

Here again we may, without violence to good usage, combine 1b and 2b to form a single, simple normative. Thus for each contradictory pair of descriptive declaratives we have a trio of normatives which are exclusive and (as regards the subjects and predicates involved) exhaustive of the normative possibilities.

The conclusion of Section 5 found us seeking value-sentences that would differ syntactically from factual sentences. We had considered favourably the view, most explicitly formulated by Brentano, that value is the referent of a semantical predicate. Brentano had suggested that good is the object of a right love: we had reformulated this to say that value is the referent of a legitimate value-sentence, that which makes it legitimate (being parallel to fact as the referent of a true descriptive sentence, that which makes it true). We had found this line of analysis attractive, in view of the various difficulties involved in other positions on the status of value, and in relation to the desiderata which the discussion of these difficulties had brought to our attention. Our trouble was that if we consistently read beyond Brentano's psychologisms there seemed no way of distinguishing between the rightness of a right love and the rightness of a right judgment, nor even, indeed, between a love of and a belief in the same matter. So we needed a formal (syntactical) distinction between value-sentences and factual sentences with which a semantical distinction between legitimacy-value and truth-value might correlate.

If the present section has been successful in showing that at least some value-sentences (normatives) differ syntactically from at least some factual sentences (declaratives), we have made a little progress. I would like to think we have done more, that we have found it plausible to suppose that all value-sentences may be replaced by normatives differing syntactically from every factual sentence. Be that as it may, I now suggest a further step. For at least those value-sentences that differ in syntax from ordinary factual sentences along the lines indicated there are legitimacy-values that, though analogous to the truth-values of factual sentences, are distinguishable from truth values. Is it not reasonable to suppose that if a normative sentence can be negated in

current. 'Doesn't need to' might be declarative, or again might be specifically imperative (indicating the agent as well as the subject): the same could be said of 'doesn't have to.' 'There is no ought' is bad in that it seems to require the inclusion of the corresponding declarative in the normative.

two different and mutually irreducible ways it can fail to be legitimate in two different and mutually irreducible ways? If 'Donald ought to wear his rubbers' has two different negatives ('Donald ought to refrain from wearing his rubbers' and 'There is no ought about Donald's wearing or not-wearing his rubbers'), is it not reasonable to suppose that it may fail to be legitimate in two different ways?

Let us suppose, then, that normative sentences are three-valued. With this supposition we can escape a difficulty in Brentano's position. That difficulty, as we have just recalled, was that, apart from the psychological overtones, the rightness of a right love was indistinguishable from the rightness of a right judgment, We now see that 'legitimate,' though a semantical term and specifically a semantical predicate assertable of sentences, yet differs from 'true.' Thus when we say that value is that which makes a legitimate sentence legitimate we are saying something analogous to, but not to be confused with, what we are saying when we say that fact is that which makes a true sentence true. Moreover we now have something more than a psychological difference between sentences which can be true and sentences which can be legitimate: we have a syntactical difference. We can now say that the same sentence cannot be both true and legitimate (or more generally, cannot have both a truth-value and a legitimacy-value).

Having met in this fashion certain difficulties that stood in the way of the type of analysis suggested by Brentano, we can now consider a further proposal. It is extremely radical and if it merits any consideration at all will call forth vehement opposition. It is to the effect that just as we can properly locate or refer to fact and value as the referents, respectively, of a true declarative and a legitimate normative, so we can find the nature, the categorial status of fact and of value reflected in the basic structure of the declarative and the normative sentence, respectively, so far as this can be found or seen by us at all. This of course makes the radical assumption that syntax can have semantical significance, though 'semantical significance' must here be given a categorial not an empirical interpretation. The very form of our sentence can say something about extra-linguistic fact, though not something that can be said apart from the content and not anything nameable.

To give some semblance of plausibility to this strange proposal will be the task of the final section of this essay.

7

WHAT IS THE SIGNIFICANCE OF LINGUISTIC ANALYSIS FOR VALUE-THEORY?

RUNNING through all of the present essay is an assumption the reader may wish to challenge. This assumption is that an analysis of our valuational language can furnish reliable insights into or at least clues as to the status of value in the world. I must confess that if this assumption, thus generally put, be questioned there is not much I can do by way of justification. One must start somewhere and have some methodological principles or the philosophic task simply cannot get under way.[1] Moreover, some propaganda value, at least, derives from the consideration that something like this assumption is apparently embedded in all recent philosophic discussions of value.[2] The naturalists almost universally base their denial that value has any categorial status on a form of linguistic analysis—one which involves I think a union of

[1] Bradley has stated this in a perverted fashion. "In theory you cannot indulge with consistency in an ultimate doubt. You are forced, willingly or not, at a certain point to assume infallibility. For otherwise, how could you proceed to judge at all?" (*Appearance and Reality*, p. 512). This is perverted because doubt and infallibility are irrelevant to the status of first principles, whether substantival or procedural, in a philosophical system, and the appearance of their relevancy leads on to just the sort of confusion of which Bradley is guilty: that between the legitimate position that every philosophic system rests on first principles which cannot in that system be established and the illegitimate assumption that the first principles of a given system (the author's, of course) must, if one is to be rational, be accepted. In some sense it must be possible to compare the reasonableness or plausibility of the first principles of different systems. And if it be retorted (I think quite reasonably) that this desideratum already to some extent commits one philosophically, I would reply that no position that destroys this possibility is itself reasonable. On *this* matter I find myself unable to get outside my own position. But even here I would refuse to muddy the waters by speaking of "infallibility" and "the impossibility of ultimate doubts."

[2] There is the possible exception of the pragmatists. A book like Lepley's *The Verifiability of Value* seems to suggest that axiology is just a part of empirical science. But then such philosophers are not discussing our type of question—What is Value? What is its categorial status? Hence perhaps they do not furnish any real exception to my generalization.

some sort of meaning criterion and some principle as to the legitimacy of reduction.[1] The objectivists with whom the early part of this essay is concerned, *viz.*, those who either explicitly claim or implicitly assume that value is a property, likewise, so it seems to me, make use of the assumption in question. Many of them specifically admit as much, but even where they do not I think they can be said to presuppose it. The very notion of a property (whether a quality or a relation, and of whatever type-level) depends upon that of a predicate and therefore upon at least a rudimentary linguistic analysis. And by 'depends upon' I mean to indicate something more than an empirical law. Perhaps it would be putting it too narrowly (and committing oneself too definitely to a specific point of view) to say that in an acceptable definition of 'property,' 'predicate' (or some equivalent) must occur in the definiens. So I shall simply say that one cannot point out at all clearly what one means by 'property' (cannot specify the grammar of the word, as the neo-Wittgensteinians would say) without reference to the structure of sentences and thus without some linguistic analysis.

If this is so then there should be few, if any, among the professional philosophers who would dispute my assumption in the very general form in which I have put it above. But the position towards which this essay is now moving, so far as it can be formulated at all, relies more specifically upon linguistic analysis. It assumes that linguistic analysis of the structure of value-sentences is of use in revealing the status or nature of value. In one sense, perhaps, this amounts to little more than the general form of the assumption. Take properties, again, for an example. I have argued[2] that it is improper to name a property as a property. The characteristic nature of something that also is a property, *i.e.*, that can be exemplified by something else, *is* properly named. Thus 'carmine' may be taken as the proper name of a certain red. As such, this naming does not put the certain red in any categorial place save that of being an entity in the world. To categorize it further, say as a property, requires the analysis,

[1] The "evocative theory" in its extreme form (which claims that value-sentences do not say anything at all, but only express or evoke emotions) might not need the latter. So far as supposed value-sentences are not linguistic expressions at all but only events, they need not be reduced to sentences of a different kind. In the present context no definition of 'meaning criterion' or 'reduction' seems called for.

[2] See footnote [1], p. 22 above.

of the structure of a sentence, so that we put 'carmine' in the predicate-place, or, more formally, we make a rule as to the sentence-place 'carmine' can occupy.[1] In this respect then the proposal of the present essay is not as radical as it may have seemed. It maintains that the status of value is not properly shown by the predicate-place in an ordinary, zero-level declarative sentence, but is far more adequately revealed by the total structure, by the "relation" of predicate to subject or subjects, in a zero-level normative sentence. This, I repeat, is not a whit more radical than the view that finds in the predicate-place of the declarative sentence the appropriate indication of the status of value (or of some form of value, such as goodness). Except for its value-objectivism, *i.e.*, in its finding in the syntax of sentences a revelation or at least a clue to the status of extra-lingustic entities, it is not more radical than the view that takes undefined predicates to designate universals and proper names to designate particulars. Any appearance to the contrary is due to a confusion. It has been repeatedly said—it has indeed become part of logistic ritual—that logical constants, such as connectives uniting atomic sentences into molecular sentences and sentential forms such as the copula uniting proper names and predicates into atomic sentences, do not designate anything. This is entirely correct within the sort of logically formalized language indicated by the contexts of such statements. But it is not such an open and shut matter when one is concerned with that congeries of philosophical questions often slipped in under the innocuous-appearing heading, 'the adequacy of a (given) formalized language.' Even here of course it might well be maintained (as I would myself maintain) that logical constants do not *designate* anything. But then, this would not be tantamount to saying that they in no sense refer to or reveal anything extra-linguistic. Indeed, if the names in such a language designate specific and observable entities it would seem that, granting the categorial adequacy of the language, it must be precisely the constants that in some fashion show the categorial features of the world. This perhaps is a somewhat rash statement unless one is willing to use 'logical constant' here in a broad fashion to refer not only to those structural features that are exhibited to the eye by special marks but also those which are

[1] All of this is extremely misleadingly put. It looks as though I were either describing games or laying down rules for the making of rules for games. Perhaps to some extent the sequel will help to straighten matters.

not. *E.g.*, the very difference between a name and a sentence-form is, in this sense, of significance for the philosopher.

This reference to the adequacy of a formalized language suggests an even narrower and more suspect form of the assumption with which we are concerned. It would be to the effect that linguistic analysis of the structure of value-sentences in an "ideal language" will assist in revealing the status or nature of value. The notion of an ideal language is a familiar one. It arose and spread in the second and third decades of the present century partly as an attempt to develop a tool of philosophical analysis that would avoid the ambiguities and misleading associations of ordinary grammar. It was also meant to solve or rather to avoid the occurrence of certain logical paradoxes. But more important for us, from the very beginning it was felt that in its structure it would reveal the categorial structure of the world. Perhaps the destructive aspect of this enterprise was at first most in evidence,[1] but it was not long before its constructive possibilities were exploited.[2] The vocabulary of an ideal language will show what simple entities are in the world; its true elementary sentences will tell us the facts; the forms of its elementary sentences will give us the structures of the facts, which are made up of the referents of the names in the sentences exactly as the sentences are made up of the names.

This whole programme has of late fallen into disrepute. The attack has been led from within, by a sort of palace-revolution on the part of the neo-Wittgensteinians (although there is evidence that both Wittgenstein and Russell have also given up the position). Since something like the assumption that the structure of fact is to be found in the structure of elementary sentences in an ideal language, and further that a similar isomorphism holds between value and normative sentences—since this is involved in the view toward which this essay has been moving, some sort of review of the arguments against what may be called "the ideal language method in philosophical analysis" seems called for, even though it will turn out that the present author does not, unqualifiedly, adopt that method.

[1] For example, Russell's theory of descriptions was meant to destroy a host of entities in the metaphysics of Meinong, and Russell's fulminations against subject-predicate logic were in part directed against the metaphysics of Bradley.

[2] I have in mind Russell's lectures, "The Philosophy of Logical Atomism" in the *Monist*, to which reference has already been made, and Wittgenstein's *Tractatus*.

7a. Can the syntax of an ideal language show the status of value?

At the very beginning it might we well to dispose of an objection from the outside. It is that this method is circular. One must already have a knowledge of the structure of the world in order to tell whether a proposed language is ideal and thus to use the structure of the latter to gain insight into the structure of the world.[1] I do not want to say that proponents of the ideal language method have never given cause for this (as it seems to me) misinterpretation. Russell has spoken as though he knew, quite independently of linguistic analysis, that the world contained no round square, and that the whole of Reality was not present in every part. And Wittgenstein, quite independently of the proper form of language, manages to know that the world divides into facts, any one of which could be the case or not the case and everything else remain the same.[2] The specious appearance of a direct, non-linguistic philosophical knowledge that such statements might suggest rests on a failure to bring out sufficiently clearly two distinctions: that between empirical and categorial features of the

[1] An example of this line of criticism is furnished by Irving M. Copilowish, "Language Analysis and Metaphysical Inquiry," *Philosophy of Science*, vol. xvi, 1949, pp. 65–70. Professor Copilowish writes, "The essence of an 'ideal' language, as conceived by the proponents of the program under discussion, is that its logical structure, 'correspond with' or 'mirror' in some sense the ontological structure of fact. Hence a language can be known to be 'ideal' only by comparing its logical structure with the ontological structure of the world, which must be known independently if the comparison is to be significant" (*loc. cit.*, p. 70).

[2] In a strange paper, "Some Remarks on Logical Form," published in 1929 (*Aristotelian Society Supplementary Volume IX*), Wittgenstein wrote: "It is the task of the theory of knowledge to find them [atomic propositions] and to understand their construction out of the words and symbols. . . . What method have we for tackling it? The idea is to express in an appropriate symbolism what in ordinary language leads to endless misunderstandings. That is to say, where ordinary language disguises logical structure, . . . we must replace it by a symbolism which gives a clear picture of the logical structure. . . . Now we can only substitute a clear symbolism for the unprecise one by inspecting the phenomena which we want to describe, thus trying to understand their logical multiplicity. . . . An atomic form cannot be foreseen. And it would be surprising if the actual phenomena had nothing more to teach us about their structure" (*loc. cit.* pp. 163–4). This certainly appears to leave Wittgenstein wide open to the sort of criticism Copilowish makes of the ideal language method. It obviously fails to distinguish categorial from empirical problems (the difficulty of philosophy lies in the subtlety of the empirical phenomena it observes?). I can only explain it on the hypothesis that it was written during a transition period; the ideal language method of the *Tractatus* was not yet abandoned, but the psychologism and literary introspectionism of the "Blue Book" were already present.

world and that between everyday language and an ideal language. An ideal language may help to avoid ambiguity, vagueness and other defects in the making of empirical statements. But it does not furnish the grounds for the latter; these are furnished by direct observation of extra-linguistice ntities. It is otherwise with categorial statements, statements, *e.g.*, as to the structure of the world or of fact. Here we have nothing comparable to sensory perception to give us the knowledge (if one wishes to call it "knowledge") that we seek. Here we must rely on the syntax of an ideal language for guidance. But then how do we know whether a proposed language is ideal? Here we must distinguish and yet relate the rôles of an ideal language and everyday language. The ideal language is not reared in a vacuum nor are its foundations laid in the clouds. It is constructed to assuage the internal difficulties of every day language, difficulties which arise from the unregenerate structure (the "misleading grammar") of the latter and lead to absurdities which it itself rejects. Perhaps this is making the division of labour a little too rigid. One of the functions of an ideal language is to show just where the sources of absurdity in everyday speech lie as well as to eliminate them. It is even of some help in bringing to our attention certain absurdities. But the ultimate test, for the ideal language method, whether some supposed statement or set of statements is absurd is not the ideal language but everyday language. Everyday language is in conflict with itself; it allows the formulation of that which it itself disowns.[1] There is thus *something* arbitrary in an ideal language; it is no mere reproduction (even with ambiguities and vaguenesses removed) of everyday language. Certain basic features of everyday language have been removed in order that the remainder may be consistent with itself in a sense which everyday language itself approves by implication (for it rejects the inconsistencies that have been removed).[2] But by eliminating the

[1] An example is the permission of 'exists' as a predicate. *Cf.* above, pp. 17–18. I think in the final analysis even such supposedly purely logical desiderata as the elimination of the "logical paradoxes" are based on the sound instinct to conform to good common sense. Why should contradiction be avoided? Not for merely technical reasons—*e.g.*, because we have so defined 'implies' that a contradiction implies everything. This is putting the cart before the horse. We set up our logic so that, *as far as possible*, what is absurd for everyday language is prohibited in our logic.

[2] It is this sense that we find expressed in Russell's frequent claim that so-and-so is the "real" meaning or the "proper" form of a commonsensical statement. I give just one example. "It is not accurate to say 'I believe the

nonsense, an ideal language is not to remove the sense, All that is significantly sayable in everyday language is to be sayable in the ideal language.[1]

Now all this does make an assumption—a "whopper" if you please. But it is not that there is any knowledge of the categorial features of the world wholly independent of linguistic analysis. It is rather that the language of common sense, purified of the nonsense it itself recognizes to be such but yet retains, shows us, in the ways in which it says things about the world, the categorial features of the world. And this assumption, so far from being circular, so far from starting with a supposed knowledge of the categorial features of the world, is rather an acceptance of a "lingua-centric predicament." So far as our categories are concerned, we can never escape from a domination of our thinking by the forms of our language.

In place of the question, How can we know independently of language the structure of the world? we can now see that the fundamental question for the ideal language method is, How is the ideal language related to everyday language? It is largely on the basis of this sort of question that the neo-Wittgensteinians have challenged the ideal language method. Perhaps two papers by Professor Max Black (whom I may venture to classify as a moderate neo-Wittgensteinian) will serve to introduce objections from this

proposition *p*' and regard the occurrence as a twofold relation between me and *p*. The logical form is just the same whether you believe a false or a true proposition. . . . Therefore the belief does not really contain a proposition as a constituent. . . ." (*Monist*, vol. xxix, 1919, p. 58). Something like this, it seems to me, is also involved in the apparent contradiction in Wittgenstein. "All propositions of our colloquial language are actually, just as they are, logically completely in order" (*Tractatus* 5.5563). "In the language of everyday life it very often happens that the same word signifies in two different ways. . . . Thus there easily arise the most fundamental confusions. . . . In order to avoid these errors, we must employ a symbolism which excludes them, . . . which obeys the rules of *logical* grammar—of logical syntax" (*ibid.*, 3.323–3.325).

[1] Professor Gustav Bergmann, in a reply to Mr. Copilowish's paper just cited, says, "The ideal language, as I conceive it, is not a language actually to be spoken but a blue print or schema, complete only in the sense that *it must show, in principle, the structure and systematic arrangement of all the major areas of our experience*" (*op. cit.*, p. 73). The only objection I have to this is its suggestion that experience comes already categorized, and the ideal language thus needs only to square in its structure with this phenomenologically given structure. I cannot convince myself that this is so. In fact, such an experience seems to me already to show the handiwork of Professor Bergmann's categories. It is precisely because we cannot get at categorial features of the world by themselves that linguistic analysis is such an important tool for the philosopher.

school of thought. They are "Some Problems Connected with Language"[1] and "Russell's Philosophy of Language."[2]

The first of Mr. Black's criticisms that I shall mention can be easily disposed of. It is to the effect that an ideal language of the kind envisaged could not actually replace everyday language, being unsuited for purposes of communication.[3] This it seems to me is quite irrelevant, since the advocates of the ideal language method have not proposed that their ideal language be used for communication even among philosophers, as though it were a sort of philosophical Esperanto.[4] It is sufficient if the ideal language enter as a subject of discourse, that philosophers be able to show how in it their analyses could be carried out. Mr. Black might, of course, object even to this; but one ground for doing so[5] seems clearly to involve a matter essentially irrelevant to the point at issue. It is Russell's alliance of the ideal language with his principle of acquaintance. This union has the strange consequence that the only names in an ideal language are those which name entities the speaker is directly acquainted with. Hence (so Black would argue) no two philosophers could have in common even small fragments of an ideal language which could be talked about (with a view to showing how analyses could be carried out). I have already argued[6] that Russell's principle of acquaintance has no necessary connection with the concept of a name (it brings in the notion of the user of a name, which is something extraneous to the purely semantical idea of the designation of a name). It is,

[1] *Aristotelian Society Proceedings*, vol. xxxix, 1938–9, pp. 43–68; reprinted in *Language and Philosophy*, pp. 139–65.

[2] *The Philosophy of Bertrand Russell*, ed. by P. A. Schilpp, pp. 229–55; reprinted in *Language and Philosophy*, pp. 109–38.

[3] Referring to the sort of philosophical language proposed by Russell in the *Monist* articles, Black writes, "Such a system . . . would be so remote from our present means of expression and so unsuited to perform the functions of unambiguous and logically accurate communication which may be desired of an efficient language, that to urge its capacity to provide 'a grammatically correct account of the universe' is to be extravagantly implausible. The 'ideal language' in practice would resemble a series of involuntary squeaks and grunts more closely than anything it is at present customary to recognize as a language" (*The Philosophy of Bertrand Russell*, p. 253).

[4] Russell himself makes essentially this point in his reply to Black. He says, "I have never intended to urge seriously that such a language should be created, except in certain fields and for certain problems" (*ibid.*, pp. 693–4). Perhaps Russell is not too clear just how the ideal language should enter philosophical discussions, but it is not incompatible with his views that such a language be not *talked* but *talked about.*

[5] *Cf.* the context of the passage quoted in the footnote above.

[6] *Cf.* footnote, p. 23 above.

then, quite possible to utilize the concept of an ideal language otherwise essentially similar to what Russell had in mind but without the principle of acquaintance. Then the basis of the objection we are now considering would be eliminated. Moreover, even if we acknowledge the principle of acquaintance to be a requirement that must be satisfied by an ideal language, Black's objection is not correctly formulated. For any ideal language would then be solipsistic. Hence any analysis of a discussion between different philosophers, carried out or even suggestively illustrated by means of it, would have to be in terms of a single such ideal language. *This* language would need to satisfy the principle of acquaintance. But the talk, mentioned within it, between the various philosophers would not. The question whether and how well they communicate would then resolve itself into a descriptive problem about their psychological behaviour. The significant question then, granting the principle of acquaintance to be a requirement an ideal language must meet, is not: Could communication occur if people tried to use such an ideal language? but rather, Does the solipsism that such an ideal language requires rule out the saying of things that common sense manages to say and would not deem nonsense?

Allied with this objection that an ideal language could never be actually substituted for everyday language for purposes of communication is a second objection offered by Professor Black. In his own words, if "the ideal language is not capable of realization, it becomes impossible seriously to defend indefinite progression towards such an 'ideal' as a desirable procedure for the philosophical criticism of language."[1] The criticism, which is left in this cryptic form, is hard to interpret. It clearly assumes that the job of creating an ideal language will never be finished. In the sense of having one but only one name for each nameable entity and one but only one grammatical form for saying each significantly different sort of thing that can be said, a complete[2] ideal language will never be attained. But what of that? By saying that "it becomes impossible seriously to defend indefinite progression toward such an 'ideal'" Mr. Black suggests that he is entertaining a pseudomathematical concept of the ideal

[1] *The Philosophy of Bertrand Russell*, pp. 253–4.

[2] This meaning of 'completeness' is obviously to be distinguished from that used by the logician to describe certain formal calculi. Professor Bergmann, in his reply to Mr. Copilowish cited above, very clearly though somewhat irrelevantly brings this out.

language—as the ideal limit of an indefinite series, the series of attempts to construct it. Personally I cannot avoid the feeling that to describe any of the groping procedures of philosophers—even those of the best of the analysts—in terms borrowed from the mathematical calculus is only to promote one of those misleading grammatical analogies which philosophical analysis has made it its business to help clear away. But even with such a notion of the philosophical rôle of an ideal language, I am not clear as to the reason for Mr. Black's condemnation of the project. Is it that the limit lies outside the series?—but to recognize this is only to admit again that the objective is in practice unrealizable. Is it that the series is indefinitely extended?—this might be discouraging to perfectionists but hardly discomforting to those of us who would be extremely pleased to find a philosophic method we could accept in principle. Is it that the series cannot be defined except in terms of its limit, which cannot itself be formulated (for to do so would be to have a completed ideal language)?—this possibility deserves further exploration.

In a paper[1] critical of the assumption that Tarski's semantical definition of truth illuminates the "*philosophical* problem of truth," Mr. Black points out that that definition involves the requirement that there be a complete inventory of names in the object-language. This furnishes no difficulty in the case of artificially constructed languages. But if the definition is to have philosophical relevance it must be applicable to such natural languages as English. These are however "open" in the sense that new names are entering them. Therefore any definition of truth like Tarski's would become obsolete practically as soon as formulated.[2] That definition does not state what it is *in general* for a sentence to be true, nor can any definition in a language such as Tarski's do so.[3] The same thing can be said for the designation of names.

[1] "The Semantic Definition of Truth," *Analysis*, vol. viii, 1948, pp. 49–63; reprinted in *Language and Philosophy*, pp. 89–107.

[2] "Every time an infant was christened, or a manuscript received a title, the inventory (of primitive terms) and, consequently, the definition of truth depending upon that inventory, would become inaccurate. The 'open' character of a natural language, as shown in the fluctuating composition of its vocabulary, defeats the attempt to apply a definition of truth based upon enumeration of simple instances. The attempt is as hopeless as would be that of setting out to define the notion of 'name' by listing all the names that have ever been used" (*loc. cit.*, p. 58).

[3] This I take it is the significance of Black's denial that any generalization of Tarski's truth-condition (*e.g.*, in the form, "(θ) For all x, if x is a sentence, then 'x' is true$\equiv x$" (*ibid.*, p. 51)) is possible.

This indicates what Black may mean in the objection we are now considering. An ideal language, to be ideal in the way necessary to the task of philosophical analysis, must be completed, not just sketched out, in the fashion of a model. It must have a full repertory of names and grammatical forms. If it omits any it cannot say just those things the philosopher desires to say. Thus no approach to it that does not attain it is of any value whatever to the philosopher.

Now this criticism, it seems to me, does make sense, but only on the assumption that in the ideal language method what *the philosopher* says, though not necessarily actually formulated in the ideal language, must be capable of such formulation. Here it is important to admit that the advocates of that method have not been themselves too clear. Some, it would seem, have felt satisfied that all proper statements of philosophers could be made in an ideal language if that language were to include sufficient semantical meta-levels, perhaps an infinite hierarchy of them.[1] On the other hand, one possible and I think even plausible interpretation of Wittgenstein's enigmatic concluding remarks[2] in his *Tractatus* is just the denial that philosophical statements can be made in the ideal language. He has made such statements throughout his book—but in the non-ideal language of everyday speech (German and English). Now he would have us see how the ideal language shows these things without itself being able to say them. I think this is a perfectly legitimate position which only the perversity of Wittgenstein's oracular style has caused to be presented in the guise of some inscrutable paradox. I do think that Wittgenstein was unfair to the rôle of everyday language in his own procedure:[3] it is clearly just as integral to his method as is its grammatical reform. Conversely, when the ideal language is set up and, through proper talk about it in everyday language, we come to see the structure of the world, the ideal language has

1 This seems to be Russell's suggestion in his "Introduction" to Wittgenstein's *Tractatus* (p. 23).

2 "The right method of philosophy would be this. To say nothing except what can be said, . . . *i.e.*, something that has nothing to do with philosophy. . . . My propositions are elucidatory in this way: he who understands me finally recognizes them as senseless. . . . (He must so to speak throw away the ladder, after he has climbed up on it). . . . Whereof one cannot speak, thereof must one be silent" (6.53–7).

3 If denied normal recognition everyday language, like any basic instinct, has a way of reasserting itself, even when necessary in perverted forms. Something like this happened when the *Tractatus* was followed by the "Blue Book" and the writings of the therapeutical neo-Wittgensteinians.

served its philosophic purpose. However correct it may be, it too is a ladder to be cast aside. As I see it, in the method of the *Tractatus* each language is necessary, but neither one is adequate to the task, nor indeed is their combination. Everyday language furnishes the talk about the world. The ideal language purifies this of misleading grammatical analogies. In doing so, however, it finds itself confined to empirical statements; it cannot formulate philosophical questions or answers. Everyday language then returns and, with its improper forms, speaks of the categorial aspects of the world by means of talking about the forms of the ideal language. But finally it finds that this talk is itself carried on by means of misleading grammatical constructions. There then supervenes, if the gods are willing, the vision, the insight.

Whether this be at all sound as an interpretation of the *Tractatus* (and I think it is not without some merit), it at least shows how one who adopts the ideal language method could meet the objection we have attributed to Mr. Black. Granted that the construction of an ideal language can never be completed. Granted also that, unless it be complete, definitions of key philosophical concepts (for our purpose, 'fact' and 'value' as well as 'truth' and 'designation'), as used by philosophers, cannot be given in it. Yet it does not follow that the partial construction or the suggestive sketch of such a language is philosophically barren. For we may talk in ordinary language about the structure of such an ideal language, pointing out, in admittedly incorrect form, how various aspects of that structure do reveal what we mean *in general* by 'truth' or 'value' or whatever category it may be, while hastening to add that such indications do not constitute "definitions" in a logically proper sense.[1] I

[1] Thus I disagree with Black when he writes: "We seem to see quite clearly that what Tarski is doing is so to define truth that *to assert that a sentence is true is logically equivalent to asserting that sentence*. And in so doing, we feel that we *understand* the definition, besides being able to apply it. But if we try to *say* what we think we understand, we sin at once against the canons of syntactical propriety. The phrase 'to assert that a sentence is true is logically equivalent to asserting that sentence', which is intuitively so clear, is in fact, a crude formulation in colloquial English of the inacceptable formula θ . . ." (*loc. cit.*, pp. 58–9). The source of error here is an incorrect view of the relation between colloquial English and an ideal language. The ideal language is not even in principle to replace colloquial language, for the latter has a function the former cannot take over—to point out features of the ideal language which cannot be stated in it. It is precisely in the performance of this function that philosophical clarification occurs. Thus the sentence Black italicizes and also puts in quotation marks is not something that in *any* sense seeks admission into an ideal language such as Tarski's.

might add parenthetically, though no doubt it is quite unnecessary, that the apparatus of semantical meta-levels within the ideal language does not avoid the need for ordinary language to say the philosophical things. To avoid the semantical paradoxes it is necessary, in the ideal language, to permit expressions to refer only to that which is below them to prohibit self-reference. But it is characteristic of philosophic concepts and standpoints that they be all-inclusive, that they involve self-reference. We are thus forced to put them in the misleading mould of ordinary language, though this may be about an ideal language (about, for example, features of the latter at *all* semantical levels).

Thus if an ideal language is not itself to serve as the language in which philosophical statements are made, the criticism that no ideal language will ever be completely constructed is not fatal to the ideal language method of analysis. On the other hand, there is a sense in which an ideal language must be complete if it is to serve philosophers. It must be complete, not in the sense that it can say everything, or merely everything non-categorial,[1] but in the sense of having a unique form for every *sort* of non-categorial thing that everyday language manages to say. It is extremely difficult to determine whether this requirement has been satisfied. It is so easy to say that something non-categorial that appears to be said in ordinary speech is not said at all, that it is just nonsense. This is easy because of the philosopher's laudable desire to simplify. Simplification is, of course, involved in the process of purification of common sense, of eliminating those grammatical forms which lead to the sort of nonsense which common sense itself recognizes to be such. But simplification can easily get out of hand and set itself up as a goal in its own right. Then we leave philosophical analysis and start constructing verbal games. I fear that something like this happened to Russell in his period of logical atomism when he thought that the analytical method involved the assumption that the world is made up

[1] I would like to write 'empirical' instead of 'non-categorial' were it not that I would be interpreted as meaning factual. But it is one of my main contentions that a great portion of the non-philosophical part of everyday speech is valuational. It is no more philosophical to say 'Donald ought to wear his rubbers' than 'Donald is wearing his rubbers.' Philosophical analysis, itself carried on in ordinary language, should attempt to put the former as well as the latter in its ideally proper form and should then ask what this allows us to see as regards such categories as value and fact.

of simples.[1] It also animated Wittgenstein in the *Tractatus*[2] and led Susan Stebbing and John Wisdom into that wild goose chase of "directional analysis" which was to lead, *via* a "Direct Display of a Fact," right up to the ultimate elements of facts.[3] This, to my mind essentially mischievous, tendency does not grow out of any straightforward attempt to clarify and purify the grammar of common sense; it has its roots in the Cartesian desire for certainty. There *is* a sort of simplicity to which an analysis of everyday language leads us: the simplicity reflected in a name as contrasted with the complexity of a sentence. Unless we make this distinction we are led into nonsense, nonsense recognizable by common sense itself and admirably pointed out by Russell, as has already been sufficiently noted. But that a proper name should name something simple in any other sense than that it lacks the complexity of fact is no requirement of the sort of linguistic analysis the ideal language method essentially commits one to.

Another objection Mr. Black urges against the ideal language method, here in the specific form found in the *Tractatus*, is that "It is not possible to produce a single 'name' in Wittgenstein's sense from our current vocabulary. Nor have we definite criteria for deciding whether any examples which might be produced in fact satisfy the requirements.[4] Black's argument is that for Wittgenstein a name is a "logical construction" out of a set of perceptible name-tokens ("signs," in Wittgenstein's terminology), but that in every language there can be found cases of different names such that there are common members to the sets of perceptible tokens of which the names are logical constructions; "*i.e.*, difference in the 'name' does not imply mutual exclusion

[1] "One purpose that has run through all that I have said, has been the justification of analysis, *i.e.*, the justification of logical atomism, of the view that you can get down in theory, if not in practice, to ultimate simples, out of which the world is built, and that those simples have a kind of reality not belonging to anything else" (*Monist*, vol. xxix, 1919, p. 365).

[2] *Cf.* 3.25–3.261.

[3] *Cf.*, L. S. Stebbing, "The Method of Analysis in Metaphysics," *Proceedings of the Aristotelian Society*, vol. xxxiii, 1933, pp. 65–94; "Logical Positivism and Analysis," *Proceedings of the British Academy*, vol. xix, 1933; Eugene D. Bronstein, "Miss Stebbing's Directional Analysis and Basic Facts," *Analysis*, vol. ii, 1934–5, pp. 10–14; L. S. Stebbing, "Directional Analysis and Basic Facts," *ibid.*, pp. 33–6; John Wisdom, "Ostentation," *Psyche*, vol. xiii, 1933, pp. 164–77; "Is Analysis a Useful Method in Philosophy?" *Aristotelian Society Supplementary Volume XIII*, 1934, pp. 65–89.

[4] *Language and Philosophy*, p. 154.

of the correlated sets of name tokens."[1] I presume that Black considers this objectionable on the ground that 'the same name' is to be defined in terms of the common features of the associated tokens, and thus that a token's belonging to two such sets destroys the possibility of univocality which is a characteristic of names in Wittgenstein's system. If this is Black's objection, I fear it is misplaced, for Wittgenstein specifically says that two different names may have a perceptible sign in common.[2] And he urges that as this is a frequent occurrence in everyday language and gives rise to fundamental confusions, a symbolism should be developed which does not allow it to occur.[3] In short, Wittgenstein would admit that we cannot unequivocally point out instances of the same name in "current" vocabularies. This is precisely one of the deficiencies of any natural language method of analysis. To point out (in ordinary language) what designation is and thus the sort of thing that can be named, we must have instances of names in an ideal language.

But the issue cuts even deeper. When Wittgenstein says that the symbol, say a name, is that which its perceptible signs have in common, what he clearly means, in my reading of him, is not some perceptible feature of the signs but their way of signifying.[4] Thus though it is an aid to psychological processes of recognition that the set of perceptible signs of a given name should have some unique, common, perceptible feature, this is not what Wittgenstein is really concerned with: it would be at best an "accidental"

[1] *Op. cit.*, p. 157.

[2] "Two different symbols can therefore have the sign (the written sign or the sound sign) in common—they then signify in different ways" (3.321). "It can never indicate the common characteristic of two objects that we symbolize them with the same signs but by different *methods of symbolizing*. For the sign is arbitrary. We could therefore equally well choose two different signs and where then would be what was common in the symbolization" (3.322).

[3] "In order to avoid these errors, we must employ a symbolism which excludes them, by not applying the same sign in different symbols and by not applying signs in the same way which signify in different ways. A symbolism, that is to say, which obeys the rules of *logical* grammar—of logical syntax" (3.325).

[4] "In order to recognize the symbol in the sign we must consider the significant use" (3.326). "One could therefore say the real name is that which all symbols [signs?], which signify an object, have in common" (3.3411).

I think it is something like Wittgenstein's "significant use" that Professor Wilfrid Sellars has in mind when he writes, "that which is common to a word as written and the same word as spoken is a *linguistic rôle*, a rôle which can be performed by the members of more than one token-class" ("The Identity of Linguistic Expressions and the Paradox of Analysis," *Philosophical Studies*,

not an "essential" feature[1] of the name. What common features had Wittgenstein in mind? Not, I believe, anything observable at all. He clearly thought he had in mind purely syntactical features (as excluding semantical).[2] He may well have been mistaken in this. But it seems unquestionable that he was thinking of semiotical features. Thus the common features that all perceptible signs of the same symbol must have are features with which they are endowed by the rules of the language.

This raises the question, What is a rule of language? It is one of the exasperating characteristics of any genuine philosophical inquiry that it leads you from your initial question into all manner of other questions—perhaps into *all* truly philosophical questions. Thus any concentration involves an arbitrary restriction. I think I must indulge in one of these now. But although I shall not in the present context propose any positive answer to the question, What is a rule of language?, I do wish to deny that a rule of language—so far at least as that concept is used in the ideal language method—is itself anything observable, or that it asserts or even implies anything observable. Now of course a rule may, in some sense, be recommended, adopted, printed, enforced, etc., but these events are adventitious to it *as* a rule. Moreover, though a linguistic rule may mention or even actually include entities

vol. i, 1950, p. 25). Let me add that I agree heartily with Professor Sellars when he says, " 'Type' has become a familiar technical term in current discussions of language. Unfortunately, it has come to connote both (1) the most significant sense in which two expressions can be said to be 'the same expression' ('they are tokens of the same type!') and (2) qualitative resemblance of linguistic events. This double connotation is possible only so long as linguistic rôles are not clearly distinguished from the token-classes which enact them" (*op. cit.*, p. 31, footnote 2). However. I am rather puzzled by one outcome of a use that he makes of this distinction. He speaks of types (not tokens) as designating, *e.g.*, of the type '·Bitter·' as designating the quality, bitter. But the type is just the linguistic rôle that members of the associated token-class play; in this case, the rôle is obviously that of designating the quality, bitter. What is it then that designates bitter? It would seem that it is the linguistic rôle of designating bitter. This looks like nonsense. I do not wish to say it is. Moreover, I do wish to say that even if it is nonsense it is important nonsense in that it is attempting to bring to bear upon a fundamental issue (What is a linguistic expression?) a very significant distinction (that between type as linguistic rôle and as physical design).

[1] *Cf.* 3·34 ff.

[2] "What signifies in the symbol is what is common to all those symbols by which it can be replaced according to the rules of logical syntax" (3·344). "In logical syntax the naming of a sign ought never to play a rôle . . ." (3·33).

that are in the world, such as particulars (tokens) or universals (types),[1] this is not essential to it *as* a linguistic rule. *E.g.*, semantically considered a name is whatever designates anything. The 'whatever' here places no restrictions on the ontological status of names.

All this may sound shocking. Has a linguistic rule, thus considered in its essence, no relation to observable fact? It has no *observable* relation. It does have a "relation," *viz.*, whatever relation is set up by the linguistic rule itself (or higher-level rules about rules). Does this imply that linguistic rules have some sort of peculiar non-observable being of their own? Not in any other sense than that common to all abstractions, or more accurately, abstractions of that odd variety I have spoken of as "categorial." But enough! I said I was not going to launch into the inquiry, What is a rule of language?, and I shall not.

It is really, I think, just another form of the last objection when Professor Black says that Wittgenstein has no criterion for identity of the logical form of propositions. Mr. Black is seeking some common perceptible feature of the propositional tokens and (save in a hypothetical notation set up precisely to furnish this) no such property is in general to be found even in the sets of tokens of single propositions, and thus *a fortiori* not in those associated with groups of propositions of the same form. And here again the answer to Mr. Black is that the common feature is nothing observable; it has its "existence" only in and by virtue of the rules of the language. Perceptible propositional tokens of the most diverse physical structure can in this sense have a common "logical" structure: according to the rules of the language they have the same syntax, *e.g.*, with the appropriate substitution of names they entail and are entailed by the same propositions.[2]

[1] Wittgenstein has made the bold suggestion that propositional signs are facts (*Tractatus* 3.1432). Perhaps the token-type distinction should be replaced by a fact-law distinction. But the point of the text holds: that all this is extraneous to questions of symbolization *as such*.

[2] It might look as though Black had seriously considered this interpretation, which seems indeed to be the plain sense of Wittgenstein's statements. "If it is objected that propositions may nevertheless have a structure which is not exhibited in the physical relationships of their associated sets of tokens, we must ask for a *definition* of this alleged structure. It is not sufficient to say that the structure *is* the common feature of all symbols which can fulfil the same purpose; it must first be demonstrated that there *is* such a common feature" (*op. cit.*, p. 160). 'Purpose' and 'fulfil' are highly misleading here. They suggest psychological motivation and its satisfaction, and thus lead us to look for

'A proposition has structure whereas a name does not' means that a proposition has complexity whereas a name does not. We may say that a proposition contains names (or variables for names) whereas names do not. But we must be careful here. 'Contains' must not be interpreted as referring to a spatial relation, so that our assertion becomes, 'Every propositional token is a spatial (or temporal) whole having name-tokens as parts.' The containing here meant is one of linguistic rule not of perceptible fact.[1] Thus to say that a proposition, *p*, is a function of the names, '*a*' and '*A*,' which it contains is misleading in that it says the same thing twice. It might be better, for example, just to say that the proposition *p* is a function of the names '*a*' and '*A*.'

But now to the misleading associations of spatial imagery of such words as 'contains,' 'structure,' 'arrangement,' constituents,'

something perceptibly common to those things that will satisfy the same motive. That this analogy was present in Black's thinking seems borne out by the footnote to the passage just quoted: "*Cf.* the argument that all objects which can open a door must have common features. This is plausible so long as we think of keys. But what is there in common between a key, a door handle, and a battering ram? Only that they can fulfil the same purpose." This analogy fails (to put my point paradoxically) not because a key, a door handle, and a battering ram have for observation too little in common but because they have too much—their common association with the behaviour of getting past a closed door. Propositions having the same syntactical structure need not have even this observably in common, that their occurrence serve some common motive on the part of anyone using them.

[1] Consider 'fire.' In 'The fire is burning brightly' it is a name. In 'Fire!' exclaimed by one who sees a burning building and in 'Fire!' commanded by a captain of a battleship, it is a sentence—in the former case declarative, in the latter imperative. You cannot *see* any names (or name-variables) in these sentences, but the tacit rules of ordinary English grammar put them there. I hope Mr. Black will take no offence at a personal allusion. I was once discussing this point with him. He desired to show that a sentence need have no more complexity than a name. So he invented a simple language our prehistoric ancestors spoke. It consisted in directional pointing. Pointing north named one's mate. Pointing west, one's cave. Pointing south named oneself, pointing east the world outside one's cave. Then pointing north-west asserted that one's mate was in one's cave. Pointing south-east said that one was oneself outside one's cave, and so on. Mr. Black quite correctly claimed that the act of pointing north-west was just as simple an act as was that of pointing north, yet to these primitives the former was a sentence the latter a name. This, I felt and still feel, failed to distinguish physical act and linguistic element. In the language of these savages, *i.e.*, in its tacit rules, pointing north-west was complex in a way pointing north was not, and indeed included pointing north and west, not as perceptible acts but as linguistic constituents. This can be shown by noting that in this language pointing north-west remains a perfectly good part of the language when one's mate is not in one's cave; but pointing upward, for example, is no expression in the language.

etc., must be added another source of confusion, particularly when we go from the simple notion of complexity to that of various degrees of complexity. Here the trouble is caused, I think, by the Cartesian desire for certainty (and linked with it for that sort of tidiness, which is to be found in logic and mathematics but not in philosophy). The notion that propositions may be of different degrees of complexity and that such differences constitute one form of structural difference seems eminently plausible (that there are others is important for me, since, for example, I wish to distinguish the structure of a normative from that of a declarative of the same complexity). But then, to many we appear to run immediately into an insuperable difficulty. It seems we cannot tell what the real complexity of any given proposition is: we cannot tell how many names it contains because we cannot tell which names in it are simple. 'John is running' seems to contain just two names, *viz.*, the name of a person and the name of a behaviour-pattern. But perhaps 'John' really names a multiplicity of sense-data and 'running' a multiplicity of patterns of sense-datistic changes. How can we tell, and if we cannot tell, then how can we determine the complexity and thus the structure of 'John is running'?

I think we can gain help here from the principle, already stated, that strictly a name just names, that the question what categorial sort of entity it names is one to be answered by reference not to its function of naming but to the place or places it is allowed to fill in various sentence-forms. It is agreeable to this principle (though perhaps not implied by it) that a name should not, as such, require the simplicity of that which is named. We have seen that a fact cannot properly be named. Thus nothing with the sort of complexity characteristic of a fact can be named. But no other sort of complexity rules out the propriety of naming the entity possessing it. It follows that the complexity of the entities named in a sentence is irrelevant to the complexity of the sentence, which is wholly a matter of the number of name-places its form involves. There is a problem concerning the complexity of any given sentence, but it is just this: What is the form of this sentence? How should it appear in our ideal language? For various extra-categorial desiderata affect the apparent form of sentences in everyday language. The problem of a sentence's complexity should not, I am contending, be formulated, Do the names in this sentence name simples; if not, just how many names would be needed to replace them if we were to allow names of simple entities only?[1]

On this point of view questions as to the propriety of reduction or of logical construction are not integral to the problem of the syntax of an ideal language. A philosopher using the ideal language method may desire, on grounds ulterior to the demands of the correct linguistic analysis of an adequate ideal language, to reduce physical-thing sentences to sense-data sentences or to "construct" nations out of individuals. And of course such a programme will be reflected in the syntax of the ideal language he proposes. But he is not forced into any such programme by adopting the ideal language method. That method involves no assumption to the effect that ontologically the world is made up of simple entities. Indeed, such an assumption seems difficult to square with the ideal language method, since it would require the translation of all sentences in everyday language into sentences in the ideal language whose only names were names of simple entities, and such a radical transformation of everyday sentences seems more than is necessary to the elimination of extra-categorial influences, such as good etiquette, pleasing style, economy of effort, and so on. If the test in categorial matters really is the forms of everyday speech we have no warrant for the assumption of ontological atomism.

Let us then eliminate from the ideal language method all trace of the Cartesian demand for a certainty which requires that only names of absolutely simple entities be allowed in the ideal language. But Mr. Black would still have an objection. It would

[1] A sense of this ambiguity of 'complexity' and its bearing upon the problem of the objective of philosophical analysis may well have been a source of that blockage, that speech impediment, which characterized Wisdom in the period when he embraced the method of Ostentation (*e.g.*, when he speaks of "the paradox that the facts displayed by a non-Ostenstive sentence S′ and its Ostentation S, though not two, are not identical," *Aristotelian Society Supplementary Volume XIII*, 1934, p. 79). In any case, he makes it clear that a more ostensive or philosophically more analytical sentence does not state as a fact about a fact what the less ostensive sentence states as a fact. "From the view that philosophic analysis consists in revealing the elements of a fact which are simple in the sense of not having elements, it would follow that philosophic analysis is applicable only to facts of the second or third or fourth or etc., order. But *England fears France* is of the first order—it is not a fact about facts. The ultimate elements of a fact are, when they are not its elements, simpler in some sense than its elements; but they are not simpler in the sense that non-ultimate elements are facts of which the ultimate elements are elements. England is not a fact of which Tom, Dick and Harry are elements" (*Psyche*, vol. xiii, 1933, pp. 173–4).

be that even without this assumption we have no reason to suppose that there is anything common to the structure of a sentence in the ideal language and the fact which that sentence asserts. His actual argument here, so far as I gather it, adds nothing to what we have already seen him say, namely that just as in current usage there need be nothing common to the perceptible tokens of the same name, so there need be nothing common to the perceptible tokens of propositions which for Wittgenstein have the same structure. He concludes, "Accordingly, there need be nothing in common between the physical structure of the system of tokens used in the language and the 'states of affairs' to which the language refers."[1] To clinch my contention that Black is really only considering perceptible properties, I need simply refer to a hypothetical language-world situation which Professor Black constructs to illustrate what would have to be the case were the structure of the proposition to be the same as the structure of the fact it asserts. It is a world of dots and bars and a language of dots and bars. "In this symbolism there *is* something in common between a proposition and its referent; for the state of affairs and the correlated propositional token are geometrically congruent."[2]

It is of course to be admitted that such words as 'pictures,' 'mirrors,' 'represents,' which Wittgenstein uses in speaking of the relation between a sentence and the fact which it asserts, are exceedingly misleading in precisely the way they have misled Professor Black—into supposing that what is common to the sentence and the fact must be some perceptible property. We have already suggested that what is common to two sentences having the same form in an ideal language is a structure they have only in and by virtue of the rules of that language. It may be objected, however, that this escape is not allowed us when we speak (as Wittgenstein does) of a sentence and a fact as having the same structure. Something similar nevertheless seems not wholly implausible. It is that the structure of a fact is not itself observable, only the fact is. On the other hand, 'the structure of the sentence' as here used refers to nothing perceptible but to certain rules or certain aspects of rules of the language. Thus the structure which the sentence and the fact it asserts are said to have in common would be nothing observable. But now a new problem, or perhaps a new form of our old problem, arises. How can we ever verify our claim that the sentences and the fact have

[1] *Language and Philosophy*, p. 160. [2] *Ibid.*, p. 162.

a structure in common? The common structure of two sentences can be determined by reference to the rules. But this test is unavailable to us when we are concerned with determining whether a sentence and a fact have a structure in common. And we cannot say (as I would say of a name and its designatum) that the rule can embrace the very referent of the sentence as well as the sentence, since there are false sentences, there are sentences that accord with the rules but to which there are no corresponding facts. Nor can we properly treat the form of a fact as itself a relation, abstractable from the fact and thus nameable. If it were this sort of thing it could be itself exemplified and we would run into the paradoxes involved in treating exemplification as a property.[1]

How then can we ever establish that a descriptive sentence and the fact it asserts have a structure in common? My answer, though probably anticipated, is none the less disappointing. We cannot establish it. It is an ultimate on the point of view I am trying to elucidate. To challenge this is to challenge the whole point of view. However, this may be said (I do not know whether it will have any persuasive power). Within this sort of view, the principle in question is basic for without it it becomes impossible to specify the fact to which a given true descriptive sentence refers. The fact asserted by such a sentence, *p*, is the fact whose constituents are the designata of the names in *p*. Now a fact is not a whole with its constituents as parts. If it were, it could be named equally with its parts; it would have no different status from its constituents. There could then be no false sentences (there are no false names). It might be objected that we can invent names by definition, and these names may be false in that they are said to be names of wholes made up of such and such parts (the entities whose names appear in the definiens). I think, however, it is impossible to do anything of this sort without the use of a descriptive sentence. (There is a remark which it is hardly necessary to make: that there is a whole with such and such parts, or that *a* is a whole having such and such parts, is not itself a whole but a fact.) A purely syntactical definition is not true or false and by its form shows nothing as to what is in the world. If it is assumed that the definiendum names something in any sense different from the set of things named by the names in the definiens, that it names a whole with distinctive whole-properties, this assumption must properly be expressed by a descriptive sentence.

[1] See Section 3b above, especially p. 19.

A fact is a different sort of thing from a whole. It is made up of its constituents in a way no whole is made up of its parts. A whole has parts in spatial or temporal (or possibly other observable) relations. It has therefore properties (empirical relations, possibly even qualities on occasion) of its own. Comparable things cannot be said of a fact. A fact can be linguistically located only by a sentence containing names of the constituents of the fact. And these names must be in the right places in the right form or the fact is not picked out by the sentence. 'John hit George' and 'George hit John' contain the same names and have the same form. Suppose them both true. They assert and thereby refer to different facts. Therefore what fact it is that is picked out by a given true sentence is determined not merely by the names in that sentence but also by the form of the sentence and the places in that form which the different names occupy.

Now this, to me, makes sense. It tells me (in improper everyday language) how a fact can be referred to (in an ideal language) and thus, indirectly, what it is to be a fact. Mr. Black can say that it has not been established, and I agree. But I would add that at least it *is* a definite account. I cannot find *any* account in Mr. Black's writings of what it is to refer to a fact. I suppose (and he occasionally seems to say as much) that he would reply that such questions are not real questions, but only sources of unnecessary perplexity. He might admit the propriety of asking, in a particular context, how a certain sentence managed to refer to a certain fact, but the answer to this question would be furnished by the context itself and the question would thus be seen to be empirical. Here is an observable sentence-token, there a fact which the utterer of the sentence and perhaps also some hearer take to be asserted by the sentence; now just what observable relations are there between the two whereby the users of the sentence can determine that the sentence does refer to the fact in question? There is no general problem here, and surely no non-empirical problem, with which the philosopher need torture himself, I can imagine Mr. Black might say.[1]

[1] "When we are engaged in clarifying genuine philosophical difficulties, the author of the paradox may be the best judge of the success with which his linguistic and epistemological intentions are made plain to him. But the methods he uses in detecting his own meanings are the ordinary empirical ones which can in principle be employed by any lexicographer, or translator, or linguist" (*Language and Philosophy*, p. 22).

This leads to the last line of objection to the ideal language method which I shall consider. Although I think it is present in Professor Black it is perhaps more explicit in certain other neo-Wittgensteinians.[1] The ideal language method, so this objection would run, was designed to answer a type of question which is not legitimate (or perhaps I had better say, to gain insight into matters presenting no genuine problems). It supposes there are meaningful questions concerning the structure of reality—*e.g.*, concerning the structure of fact, What is fact?, and now, in the present inquiry concerning the structure of value, What is value? —whereas such questions are just verbal confusions. They arise through the naïve assumption that the grammars of sentences that look alike are really alike. Thus 'What is a fact?' seems to have the same grammatical form as 'What is a chimpanzee?' and 'What is the structure of a fact?' seems to have the same syntax as 'What is the structure of a chimpanzee?'[2] But then it is found that the same methods cannot be used in the two cases. We can look at a chimpanzee and study his structure observationally. Not so a fact. So it is thought that the nature of a fact, its structure as a fact, is something there in the world but mysteriously hidden. Hence a new method, other than that of ordinary observation, must be devised to get at this queer entity. But all the time there is nothing but misleading grammatical analogy at work, engendering a puzzlement. So instead of asking, What is a fact? What is truth? What is a value? What is . . . ?, in cases where we are not concerned with observable phenomena and their classification, we should rather ask, What is the grammar of the word 'fact'? *etc.* When we answer *this* question we find the source of our puzzlement (the grammar of 'fact' is like that of 'chimpanzee' but also unlike it) and thus are cured

[1] I have in mind certain later writings of John Wisdom, such as "Philosophical Perplexity," *Proceedings of the Aristotelian Society*, vol. xxxvii, 1937, pp. 71–88, and "Philosophy, Anxiety and Novelty," *Mind*, vol. liii, 1944, pp. 170–6. There is also the "Blue Book." Since the authenticity of this work is, so it is reported, denied by the reputed author himself (with what grounds I am in no position to judge), I shall not ascribe its statements to Witt. . . . but just to the Blue Book, as though it managed to write itself. See also, B. A. Farrell, "An Appraisal of Therapeutic Positivism," *Mind*, vol. lv, 1946, pp. 25 ff. and 133 ff.

[2] ' 'Isn't the structure of a fact somehow analogous to but to be differentiated from the structure of a value?' seems to have the same grammar as 'Isn't the structure of a chimpanzee somehow analogous to but to be differentiated from the structure of a man?' ' would be an illustration relevant to the present inquiry.

of it.[1] And *this* question, and its answer, can be formulated in ordinary language.

Now this all sounds very sane and hygienic. I am sure that any reader of the present essay must feel its attractiveness, as, indeed, the author does himself. But I fear that like all systems of psychiatry it harbours within it its own peculiar sources of morbidity; it engenders its own puzzlements. We are to look for the grammar of the words and sentences that give rise to philosophical questions. What grammar? Not that of an ideal language but, ostensibly, the grammar of common usage. But this answer won't do as it stands. It was precisely something misleading in ordinary grammar, some wrong appearance, that misled the philosopher originally. It would seem we must distinguish between the apparent grammar and the real grammar of expressions in everyday usage.[2] And often this real grammar has not been specified; that is why it is so frequently confused with the apparent grammar.

1 "Our problem, in other words, was not a scientific one; but a muddle felt as a problem." "Philosophy, as we use the word, is a fight against the fascination which forms of expression exert upon us" (the Blue Book). The exposition of the text largely follows the Blue Book. Wisdom still suspects that there may be something more than confusion in the philosopher's perplexities over categorial matters. He says, Wittgenstein "too much represents them as merely symptoms of linguistic confusion. I wish to represent them as also symptoms of linguistic penetration" (*Proceedings of the Aristotelian Society*, vol. xxxvii, 1937, p. 77). This does not, however, lead him into the admission that the ideal language method may be useful. The philosophical paradoxes, he writes, persist "not merely because they are symptoms of an intractable disorder but because they are philosophically useful. The curious thing is that their philosophical usefulness depends upon their paradoxicalness and thus upon their falsehood. They are false because they are needed where ordinary language fails though it must not be supposed that they are or should be in some perfect language. They are in a language not free from the same sort of defects as those from the effects of which they are designed to free us" (*ibid.*, p. 87).

2 "When words in our ordinary language have *prima facie* analogous grammars we are inclined to try to interpret them analogously. . . ." ". . . but we must not be misled by the similarity of their linguistic form into a false conception of their grammar. . . ." "We don't say that the man who tells us he feels the visual image two inches behind the bridge of his nose is telling a lie or talking nonsense. But we say that we can't understand the meaning of such a phrase. It combines well-known words but combines them in a way we don't yet understand. The grammar of this phrase has yet to be explained to us" (the Blue Book). In connection with this last passage, what I don't understand is, What is it the Blue Book doesn't understand? Why are we to suppose that the grammar of 'I feel a visual image two inches behind the bridge of my nose' isn't exactly the same as the grammar of 'I feel a pain two inches behind the bridge of my nose'? Because such a supposition gives rise to paradoxes? Are we then to suppose there is a real grammar of common usage that doesn't give rise to paradoxes? Just where is it? And when can we be sure we have found it?

Here the warning of one of these neo-Wittgensteinians himself is apposite: "when a philosopher says that really something is so we are warned that what he says is really so is not so really."[1] The real grammar of the perplexity-producing phrases cannot be their apparent grammar, the grammar they actually display in everyday usage. For that is what gives rise to the paradoxes. Thus we seek most painfully and tortuously and with frustration (since we are looking for it in a place where it is not to be found) the grammar of the puzzle-producing expressions. Thus we are led into the perplexity, What and where is the grammar these neo-Wittgensteinians are seeking? It is still a puzzlement, I fear, when put in their own terminology: What is the grammar of 'grammar' as used by the neo-Wittgensteinians in their attempts to cure philosophical puzzlements?

One possible answer to this question need not long delay us. it is that the word 'grammar,' obviously not used by the neo-Wittgensteinians in the sense of the grammar of the grammar-books (in this sense the grammar of the puzzle-producing phrases is as plain as that of any expressions), is to be taken in the broad sense of correct usage in the context, and 'the context' refers not to the context of words but of the behaviour of the language user and of the environment in which that behaviour occurs.[2] This is, of course, an extremely odd and misleading use of 'grammar.' But the reason we need not be delayed by consideration of this answer is not the strangeness of this use of 'grammar' and hence the unwisdom of introducing it without warning, but rather its irrelevance to our problem (and to every philosophical problem). Whether or not philosophical puzzlings (*e.g.*, over the question, What is value?) have been *caused by* the dissimilarities in the behavioural contexts of the occurrences of words and phrases that are similar in their grammar-book grammar is an empirical question, a psychological question, which is quite different from, and not to be confused with, the philosophical questions themselves (*e.g.*, with the question, What is value?). It is of course a

[1] Wisdom, *loc. cit.*, p. 77.

[2] Something like this seems to be suggested in such a passage as the following, taken from the Blue Book: "We said that it was a way of examining the grammar (the use) of the word 'to know' to ask ourselves what, in the particular case we are examining, we should call 'getting to know.' . . . But this question ['What is it like in this case to "get to know"?'] really is a question concerning the grammar of the word 'to know,' . . . It is part of the grammar of the word 'chair' that *this* is what we call 'to sit on a chair,' and it is part of the grammar of the word 'meaning' that *this* is what we call 'explanation of a meaning'. . . ."

legitimate philosophical position to say that there are no genuine philosophical questions, but no investigation of how philosophers came psychologically to suppose there were such questions can establish this position.

Were the neo-Wittgensteinians to answer, and there is some ground for supposing they might: "There is no hocus-pocus here; we seek the actual grammar of colloquial speech. The misleading character of it is its multiplicity. Various words are used in several ways, have several grammars. The philosopher, seeking a single, consistent use, is led, by this improper objective, into perplexities"[1] —were they, I say, to answer in this fashion, our reply would not be far to seek. The ideal language method uses an ideal language not to improve *in general* upon everyday language but to improve upon it *as a vehicle of philosophical insight*, as revealing categorial features of the world. Thus it need not for a moment suppose there is only a single use in everyday speech of such terms as 'truth,' 'fact,' 'value,' 'exists,' and so on. Rather, it *chooses* a single usage as being philosophically significant. It then finds that in *this* usage there are not only unclarities but also paradoxes. *E.g.*, we have found paradoxes arising from a certain use of 'fact' (where 'fact' supposedly names the object of a true descriptive sentence). There are also other common uses of 'fact' (as in 'It is a fact that $2+2=4$'). The ideal language method need not assume that key terms and structures of everyday language are univocal in meaning or use, nor, *a fortiori*, that a proposed ideal language will give the real univocal meaning of any everyday expression. All it needs to assume, on my interpretation, is that in saying the philosophical thing ordinary language gets into trouble caused not by ordinary ambiguity, by a shift from one use to another of some word or form, but by the very sort of thing that one is trying to say, and that constructing an ideal language may help to alleviate this trouble.[2]

[1] "The man who is philosophically puzzled sees a law in the way a word is used, and trying to apply this law consistently, comes up against cases where it leads to paradoxical results." "It is wrong to say that in philosophy we consider an ideal language as opposed to our ordinary one. For this makes it appear as though we thought we could improve on ordinary language. But ordinary language is all right. Whenever we make up 'ideal languages' it is not in order to replace our ordinary language by them; but just to remove some trouble caused in someone's mind by thinking that he has got hold of *the* exact use of a common word" (the Blue Book, italics mine).

[2] Not, I have urged, because the ideal language can say the philosophical thing, but because everyday language can better say it by talking about the ideal language than by trying to say it directly.

A variant of the objection under consideration is expressed by a number of philosophers who may conveniently be called "neo-Mooreians,"[1] They would not, however, stop with the statement that the philosopher's problems are due to perplexities arising from linguistic confusions. They are much too impressed with the fact that the philosopher doesn't get over his perplexities when they are pointed out to him. The philosopher thinks he is saying something when he answers such questions as, 'What is existence?' 'What is it to know?' 'Is there empirical knowledge which is certain?' G. E. Moore has frequently interpreted philosophers' answers to such questions as though they conflicted with factual statements, as though, for example, Berkeley's '*esse est percepi*' conflicted with 'Here is a hand.' The neo-Mooreians note that if the conflict of Moore with, *e.g.*, idealistic or sceptical philosophers were of this sort, it could be easily terminated simply by ascertaining the facts. But that it has not been so terminated indicates that there must be some other issue here. What other sort of issue could there be? If the controversy is not about the facts, it must be linguistic. Specifically, it must be as to what language is to be used. The philosophers in question, therefore are making a proposal, and Moore is objecting to it. They propose a new language to describe the facts; Moore counters by defending the language of common sense as the correct language. Now in what sense, on this interpretation, is it Moore's *real* contention that the language of common sense is correct and thus that the philosopher's innovations would be incorrect? Just what is it, on this view, that Moore is maintaining? Apparently it is just that it is commonsensical language that we all ordinarily do use in describing the facts, that the philosopher's language would be absurd for the purpose since it contravenes our basic linguistic habits. Apparently the neo-Mooreians would themselves be somewhat more tolerant: the philosopher's proposed changes are all right as long as he sees that he is saying exactly what most of us say in commonsensical language, and as long as he doesn't charge us with incorrect language or with saying what is really false simply because we do not use his language.[2]

Two things seem to me rather clear in this connection. The

[1] I have particularly in mind Norman Malcolm, Morris Lazerowitz, and Alice Ambrose. See, for example, their contributions to the volume, *The Philosophy of G. E. Moore*, ed. by P. A. Schilpp.

[2] Possibly Mr. Malcolm comes somewhat closer to the position ascribed to Moore, *viz.*, that common-sense language is *really* the only correct language.

first is that this whole business of proposals as to language is being thought of in terms of the actual employment of a language for ordinary communication. Few if any philosophers have made linguistic proposals in this sense. The older philosophers did not. Berkeley, for example, explicitly disclaimed any such purpose. The advocates of the ideal language method do in a sense make a linguistic proposal, but they do not propose that the ideal language replace everyday language for ordinary purposes of communication. This is so obvious and indeed is so plainly a question of fact that we wonder the neo-Mooreians can argue it at all. It would seem that they, too, have contracted the philosopher's disease. Though few if any philosophers appear to be simply proposing a change in people's linguistic habits, nevertheless, say the neo-Mooreians, this is just what philosophers *really* or *ultimately* are doing. I shall not press this 'really,' thereby engendering the perplexity, Just where and what is this real event? Nor shall I ask the embarrassing question, What is the grammar of the word 'proposal' as the neo-Mooreians use it?—for clearly its grammar is not that of 'proposal' as ordinarily used! Rather, let me ask simply, What is the neo-Mooreians' argument? That argument is simple. It is that any *real* difference, any genuine controversy, must be either empirical (as to the facts asserted) or linguistic (as to the language proposed). Now perhaps these are the only alternatives. If so, the neo-Mooreians are right in regard to Moore and his conflict with the idealists and the sceptics.[1] More to the present purpose, however: if the neo-Mooreians are right the ideal language method collapses. That method is then a method of solving a problem which is no genuine problem. There is no issue as to the real world which is not just factual; there is no issue as to the structure of that world or fact or (to come to our problem) of value. Categorial questions are not genuine questions. No peculiar method (different from ordinary observation) is required to solve them—specifically, no method of constructing an ideal language whose forms reveal or show the categorial features of the world is needed or allowed.

But what are the grounds of the neo-Mooreian assumption that these are the only alternatives? May there not be categorial issues concerning the extra-linguistic world (which as such are

[1] Since that controversy is not over the facts, either it is not a genuine controversy or it is a conflict of proposals as to the language to be used in describing the facts.

irreducible to differences of linguistic proposals) that yet are not factual in the sense of being questions as to what are the observable facts? This no doubt is ultimate, and about all that I can say is that I would, as against the neo-Mooreians, answer this last question in the affirmative. But perhaps I *can* say just one more thing. To claim that the only genuine issues as to the extra-linguistic world are factual, in the sense indicated, *i.e.*, that there are no categorial issues, is to claim something not itself factual—the truth or falsity of such a claim cannot be determined by observations of facts. I happen to differ with the neo-Mooreians on the matter (and I believe I could find some company in so doing). On their account, this divergence must be just a conflict of proposals as to the language to be used. They could of course choose to be consistent and to hold exactly this. Then they should not say, "Those who claim there are categorial issues—as well as factual questions and linguistic proposals—are *really*, in claiming this, just making a linguistic proposal." This wouldn't do at all. They should rather say, "*We propose* that our opponent treat his claim that there are categorial issues as itself just a linguistic proposal on his part." And if that opponent should ask, "Why?" The answer should not be, "Because you are mistaken in supposing there are such categorial matters," nor even, "Because to talk your way is misleading (by being about the world, categorial statements seem to be factual, but then it is noticed they cannot be verified by observations)." For such answers presuppose there are *really* only factual statements and linguistic proposals, *i.e.*, this position would no longer be itself presented as *just a linguistic proposal.*

Moreover, if the neo-Mooreians are to be consistent one wonders if they can even make such a proposal. It would seem to require reference to a class of statements, *viz.*, those which are factual. That a statement is factual, on their standpoint, means that it asserts a fact, that it can be verified or disverified (or confirmed or disconfirmed to some degree) by observation of facts. It thus would seem that facts have something in common (if nothing more than their observability). Why cannot this be affirmed in some sentence? But if it were, *that* sentence would not be factual (could not be verified or disverified by observation), yet it would seem clearly to be extra-linguistic in significance and thus not merely a linguistic proposal.

Indeed, this last sort of difficulty seems common to the neo-

Mooreian and the neo-Wittgensteinian positions. Both manage to say a great deal about philosophers, their perplexities, their use of language, their possible confusion of linguistic and factual matters, and so on. Such talk has its own categories. There are philosophers, perplexed by language and perhaps proposing changes in it. What is such a position to say in the face of such a challenge as: There are no philosophers nor are there perplexities; there are only sense-data? Or: There is no extra-linguistic world, there are only sentences, some being protocol-sentences, others being built upon or verified by protocol-sentences? Granted, as it must be, that this issue would not be one of fact. Can we say it is one of grammar to be used, of proposals to be adopted? Not, it seems to me, without assuming there are language-users, an extra-linguistic world, *etc*. My point is not that such an assumption would beg the question. Every philosophic position must beg the question ultimately. My point is rather that by begging the question this assumption is clearly itself categorial. And some such suppressed assumption seems definitely involved in the neo-Wittgensteinian and neo-Mooreian positions.

Now it may be that I am mistaken here. It may be that the neo-Wittgensteinian and neo-Mooreian positions do not tacitly involve any categorial assumptions. Or again, I may be correct on this matter but there may be some other position, a position perhaps that no one has formulated or even thought of, which does not require that besides observable features the world have categorial aspects. But granted this, we need not admit that such sheer possibilities show that it is absurd to assume, contrariwise, that the world *has* categorial aspects and thus that some method of testing the truth of categorial statements, which of course must be different from the observational methods of verifying factual statements, is a genuine philosophical desideratum. Thus what the ideal language method is trying to do is not just absurd; it is not trying to answer an obviously meaningless sort of question.

This completes my defence of the ideal language method of philosophical analysis. I must now indicate my feeling of the inadequacy of that method, particularly in dealing with our present problem (What is value?), and specifically as that method has been actually utilized in the past.

To my knowledge, no one has used it, in any consistent and thorough-going way, to answer our problem. The ideal languages proposed have not contained value-sentences. This defect, from our standpoint, must be remedied by the sketching-out of an ideal language containing normative as well as declarative elementary sentences and an apparatus for building compound sentences from both, whether the elements be of the same kind or mixed. Moreover, in such a language it is requisite that the declarative corresponding to any given normative be marked out by an appropriate difference of form incorporating the same content. As this has already been argued I shall pass on. Another deficiency hitherto has been the failure to recognize the threefold way in which everyday language is utilized in the ideal language method. It not only furnishes the problems (the paradoxes and philosophical puzzlements which engender the demand for a clarified and purified language) and also the test (of the adequacy of the ideal language—Does it allow one to say every sort of thing sayable in ordinary language?); it likewise is part of the apparatus of saying the categorial things (the ideal language can say nothing categorial; its forms simply show the categorial things—but this latter sort of statement itself occurs, it occurs in the non-ideal language of everyday life as it speaks about the ideal language). Thus clearly the ideal language method is not just a procedure of going from everyday language to a purified language. In its very nature it involves a shuttlecock movement between the two languages. I think this was involved but not too clearly recognized in the actual use of the ideal language method in the past.

The defects, or rather the inadequacies, in the ideal language method just referred to were rather explicitly indicated in earlier portions of the present essay. Another possible deficiency in that method was somewhat indirectly suggested but not explored nor even specifically formulated. I hesitate to state it. It may not really be a defect but a virtue. And in any case its statement may have the effect of adding weight to the suspicion that that whole method, however tinkered with, deserves nothing better than to be completely discarded where philosophical analysis is being carried on. But since I am headed toward the admission that this method, though the best we have, finally breaks down, I may as well indicate the deficiency of which I am now thinking. It may be the case that no one ideal language method should admit the necessity of two or more ideal languages, which are not isomorphic (differing essentially only in notation) nor such that they can be combined into a single, richer language (such a combination issuing in contradictions, if not in the ideal language itself then at least in our colloquial statements as to what its forms reveal). To make this concrete, it is enough to recall our struggle to find a proper form for an imperative.[1] On the one hand, an imperative must not literally include its corresponding declarative. Thus, 'Donald, wear your rubbers!' is not to include 'Donald wears his rubbers.' We attempted to meet this requirement by setting the imperative up so that it would have the same content (subjects and predicate) as its corresponding declarative but a different though analogous form. But then we saw that a merely analogous form was not sufficient. *What* is commanded in 'Donald, wear your rubbers!' is precisely that state of affairs asserted by 'Donald wears his rubbers.' An *analogous* form is not enough. In this frustrating situation we suggested two basic imperative forms in the ideal language, neither of which alone adequately revealed imperativity.[2]

It may of course be nonsensical to suggest that we may have to use a battery of ideal languages, not just one, if we wish to show adequately the categorial features of reality as judged by the main sorts of things we can and do say in everyday language. I am not at all sure of myself here, except that if this is nonsense it is not because we cannot consistently use such a plurality of ideal languages to talk of the world. The ideal language method uses an ideal language to gain insight into, not simply to describe, the world. It might just be that were we to describe the world in ideal language L_1 and then again in ideal language L_2 each language, by *its* removal of paradoxes growing out of commonsensical descriptions, would give us some categorial insights the other did not. Of course if we *can* construct another ideal language, L_3, which can unite L_1 and L_2 without engendering paradoxes, we should do so. But if we cannot, it still seems to me that it makes

[1] See above, pp. 130 ff.

[2] In a suggested notation, there was both '$A_{(a)}$!' and '$A_{\{a\}}$' to represent the imperative whose corresponding declarative was '$A_{(a)}$.' See above, footnote, p. 152.

A somewhat similar situation might develop in any adequate analysis of contrary-to-fact conditionals. On the one hand, an ideal language could be set up where such sentences basically appeared as universals (or as a conjunction of a universal and a negative singular). On the other, they could appear in a different ideal language as a basic form of singular sentence. And perhaps neither form alone is adequate to say what is said by contrary-to-fact conditionals in ordinary speech, each supplying some insight that the other fails to supply. See above, p. 55 ff.

sense to allow the possibility of uniting the insights we have gained through building L_1 and L_2. This of course can only be done by using common-sense language. But by now speaking of L_1 and L_2 and of how each in its way shows up and removes unclarities and paradoxes in everyday language, we are not left where we were before the construction of any ideal language. Indeed, I cannot see any difference *in principle* in thus uniting insights gained from more than one ideal language from the procedure of constructing a single ideal language and then judging its adequacy by means of a comparison (conducted in everyday language) with everyday language. For, in the latter case, you are clearly considering it to be a meaningful possibility that the ideal language, though eliminating paradoxes of common speech, is just not adequate in certain respects to saying certain things that common speech manages to say. That is, you are admitting the possibility that certain insights might be obtained by considering certain features of everyday language that have not been clarified by incorporation in the ideal language. Thus the meaningfulness of using two different languages (in this case the ideal language and everyday speech) as object languages through which to gain philosophic grasp is tacitly admitted. And of course here too it is not supposed that these object languages are united, save as objects of analysis, in the philosophical language. That this be done with two ideal languages as the object languages, *i.e.*, with languages clarified to eliminate paradoxes within themselves, does not commit one in principle to anything further. The philosophically significant alternative is not of the kind just indicated, but rather the complete giving up of everyday language as something through whose analysis some grasp of the categorial features of the world, over and above that found through an analysis of the ideal language, is obtainable. The ideal language method could still, on this alternative, use everyday language as the medium of analysis (and of course of communication). But it would lose whatever plausibility it might have as a philosophic method. It would require some such assumption as that ascribed to it by Mr. Copilowish and Mr. Black, that the categorial features of the world are directly inspectable and can be compared, as such, with features of the ideal language (to determine the "adequacy" of the latter), in order to be of any philosophic significance. But if this assumption is made then the whole labour of constructing and analysing an ideal language becomes, philosophically, a work of supererogation. On the other hand, if we are in earnest about using adequacy to common speech as our criterion of the philosophic significance of an ideal language, it may be necessary to admit the need of a plurality of ideal languages in the ideal language method.

The ideal language method as exemplified by Wittgenstein's *Tractatus*, in the interpretation I have given it, combines a sketch of an ideal language with the use of everyday language. The ideal language sketched out contains no metasentences. It is a language in which to talk directly of the world. All the statements about it, and particularly all the categorially significant statements, *e.g.*, those to the effect that the sentence pictures the fact, are in everyday language. Since the publication of the *Tractatus* a great deal has been done in the development of the logic of metalanguages, particularly of semantical metalanguages. As already indicated, I do not believe that any development of the ideal language along these lines will allow the ideal language method to dispense with everyday language as the means of saying the categorial things, of pointing out how the forms of the ideal language show us the forms of reality. This has already been suggested in the case of factuality. Since no fact can, in a correct language, be named, no correct metasentence can say what we want to say and do somehow manage to say in the incorrect sentence, 'A fact is that which makes a true descriptive sentence true.' A similar thing can be said of the sentence, 'A value is that which makes a legitimate normative sentence legitimate.' Yet some purification of such colloquial metasentences is possible, it would seem, in an ideal language that has a place for semantical sentences as well as for object-sentences. An investigation of this possibility concludes the present inquiry.

7b. Can semantical rules for value-sentences show the status of value?

During the course of our inquiry there have emerged certain desiderata for any acceptable philosophical analysis of value. (1) There is value. Where value is, whether in the external world or only in human experience, has not concerned us. But value is not to be reduced to fact or to anything but value. This has been assumed, not argued, though it might have been argued on the basis that no other kind of sentence can say what a value-sentence in colloquial speech says. (2) Value is thus in some sense simple.

(3) Yet value is not a simple property, whether a quality or a relation. What is valuable is never just a particular or just a universal, but that some particular exemplify some universal or that two or more particulars stand in some relation. (4) However, value is not a property of fact, since it is implausible to hold that facts have properties and since moreover value seems frequently to be present in the absence of the appropriate fact. (5) Thus value is in some sense complex. It would seem to be so in a way analogous to the way in which fact is complex. This is reflected in the analogy between the structure of a normative sentence and that of a descriptive, declarative sentence. (6) Thus it may be supposed that a value may have the same components (a particular or particulars and a quality or relation) as some actual or possible fact. However, this is an insufficient characterization of the structure of value, since what is valuable is that some particular or particulars exemplify some property. (7) Hence it seems necessary to suppose that in some way the structure of a value includes (and is not merely analogous to) the structure of a fact —specifically, of the fact which would be valuable did it exist. Yet this seems to conflict with another consideration. (8) Value and fact are independent. A value may obtain where the corresponding fact (that with the same constituents) does not, and *vice versa*. (9) All the above requirements are put in the incorrect and highly misleading form of everyday language. At least some purification can be obtained by performing the appropriate analysis upon the syntax of the value-sentences in an ideal language, and even possibly upon those semantical sentences or rules in such an ideal language that deal with value-sentences.

The view toward which we have been moving measures up pretty well to these desiderata except that so far it has been stated in everyday language. It is that value is that which makes a legitimate value-sentence legitimate, that its structure is revealed by the structure of the normative sentence, that is, that value is the oughting-to-exemplify or the it-were-good-to-exemplify that obtains between a particular or particulars and a quality or relation (analogously to fact, which is the actual exemplification of a quality or relation by a particular or by particulars). What can we now do by way of clarifying and purifying this statement of its highly misleading suggestions? Can the use of semantical sentences, specifically semantical rules, in our ideal language help us to gain insight into value? I think, with many reservations, that to some degree it can. Let us start with our analogous case of factuality.

Suppose we wish to gain insight into the nature of fact. We can start by saying "Any fact is an exemplification of a property by a particular." But as we have seen, 'any fact' is an improper variable. Its values should be names of facts, but we cannot name a fact. Correct language limits us to the assertion of facts, *i.e.*, to the use of full sentences, not mere names, to refer to them, sentences which in any given case may be false, and thus fail to refer to a fact without being completely without reference (since its terms may still name entities). A given singular sentence is adequate to the assertion of some individual fact, as for example '*a* exemplifies *A*.' But now we want to get at its factuality. We can try again by saying, "The fact is that which is in the world when '*a* exemplifies *A*' is true but is absent when '*a* exemplifies *A*' is false." But again we cannot tolerate 'the fact.' If we eliminate the word 'fact' and its equivalents, what can still be done? We can still name sentences, which can be asserted to be true or false, and we can assert facts. In this situation we can get a good deal of help toward showing (not saying) what a fact is by the use of Tarski's truth-condition: "*a* exemplifies *A*' is true if and only if *a* exemplifies *A*, where '*a*' designates *a*, and '*A*' designates *A*.'[1]

Now for our purposes this must not be taken merely as a rule, for example as a technical condition to be satisfied by a definition of truth. Rather, we must look upon it as a feature of a clarified language that assists in revealing the nature of fact. It might be attractive to suppose that the facts, such as that *a* exemplifies *A*, are there from the start and that we then set up a condition for the truth of sentences asserting them. Perhaps in some sense it is possible just to *have* facts, quite independently of any true sentences asserting them, and indeed quite independently of language. I am inclined to think however, that this is not so. A world in which there are facts is a world already categorially structured, a world already shaped up in the language (however vague) of some philosophic point of view. But in any case we cannot *say* this (*viz.*, that facts can be just given quite independently of true sentences): indeed we cannot understand (in some speechless

[1] I am in complete agreement with the contention that what Tarski does with this device is not particularly enlightening in the discussion of any philosophical problem. But it seems to me that, handled quite differently and with a different end in view, it can shed a great deal of light both on the nature of truth and on the nature of fact.

way, much less analyse, the nature of fact except through true sentences.

Now of course to say that *a* exemplifies *A* is to say nothing about a sentence and its truth. Yet to say that '*a* exemplifies *A*' is true if and only if *a* exemplifies *A* is to make progress. It shows, in the equivalence it stipulates, how, *via* true sentences, we can get at the nature of facts. Our truth-condition, for the representative sentence we used, requires that '*a*' designate *a* and '*A*' designate *A*. But though requiring this the truth-condition goes beyond it. It does not merely set up the designation of a list of names ('*a*' and '*A*'). The way in which ' '*a* exemplifies *A*' is true if and only if *a* exemplifies *A*, where '*a*' designates *a* and '*A*' designates *A*' goes beyond a designation rule for '*a*' and '*A*'—this way, I repeat, shows how the structure of a sentence, as different from a list of names (and as different from the sentence as itself treated as a name[1])

[1] Note that we are not to render our truth-condition by any such form as ' '*a* exemplifies *A*' designates (the fact that) *a* exemplifies *A*.' This would involve the mistake of supposing that a sentence can name a fact. P. F. Strawson, in an article critical of those who think that "the Semantic or Metalinguistic Theory of Truth" throws light on the philosophical problem of truth ("Truth," *Analysis*, vol. ix, 1949, pp. 83–97), appears to make precisely this mistake, for he is willing to treat 'is true if and only if' of our truth-condition as synonymous with 'means that.' However, I think he really does not make this mistake but rather two others. These are revealed by his calling such a sentence as ' 'The monarch is deceased' means that the monarch is deceased' a degenerate case of ' 'The monarch is deceased' means that the king is dead,' on the grounds, apparently, that the latter is of use in telling us what 'The monarch is deceased' means, whereas the former is not. But the only difference between the two is in the sentence that follows 'means that.' Now if 'means that' is to be taken as synonymous with 'designates' or 'names' then clearly the sentence after 'means that' in each of these two cases must be taken in use. ('In use' here is to be taken as a semantical not a psychological predicate; whether its predication is correct is determined by semantical rules, not by observation of psychological fact.) But in use these expressions (namely, 'the monarch is deceased' and 'the king is dead') are not two sentences but one; they assert exactly the same thing. Thus though Strawson does not use quotation marks or other devices to indicate it, he is apparently mentioning, not using, the sentences coming after 'means that.' Now it is possible that he is mentioning them in a semantical sentence, so that 'means that' is a semantical predicate. Then, for example, the degenerate and undegenerate sentences he has in mind might be rendered, respectively, ' 'The monarch is deceased' means the same thing (designates the same fact) as does 'The monarch is deceased' ' and ' 'The monarch is deceased' means the same thing (designates the same fact) as does 'The king is dead.' ' This of course would involve the mistake of supposing a sentence can be a name. However, it is not at all clear why one would be degenerate and the other not. Moreover, the context seems to make clear that Strawson has in mind not a semantical but a psychological context in which sentences following 'means that,' in the cases quoted, are mentioned. Thus we might formulate what he has in mind by some such phraseology as ' ' 'The monarch is deceased' helps us understand 'The monarch

can reveal the way in which a fact differs from the set of its constituents.[1]

But if we admit that this sort of truth-condition helps it must also be recognized that it is inadequate and even misleading in any attempt to understand the nature and status of fact. Our predicament indeed is worse than we indicated above. Though we cannot name facts we have supposed that we can name entities that are components of facts (actually particulars and properties, but that they are particulars and properties is not revealed in their names as names). The qualification in our typical truth-condition—namely, that '*a*' designate *a* and '*A*,' *A*—is an explicit stipulation as to such naming, which, in the form of designation-rules, seems necessary, on our method, for any philosophical clarification. Without it we could still name things in our ideal language but that language could never in its own expressions show the "relation" between a name and its referent and thus allow us by analysing it to speak of what is in the world, as designated by our names, as distinguished from what is in our language. But a designation-rule is a rule of language. Let us suppose it is *wholly* linguistic in the sense that no entity which is present in the rule is extra-linguistic. Then we cannot get *a* and *A* (as contrasted with '*a*' and '*A*') into the rule, save in the rare instances where *a* and *A* are themselves linguistic expressions. Therefore, on this supposition, no designation-rule can ever tie a name (of an extra-linguistic entity) with what it names.

is deceased'' is a degenerate case of ''The king is dead' helps us understand 'The monarch is deceased.''' Thus though Strawson does not make the mistake of supposing a sentence can name a fact, he does seem to be guilty of two others: (1) he confuses the mention and the use of a sentence (as is independently corroborated by his statement, critical of the supposal that Tarski's truth-condition is a definition or part of a definition of 'true,' that ". . . part of the expression to be defined (namely, the combination of quotation marks and the phrase is 'true') *disappears* in the definiens without being replaced by anything else"), and (2) he certainly confuses epistemological issues with psychological.

[1] It may be supposed that besides the qualification noted (as to the designation of names) our truth-condition must stipulate that ''*a* exemplifies *A*'' name the sentence '*a* exemplifies *A*' (*cf.* J. F. Thomson, "Note on Truth," *Analysis*, vol. ix, 1949, pp. 67–72). I think there is such a requirement. To formulate it, however, requires a rule in a meta-metalanguage, and specifically one which does not contain a zero-level sentence in use; *e.g.*, it should not be confused with a rule to the effect that '*a* exemplifies *A*' designate (the fact that) *a* exemplifies *A*. A sentence can be named but a fact cannot. It is indeed the way in which our truth-condition avoids the necessity of saying that '*a* exemplifies *A*' designates (the fact that) *a* exemplifies *A* which gives that truth-condition its power of philosophical illumination.

There is a well-known distinction that may be thought capable of getting us out of this difficulty, namely, that between the mention and the use of linguistic expressions. It may be said that of course a designation-rule does not physically include the designatum, but only its name, but that it does include this name *as used* (it also of course mentions it). Thus, it may be thought, we are able in a designation-rule to get at, to specify, the extra-linguistic entity to be designated by some name.[1]

There is of course no objection to this distinction; in fact, its adoption allows us to escape many paradoxes. To suppose however that it permits us to solve the present problem, to escape what I have called the lingua-centric predicament inherent in philosophical clarification (or "categorial analysis"), is to put one's faith in a subterfuge. It is simple enough to show this. What our designation-rule is to do is to clarify (by a stipulation) how a name *as used* designates its extra-linguistic designatum. It is no solution to *use* the name *in* the designation-rule, for this procedure begs the clarification, since it clarifies by means of using in unclarified form precisely that which it is supposed to clarify. This is particularly true where the epistemological position supposedly supported by this sort of clarification is that of linguistic positivism. This position, I take it, holds that designation is wholly linguistic; thus theoretically all designation can be reduced to linguistic rules and their consequences. But if these rules must themselves contain names in use, *i.e.*, names *as designating*, in order to stipulate, linguistically, how various expressions shall designate, the whole position is tacitly abandoned.[2]

As it strikes me, there seem to be just two promising ways out

[1] Professor Carnap, in " Hall and Bergmann on Semantics," *Mind*, vol. liv, 1945, pp. 148–55, not only criticizes the present author as misinterpreting him (and of course on this point he is obviously the unquestionable authority), but also as not having grasped the distinction between mention and use. I do not care to argue this beyond the point relevant to the present context. Carnap obviously feels that had this distinction been grasped, he could not have been accused of falling into the lingua-centric predicament in his *Introduction to Semantics* (as he was by the present author in "The Extra-Linguistic Reference of Language, II Designation of the Object-Language," *Mind*, vol. liii, 1944, pp. 25–35). My answer to this is in the text above.

[2] The same criticism can be put differently. Suppose we only allow names in use. We can then preserve the distinction between the mention and the use of a name by the distinction between *its* name and the name itself. A designation-rule could then be formed by using such a pair, but it would not include the designatum of the name itself. It would have to assume that this names, quite independently of the rule. And it was precisely *this* naming that the rule was to specify and thereby clarify!

of this unpleasant situation.[1] One is to admit that designation-rules can never specify an extra-linguistic designatum of an expression; the other is to accept the paradox that a rule of language may literally include extra-linguistic entities. The former can build up a formal schema in which such *words* as 'name,' 'designation,' 'designatum' occur, but it cannot interpret these terms, or more accurately, it can only interpret them intra-systemically within some semantical hierarchy of languages, not by reference to anything outside language.[2] This is an "escape" from the lingua-centric predicament only by courtesy. Strictly it is a facing and an accepting of that predicament.

The other way does extricate us from the lingua-centric predicament, but only at the cost of admitting that there are rules of language which cannot be written down or spoken. This follows from the admission that a designation-rule can literally include an extra-linguistic designatum. I personally am favourably inclined toward this very radical view. I consider it a quite intelligible supposition that designation-rules giving extra-linguistic meaning to terms of an empirical language should be very different in nature from ordinary sentences in that language, that they should in a sense transcend language by literally uniting the terms in question with their extra-linguistic designata. Just what such rules themselves could be I am not prepared to say, beyond suggesting that they literally create the designations specified (though not the designata nor the names save *qua* designata and names). The present essay, however, is not the proper place to try to develop this view. All we need note here is

[1] I no longer believe we can escape *via* "empirical ties" (*cf. Mind*, vol. liii, 1944, pp. 35 ff.), *i.e.*, *via* demonstrative pronouns, and similar signs, taken in the context of their actual occurrence. For this would require that a designation-rule embrace such contexts. The fact that the context is that of a sign-token is misleading. This is just a special case of the view that a designation-rule may literally include an extra-linguistic entity. In addition it involves an implausible assumption of something like Russell's principle of acquaintance.

[2] As I understand him, this is the solution offered by Professor Gustav Bergmann ("Pure Semantics, Sentences, and Propositions," *Mind*, vol. liii, 1944, pp. 238–57). I think he rightly insists that this is the consistent outcome of linguistic positivism, in one of its senses, that is, in its anti-ontological (not in its phenomenological) aspect. It is his contention that pure syntax, pure semantics, and pure pragmatics (each of which is wholly formal in the sense of being wholly confined to symbols, of containing no extra-linguistic interpretations) show, respectively, all that is of epistemological significance in the traditional coherence, correspondence, and pragmatic theories of truth without any reference to a world beyond language.

that it has a consequence in common with the position which frankly accepts the lingua-centric predicament, namely, that the qualification we have seen to be necessary to our truth-condition, to the effect that '*a*' designate *a* and '*A*' designate *A*, cannot strictly be formulated. Thus this truth-condition, if taken as a means of gaining insight into the nature of fact, is inadequate if not downright misleading.

Moreover, our type of truth-condition may be a hindrance in another way. Its structure was supposed to show us, in some way, the structure of fact. But we must not assume that the structure of a fact is literally the structure of a true sentence asserting that fact. I am no longer referring to the impossibility of naming a fact or a fact's structure, and thus to the impropriety of a sentence that says that the structure of some fact is the same as the structure of some sentence. It is of course obvious that the spatial structure involved in the union of '*a*' and '*A*' in the written sentence, '*a* exemplifies *A*,' and the temporal structure of the spoken correlate are not structures we attribute to the fact asserted by '*a* exemplifies *A*.'[1] Nor will just any combination of *a* and *A* do. If it would, we could replace sentences by vocabulary-lists and refuse to admit false but meaningful sentences, for the entities named in such a list would in every case be combined at least in the sense of being in the universe. Nor will just any differential combination of *a* and *A* do (that is, any combination where *a* and *A* play different rôles in the structure). The rôles must be specific ones traditionally referred to by 'substance' and 'attribute.'[2] But these ontological rôles are surely not literally the same with the grammatical functions of subject and predicate, although reflected in them. Indeed, we should all agree that in some sense the way subjects and predicates enter our sentences is a matter of grammatical rules. But since the structure of fact is something objective and not determined by linguistic rules, the only way we could insure that our subjects and predicates had functions in

[1] This was Professor Black's type of mistake. *Cf.* above, pp. 207–11.

[2] I have used the terms 'particular' and 'property.' 'Particular' seems to avoid the connotation of temporal persistence involved in 'substance,' but unfortunately it has an atomistic flavour. The best terms would be no doubt be semiotic, *e.g.*, 'the function performed in a fact by the referent of a name in a subject-place in a sentence asserting that fact' and similarly for property, substituting 'predicate-place' for 'subject-place.' But such expressions beg our present issue. However, since every philosophic system must rest on concepts and principles that beg the issues between itself and its rivals, perhaps the terms just suggested may be allowed to pass.

sentences that reflected the functions of particulars and properties in facts would be to require this by our rules. To some extent, I think our rules do so require. Otherwise I cannot account for the distinguishing features of a sentence, namely, that it differs from a list (of the names it contains) simply in its structure, that this is not itself another name to be added to those it contains, and that it makes a difference where the names occur, different sentences being producible out of the same names and the same sentential structure. But this leads back to the issue we faced in connection with designation-rules for names.

To do what we want it to do, must not our truth-condition for a descriptive sentence literally embrace the fact asserted by the sentence? To answer in the affirmative would force us to admit that such truth-conditions, like the designation-rules (except in a few trivial cases of sentences about marks on paper) cannot be written down. But now an added difficulty arises.[1] If the fact asserted must itself be present in the truth-condition, then we can have truth-conditions for true sentences only. The fact asserted by a false sentence cannot be put into a truth-condition since there is no such fact. Nor will it help to try to put the abstracted structure of the sort of fact asserted into the truth-condition, along with the referents of the names occurring in the sentence. For to treat the structure of a fact as something abstractable from it and at the same time something common to a number of other facts (both stipulations being necessary on the suggestion just made), is, it seems to me, tantamount to making its structure a property of the fact. We have already seen (particularly in discussing the view that exemplification is a property) that this will not do, that it gives rise to intolerable paradoxes if consistently carried out in everyday language.[2]

Facing this unhappy outcome, we must, I think admit that we are involved in the lingua-centric predicament. Our truth-condition, for any given descriptive sentence, remains wholly

[1] Although I do not care to stress it, it may not be without significance that though 'designates' behaves like a relation-word (it is a predicate demanding two subjects), 'true' does not (it is a predicate taking a single subject). Thus we say '*a*' designates *a*' but never ' '*p*' trues *p*' or even ' '*p*' stands in the relation of truth to *p*' but simply ' '*p*' is true.' This suggests, though it does not require, the propriety of saying that designation-rules may embrace extra-linguistic referents whereas there is nothing comparable for truth-rules.

[2] See above, p. 19.

linguistic: it cannot literally reach out and embrace extra-linguistic fact.[1] But perhaps this predicament is not quite as serious as the preceding sentence might suggest. It may be, as I have suggested, that in the designation-rules for names embraced within or presupposed by such a truth-condition extra-linguistic entities are literally included. And even if not, it must be remembered that it is in the ideal language that we are in the linguacentric predicament. It is still possible to use everyday language to say (quite misleadingly, perhaps, yet in some sense meaningfully and perchance even truly) that the truth-condition for a descriptive sentence does show us something about fact, something that avoids at least some of the misleading suggestions of 'A fact is that which makes a true descriptive sentence true.'

But now, for our categorial analysis of fact, this truth-condition may be misleading in another way. It contains the sentence, ' '*a* exemplifies *A*' is true.' It might be supposed that this is an ordinary declarative and thus that if true, and our general thesis is accepted, it reveals in its structure the structure of some fact.[2] It would seem that a mistake as crass as this could not be made, and indeed it probably is not made by anyone who would admit that Tarski's truth-condition gives us philosophical insight. But some such error does seem to be involved in any position making truth an empirical property.[3] 'True' then becomes an ordinary predicate, and sentences containing it as a predicate are ordinary factual sentences, except that all the true ones among them (as

[1] It was perhaps a vaguely felt uneasiness in this predicament that helped induce Carnap, in *Introduction to Semantics* to resuscitate an otherwise largely extinct entity—the "proposition." This shared with facts the feature of being extra-linguistic, with sentences the possibility of being false. I think it is a sound instinct of the philosopher to reject such hybrid entities created *ad hoc* to meet his peculiar problems.

[2] Clearly I must distinguish between the class of grammatically declarative sentences and the class of factual sentences (only the latter revealing in their structure the structure of fact). On this difficult topic I shall make only two remarks. First, it seems obvious that declarative sentences form a class larger than factual sentences and including the latter as a subset. Second, for present purposes, at least, we need not admit any declarative sentences which are not factual except those that are semiotical. This latter subset of declaratives, however, is not to be restricted to sentences in pure or logical semiotics. For example, ' '*a* exemplifies *A*' is true' is a semiotical sentence but not logical, its truth being determined by fact, not by linguistic rules alone.

[3] It is possible for one holding that 'true' designates an empirical property to accept ' '*a* exemplifies *A*' is true if and only if *a* exemplifies *A*,' but not as a condition for a definition of 'true'—it must rather be treated as a factual assertion.

well as some of the false) have the names of sentences or of something analogous to sentences as subjects. There are many well-known difficulties in such a view, to some of which I shall merely allude.

In the first place, it would seem that sentences predicating 'true' of anything other than sentences or their equivalents are not merely false, they are strictly nonsensical. Thus we allow such sentences as 'This apple is true' only in a highly metaphorical sense which can always be rendered by other factual sentences not containing this predicate. Again, in the case of sentences that predicate 'true' of some sentence, we never attempt to verify or disverify them by observing the sentence they are about to see whether it has the property of being true. Rather, we attempt to observe the fact which the sentence they are about asserts. If we observe that there is such a fact, we immediately grant their truth without any further observations. Moreover, there is no general empirical property of truth that we observe to obtain in all cases of true sentences (and to be absent in all false ones). What we observe, in verifying the truth of various factual sentences, is as various as the sentences. If against this it be said that there is some such common property, *e.g.*, the satisfactoriness or practicality of all true beliefs, we need only point out a confusion. If in the case of every true sentence there is, besides the fact that it asserts, another fact, namely, that belief in it (or a certain correlated belief) is satisfactory, then we must distinguish *two* sentences *both* of which are true, the sentence asserting the original fact and the sentence asserting the satisfactoriness of the belief. Now, however general and invariable the correlation of these two sorts of fact, it is empirical only, as is evidenced by our verifying the one sentence by observing the original fact, the other by observing the satisfactoriness of the belief.[1]

A firm grasp of this has an important consequence. We cannot properly say that ' '*a* exemplifies *A*' is true' gives us an analysis of '*a* exemplifies *A*,' in that sense of 'analysis' in which sentence$_2$ is an analysis of sentence$_1$ if sentence$_2$ says more articulately what

[1] The above remarks are directed against a pragmatic account of truth. Similar remarks could be made regarding any position that makes truth an empirical property (*cf.* above on Professor Baylis's exemplificational theory of truth, pp. 48 ff.). Each such position requires that there be added to the facts of the world a reflection thereof—the facts of sentences' being true that assert these facts. And this addition is superfluous since we determine whether the sentences asserting the first facts are true, not by observing the facts of their exemplifications of truth but the facts which they assert.

sentence$_1$ says.[1] In some sense ' '*a* exemplifies *A*' is true' does say what '*a* exemplifies *A*' says, since they are logically equivalent, equivalent by linguistic rule.[2] Indeed, this is the real basis for claiming that the former does not have the same structure as the latter, for if it had, we would have to say that it ascribed the property, truth, to a sentence taken as a particular, and thus that it asserted a different fact from that asserted in the latter. The trouble is that ' '*a* exemplifies *A*' is true' does not strictly say more articulately what '*a* exemplifies *A*' says. The latter says as articulately as can be said what it attempts to say. It looks as though the former were more articulate, no doubt because there are more words in it.[3] Moreover, it seems to say or at least assume that besides the fact of *a*'s being *A* there is a sentence which asserts this fact and there is the truth of this sentence. But if the sentence and its truth were anything (say a fact) over and above the fact asserted in the sentence, that alone would show we do not have analysis of '*a* exemplifies *A*' in ' '*a* exemplifies *A*' is true.' For the latter would then not say the same thing as the former.

But may it not be that there is no such thing as a fact, that when we say, for example, '*a* exemplifies *A*' we are speaking elliptically and really mean to assert ' '*a* exemplifies *A*' is true'? Then it would seem that the second is (in the present sense) a genuine analysis of the first. Such a view, however, must immediately

[1] *Cf.*, *e.g.*, Wisdom, in *Aristotelian Society Supplementary Volume XIII*, 1934, p. 78.

[2] It might be thought that ' '*a* exemplifies *A*' is true' does not say what '*a* exemplifies *A*' says, since the former is about a sentence, the latter about a fact. P. F. Strawson (*cf. loc. cit.*,) has indeed constructed a paradox along these lines into which "the semantical theory of truth" falls. That theory maintains that both ' '*a* exemplifies *A*' is true' says the same thing as does '*a* exemplifies *A*' (they are logically equivalent) and that it does not (for it is about a sentence whereas the latter is about a fact). This mistake—for so I conceive it—could be caused by either of two confusions. One might suppose that when one mentions a sentence in predicating truth of it one is mentioning it as an occurrent, as written or spoken or subvocally mumbled. Thus the predication of truth might seem to be an empirical assertion—an assertion of a fact different from that asserted by the sentence mentioned. But the very use of the predicate 'true' should warn us against this error. The truth of a sentence is something quite independent of any occurrence-aspect of the sentence. The other confusion is of ' '*a* exemplifies *A*' is true' with ' '*a* exemplifies *A*' is true if and only if *a* exemplifies *A*.' The latter does talk about, in the sense of stipulating concerning, the sentence, '*a* exemplifies *A*' (it asserts, in an empirical sense, nothing at all); the former does not. Indeed, it is by virtue of the latter's making the stipulation it does about this sentence that the former can be seen not to talk about it (either by stipulating concerning it or by making an empirical assertion about it) but to assert it.

[3] It contains more marks but not more terms or names.

face the embarrassing question of a criterion of truth. How are we to establish the truth of any such sentence as ' '*a* exemplifies *A*' is true'? Not by observing the fact that *a* does exemplify *A*, since (on this view) there is no such fact and our sentence does not assert that there is. Is it to be supposed that though there is no primary fact (such as *a*'s exemplifying *A*) there are secondary facts (such as the exemplification of truth by '*a* exemplifies *A*')? And that we can directly observe the latter? To this all our procedures of empirical verification give the lie. It would seem then that we are forced into some form of intuitionism resting on the criterion of self-evidence.[1] Such an outcome is sufficient, in the present author's estimation, to condemn the view giving rise to it. We must conclude that ' '*a* exemplifies *A*' is true,' is not an analysis of '*a* exemplifying *A*' in the sense of saying more articulately what the latter says. The latter asserts a simple fact and asserts it as articulately as it can be asserted.

Now, despite all the above qualifications and warnings, I still maintain that the rule, expressed in the truth-condition stipulation, ' '*a* exemplifies *A*' is true if and only if *a* exemplifies *A*, where '*a*' designates *a* and '*A*' designates *A*,' is helpful in the attempt to gain philosophical enlightenment as to the nature of factuality. It enables us to see that factuality is a structure which unites in a certain way the referents of the subject and the predicate of a descriptive sentence. But that it enables us to see this cannot be said in a correct language.

At the end of Section 5 it was suggested that some insight into the nature of value might be attained by attributing to value-sentences a semantical property, legitimacy, analogous to but not identical with the property, truth, of descriptive sentences. It was of course noted that this involved the necessity of a "legitimacy-condition" for value-sentences, paralleling the truth-condition for descriptive sentences, which must be a consequence, for each such value-sentence, of any acceptable definition of 'legitimacy.' This legitimacy-condition, for the value-sentence '*a* is good,' was there formulated, ' '*a* is good' is legitimate if and only *a* is good.' In the following section it was proposed that in an ideal language the various sorts of value-sentences of colloquial speech be put in the normative form, illustrated by '*a* ought to exemplify *A*' or 'It were good that *a* exemplify *A*.' In accordance

[1] This we saw (*cf.* above, p. 101) to be the outcome of Franz Brentano's views as semantically interpreted.

with this proposal, the legitimacy-condition for value-sentences should be represented with a sentence in the normative, rather than the value-predicative, form, *e.g.*, ' '*a* ought to exemplify *A*' is legitimate if and only if *a* ought to exemplify *A*.' It was further suggested, in Section 6 and in the first part of the present section, that the structure of the normative sentence in the ideal language proposed, particularly in its analogy to but difference from the structure of the corresponding declarative, shows us, so far as it is possible, the structure of value as compared with that of fact. But we had to say this wholly in everyday language. We are now asking whether the form of the legitimacy-condition, as occurring in the ideal language, may not help in this process of getting as close as we can in the ideal language to what we are trying to analyse, even though finally the analysis has to be stated in common-sensical terms.

I think that such help is to be had, of a kind exactly paralleling that (such as it was) furnished by the truth-condition for descriptive sentences when we were trying to gain insight into factuality. We have, then, the rule or stipulation: ' '*a* ought to exemplify *A*' is legitimate if and only if *a* ought to exemplify *A*, where '*a*' designates *a* and '*A*' designates *A*.'[1] In this we can see (though it does not itself say) that, although necessary, it is not sufficient that the world contain *a* and *A* in order that '*a* ought to exemplify *A*' be legitimate. Thus whenever what is asserted in such a sentence as '*a* ought to exemplify *A*' does obtain, and this sentence is legitimate, there must be besides *a* and *A* something more in the

[1] This stipulation sets up a logical equivalence. There would be, I should suppose, no objection to logical equivalence in normative logic (*cf.* the article by Professor Storer, referred to above, p. 143). It might, however, be thought objectionable that a declarative be made logically equivalent to a normative sentence, as certainly seems to be the case in the sort of legitimacy-condition here under consideration. It certainly would be objectionable to make a descriptive or zero-level declarative logically equivalent to a zero-level normative; indeed it is precisely against this sort of error (from the standpoint of the desirability of constructing an ideal language adequate to everyday speech) that much of the polemics of this essay are directed. But '*a* ought to exemplify *A*' is legitimate' is not a zero-level sentence and it would seem appropriate to set up our ideal language so that it should not be equivalent to any descriptive zero-level sentence. On the other hand, there may be technical logical objections to such an equivalence as that involved in our suggested legitimacy-condition. It will of course be kept in mind that the author is favourably disposed toward retaining the two-valued form of logic for declaratives but combining it with a three- (or multiple-) valued form for normatives. But it is not immediately apparent that this involves any difficulty in the present instance. (*Cf. Philosophy of Science*, vol. xiv, 1947, footnote 21a, p. 343.)

world (which I call the value in the case in question) which somehow includes and combines them in the differential manner indicated by the sentence, '*a* ought to exemplify *A*.'

What I have just said—or rather what I have just tried to say—about what our legitimacy-condition in our ideal language allows us to see is itself put in everyday language, and is thus incorrect and misleading. Concerning it we must make qualifications and set up warnings exactly paralleling those made for our similar contention that the truth-condition for '*a* exemplifies *A*' somehow gives us insight into the nature of the fact asserted by this sentence. We must, for example, deny that legitimacy is a property, that ''*a* ought to exemplify *A*' is legitimate' gives an analysis of '*a* ought to exemplify *A*,' and so on. Let me so far presume on the good will of the reader as not to formulate remarks which would exactly parallel those given earlier. To these qualifications must be added further ones not paralleled by anything in our discussion of the insight into factuality our stipulated sort of truth-condition may furnish.

In the first place, there is something obvious in itself which we have stressed from the first. Though 'legitimacy' must be kept analogous to 'truth' it must also be kept distinct. This requires that our form of legitimacy-condition for normative sentences must itself be different from (though also analogous to) the truth-condition sort of stipulation for descriptive declaratives; and this in a respect over and above the requirement that in the one there occur normative sentences and their names, in the other, descriptive sentences and their names. In other words, 'legitimate' must behave differently from 'true' in our semantical sentences and this not merely in regard to the sorts of sentences whose names can be combined with these predicates. At first glance this requirement might not seem to have been met: our legitimacy-condition for, say, '*a* ought to exemplify *A*,' seems to have exactly the same form as our truth-condition for '*a* exemplifies *A*,' differing only in the sentences, and names of sentences contained, and in that 'legitimate' replaces 'true.' But this is a mistaken impression. For purposes of economy of effort and ease in reading we have formulated the truth-condition as though it were independent of a falsity-condition. The required distinction is brought out if we take into account the three semantical values we proposed a normative sentence should have (to correspond with the syntactical distinction between an elementary normative and the two different sentences constructed from it by the use of two different negative connectives).[1] A truth-falsity-condition has a dual form different from the triple form of a legitimacy-illegitimacy-non-legitimacy-condition. A descriptive sentence may fail to be true only by being false; a normative sentence may fail to be legitimate either by being illegitimate or by being non-legitimate. This allows us to see that the something more that must be in the world, over and above the referents of the names, when a normative sentence is legitimate is different from the something more when a descriptive sentence containing the same names is true, though the two are analogous in that they cannot properly be named, but are ways in which entities that can be named function differentially in different unities (unities we call in one case a value, in the other, a fact).

We may perhaps gain one more insight into the nature of value and its relation to fact by allowing legitimacy-conditions for normative as well as truth-conditions for descriptives to enter our ideal language as rules. We have noted that it is commonsensical to suppose that for every value-sentence there is a corresponding descriptive sentence—that which asserts as fact what it is that the value-sentence values (*e.g.*, the *what* that an elementary normative asserts ought to be a fact). This can now be seen in the occurrence of the names in the sentences (asserted and named) in the truth- and legitimacy-conditions and in the designation rules included in the latter. That is, we may suppose that for every legitimacy-condition for a normative sentence there is a parallel truth-condition for the corresponding descriptive sentence, where the same names occur and the same designation rules for those names are included. This is illustrated by our use of '*a*' and '*A*' in the formulations given above.[2]

[1] Our truth-falsity-condition for '*a* exemplifies *A*' would then be: ' '*a* exemplifies *A*' is true if and only if *a* exemplifies *A* and '*a* exemplifies *A*' is false if and only if *a* does not exemplify *A*, where '*a*' designates *a* and '*A*' designates *A*.' On the other hand, our legitimacy-illegitimacy-nonlegitimacy-condition for '*a* ought to exemplify *A*' would be: ' '*a* ought to exemplify *A*' is legitimate if and only if *a* ought to exemplify *A*, '*a* ought to exemplify *A*' is illegitimate if and only if *a* ought to fail to exemplify *A* [or *a* ought to non-exemplify *A*] and '*a* ought to exemplify *A*' is non-legitimate if and only if there is no ought about *a*'s exemplifying *A* [or *a* non-ought to exemplify *A*], where '*a*' designates *a* and '*A*' designates *A*.'

[2] An actual case, omitting such typical or pseudo-abbreviations, is furnished by the parallel between ' 'The shutters ought to be green' is legitimate if and only if the shutters ought to be green, where 'the shutters' designates the shutters and 'green' designates green' on the one hand and, on the other, ' 'The shutters are green' is true if and only if the shutters are green and 'the shutters' designates the shutters and 'green' designates green.'

This, I think helps us a little to see how a value is related to the fact that corresponds (or would correspond) to it. Its inadequacy becomes obvious when we note that it simply shows us that the fact has the same constituents as those to be found in the value in a different but analogous structure. Thus it might easily but erroneously be supposed that the correspondence between a fact and a value is symmetrical. I think actually the world is so made up that there is such a symmetry: that for every actual and possible fact there is a corresponding value (positive or negative in one or the other of the two forms of negativity) and *vice versa*. But in the nature of factuality and value we find an asymmetry. This can be expressed by saying that it makes sense to suppose there might have been a world of facts without values but doesn't to suppose a world of values without facts. It might be slightly less misleading to say that value internally bears reference to fact, but not contrariwise. This we have in various ways repeatedly emphasized. It is always some possible fact that is valued. This has been expressed by the use of the infinitive of the copula in our normative example, '*a* ought to exemplify *A*.' In common usage this is analogous to a sentence expressing purpose, *e.g.*, 'I plan to exemplify the utmost caution,' which neither literally (in use) nor by name (by mentioning) includes the declarative 'I do (or shall) exemplify the utmost caution,' yet clearly depends upon the latter (in respect of its sentential form not merely of the names it includes) for its meaning. The same sort of thing can be said as regards the use of indirect speech in our type-case, 'It were good that *a* exemplify *A*.'

However, these two typical normative sentences have been taken over from ordinary speech. It is through some tacit but unformulated rules of everyday usage that they allow us to see that a normative sentence is not merely analogous to the declarative corresponding to it but in some peculiar way includes the latter without asserting it. Our ideal language has not yet been made to do this.[1] For its accomplishment the only likely vehicle would seem to be a semantical sentence.[2] But this would require that

[1] This is revealed in the notation suggested above, namely, '$A_{\{a\}}$' for the normative whose corresponding declarative is '$A_{(a)}$.'

[2] To make it occur at the zero-level would require that normatives literally include their corresponding declaratives, thus that they be compounds, one element in which is the corresponding declarative. Clearly, however, there is just as much basis in everyday speech for accepting elementary or simple normatives as for accepting elementary declaratives. To make it occur at a

there be a semantical sentence which referred to a declarative and yet was itself a normative or logically equivalent to a normative. Moreover, it would require that this semantical sentence be logically equivalent to a zero-level normative, since, as we have seen, everyday language requires sentences of this latter sort.

In this situation I am going to make a suggestion that no doubt is simply ridiculous. It may have consequences that are intolerable. Still, I'm not *sure* that it does, and it may help meet our present need.

In ordinary speech we frequently find such semantical, normative sentences as the following: 'Whether or not it is true that John still loves her it certainly would be good were it true.' 'It ought to be the case that every good man is happy; unfortunately it is false.' ' 'There are no spies among our top scientists' happens to be false; it ought to have been true.' 'It ought to be the case that every suspect is arrested; I am glad to report that this is the case.' Such sentences, it seems to me, can without impropriety be put, so far as their normative components are concerned, in the following form, '*s* ought to be true,' where '*s*' is the name of a declarative sentence.

My suggestion has two parts. First, let us allow in our ideal language normative sentences having the form just indicated, that to be found in '*s* ought to be true.' Second, let us add to our type of declarative truth-condition for declarative sentences as already discussed a normative truth-condition for the same sentences. This can be represented by the following type-instance: ' '*a* exemplifies *A*' ought to be true if and only if *a* ought to exemplify *A*, where '*a*' designates *a* and '*A*' designates *A*.' Let me point out that such a rule would not depart too radically from good usage. The sentence, ' 'The State Department has a definite far-eastern policy' surely ought to be true,' would, I think in journalistic debate be treated as logically equivalent to, as saying just the same thing as, 'The State Department surely ought to have a definite far-eastern policy.' Third, let us suppose that for every normative sentence in our ideal language for which such a normative truth-condition obtains there is a corresponding declarative (having the same content).

pragmatic meta-level would be to reduce all normatives to declaratives about the occurrence of linguistic expressions, which would conflict with the objectivism of the present essay, or at least would reduce all normatives to statements as to the value of the occurrence of linguistic expressions (thereby confining value to what should be *said*), which surely would sacrifice all affinity to common usage.

Now let us see what this odd suggestion, if carried out, could do for us. The obvious pecularity of this normative truth-condition is that it includes the name of a declarative sentence but not the sentence so named, and, contrariwise, a normative sentence but not that sentence's name. It clearly sets up a logical equivalence between two normatives, one of which is in the object-language and, when that object-language is at zero-level, asserts directly some extra-linguistic value. It thus stipulates that an apparently different sentence, an ostensibly metalinguistic sentence, is to say the same thing as a normative sentence which speaks directly of the world. But the ostensibly metalinguistic normative sentence in our stipulated equivalence does not contain the name of the normative sentence in the object-language with which it is made equivalent; rather, it contains the name of the declarative that corresponds with this normative. Since only the name of this declarative, and not the declarative itself, is included, it is clear that the rule does not require that a normative assert the fact its corresponding declarative asserts. This shows how value is independent of fact.[1] On the other hand, by stipulating that the name of this declarative be included in the metalinguistic sentence equivalent to a given normative, our normative truth-condition shows how a reference to fact is included in value.[2]

[1] Specifically how value is independent of the fact which would need to be the case if what is valuable were actual.

[2] Our suggested normative truth-condition raises the interesting but somewhat tangential question, what is to be meant by the equivalence of two normative sentences? As a technical problem we must put it aside; an unobjectionable answer must await the development of a normative logic. But I suppose we may say that common usage would make certain vague but not wholly unintelligible demands. The equivalent normatives must say the same thing, must mutually imply one another, and thus be mutually substitutable. This seems to indicate that whatever legitimacy-value one has the other must have also.

It should be noted, however, that granted this our suggested normative truth-condition for '*a* exemplifies *A*' does not have the consequence that we can substitute ' '*a* exemplifies *A*' ought to be true' for '*a* ought to exemplify *A*' in the sentence ' '*a* exemplifies *A*' corresponds to '*a* ought to exemplify *A*,' ' for in this last sentence it is not '*a* ought to exemplify *A*' that occurs but rather its name. If we could correctly say that a certain fact corresponded to a certain value, *e.g.*, that *a*'s exemplifying *A* is the fact that corresponded to the value, *a*'s oughting to exemplify *A* (if the reader will permit the solecism), then such a substitution as that just suggested might occur and we would have the sentence, '*a*'s exemplification of *A* is the fact which corresponds to '*a* exemplifies *A*' ought to be true.' But this sentence, which would help us immensely in seeing how value includes a reference to fact, must remain in incorrect colloquial speech.

There is danger of a mistake here. It is certainly true that the name of something is not the thing itself. Thus suppose '*a*' names *a*. Then the name of '*a*' is not itself '*a*,' that is, is not the name of *a*. But now a serious mistake arises if it is supposed that ' '*a*' ' (the name of '*a*') *in no sense whatever* refers to *a*. The mistake arises because we can think of '*a*' in two ways—as the name of *a* and as an entity in its own right (whether as a particular or a property, a "token" or a "type" is here quite irrelevant). If '*a*' is taken, for example just *as* a design on paper, then ' '*a*' ' as a name of '*a*' has no reference to *a*. So far, however, as we take ' '*a*' ' to name a *name*, to name '*a*' *in its function* as a name of *a*, then ' '*a*' ' does have some sort of reference to *a*. Though ' '*a*' ' does not name *a* it does name the name of *a* (and names it *as* the name of *a*). Beyond this it is perhaps impossible but also unnecessary to go. So when we name a sentence, the name is not the sentence and so does not assert what the sentence asserts. Still, if we name the sentence *as* a sentence our name does in some sense refer to that which the sentence asserts.[1] After all, the name of a sentence is a name *of a sentence* not of a cow or a centaur or even a set of ink-marks on paper. Moreover, the apparently metalinguistic normative in our ought-condition contains the predicate 'true.' Of course it does not say that the declarative sentence it names *is* true; it says it *ought to be true*. But by uniting the name of this declarative with 'true' it is indicated that some sort of reference to fact is involved in value.

Thus our normative truth-condition, by stipulating that a sentence naming a declarative and "oughting" its truth is to say the same thing as the normative corresponding to that declarative, does give us some help in seeing (but not in correctly stating) how the structure of value involves the structure of fact. And it even gives some help in seeing that this does not destroy the simplicity of the structure of value. Although it might not appear so at first glance, ' '*a* exemplifies *A*' ought to be true' is as truly a simple sentence as its equivalent, '*a* ought to exemplify *A*.' For its subject is a name, not a sentence, and the simplicity or complexity of a sentence is a matter of *its* structure, not of the structure of that which its terms designate.

Warnings and restrictions parallel to those connected with our use of the declarative truth-condition in trying to understand

[1] The matter is complicated in that the sentence itself does not name but refers in the peculiar true-or-false manner we have called "assertion."

factuality should be posted here in connection with our use of the normative truth-condition in attempting to gain insight into the way value includes fact. I shall leave their formulation to the ingenuity of the reader. Let me specifically call attention, however, to one way in which the normative truth-condition may, for this purpose, be seriously misleading. We saw that, on the equivalence stipulated by the declarative truth-condition, the sentence, ' '*a* exemplifies *A*' is true,' was not to be taken as asserting a property (truth) of a sentence—as though it said anything more than that *a* exemplified *A*. Similarly, on the equivalence stipulated by the normative truth-condition the sentence, ' '*a* exemplifies *A*' ought to be true,' does not assert some value (attaching to a sentence) over and above the value that *a* ought to exemplify *A*. It follows that the 'ought to be' of ' '*a* exemplifies *A*' ought to be true' is not the same as the 'ought to be' of '*a* ought to be *A*.' The only "oughtings" we really ever assert are of the latter sort (which I take it is part of what the normative truth-condition reveals). We may formulate this, if we please, by saying that the former 'ought to be' is "pseudo," that the sentence, ' '*a* exemplifies *A*' ought to be true' does not really have the structure of a normative. But this would be misleading. It would be like saying that the sentence, ' '*a* exemplifies *A*' is true' is not a declarative, that its 'is' is only "pseudo," for it does not predicate a property, truth, of a sentence. It is less misleading to say that the sentence ' '*a* exemplifies *A*' ought to be true' is a normative, but that it only appears to "ought" the exemplification of truth by the sentence it names; what it really "oughts" is the exemplification of *A* by *a*. (A parallel statement could be made for its corresponding declarative.) Yet this appearance is, for our categorial purposes, vital: it helps us see how a normative is related to its corresponding declarative, and thus how value includes fact. So we must keep up the appearances even when, and in fact because, they are only appearances.

But even yet we are not done with the necessary warnings. Value intentionally includes fact. We can, to some degree, see this in a certain type of sentence, *viz.*, a sentence that is equivalent to a normative that is directly about the world and that names that normative's corresponding declarative and "pseudo-oughts" the truth of the latter. Thus the inclusion of fact in value, if we are to go by this appearance, would seem to be literally intentional or referential. But no value, in the extra-linguistic world, names any fact, both because facts are unnameable, and because names occur only in language, not in the extra-linguistic world. Our apparent normative, ' '*a* exemplifies *A*' ought to be true,' thus seems finally to have failed us. In fact, it *has* failed us. But this is no new or additional failure. It is just the one we have been struggling with when we noted that, by our normative truth-condition, ' '*a* exemplifies *A*' ought to be true' is not "oughting" anything of the sentence, '*a* exemplifies *A*,' nor of the fact of *a*'s exemplification of *A*. There is a simple value-structure. Not only do values with this structure not include their corresponding facts, they do not include a name of them or any reference to them (in the correct use of 'reference' which requires linguistic elements created by semantical rules). Just how then does our normative truth-condition help us to see the relation a value bears to its corresponding fact? This cannot be correctly formulated. It can only finally be experienced. But the incorrect formulations which we have given, together with the recognition of how they are incorrect, may not be useless in inducing this experience.

CONCLUDING REMARKS

Our essay has ended with the unsayable. We cannot in a correct language formulate an answer to our question, What is value? In many ways it might be appropriate (though it would also be misleading in many ways) to characterize our position as that of the Wittgenstein of the *Tractatus*, but with his world extended to embrace whatever ought to be the case as well as whatever is the case. But does this not suggest that we ought to follow the example of the neo-Wittgensteinians (and perhaps of Wittgenstein himself, supposing he did espouse the position of the Blue Book)? Should we not give up the whole undertaking as unnecessarily self-frustrating? I think not. I need not and I shall not conceal the fact that I have my own moments of despondency when I am tempted to throw aside the whole philosophical endeavour to find an answer to such questions as, What is value? What is fact? What is truth? What is entailment? What is designation? And I suspect that this despondency is not peculiar to me and my individual inadequacies as a philosopher; I suspect that everyone who has seriously wrestled with these issues must have at some time experienced it. But I am convinced that the perplexities that give rise to such despondency are not merely psychological in origin. There are real problems concerning our world to which an empirical solution is not possible because not relevant, problems I have designated "categorial." These cannot be given a psychological solution because they are not psychological. They can be set aside through psychiatric treatment only in the way that any real problem can be so set aside. They cannot be destroyed by seeing through them and noting that they are not real problems at all but just ways in which the human mind inflicts torture on itself.

In raising categorial issues we are attempting to clarify and to find the extra-linguistic significance of concepts that are involved in everything or nearly everything else we say. It is not then to be wondered at that we end with the unsayable: This we should expect. The objective should be to postpone this inevitable result as long as possible, to push the unsayable as far back as we can, to let the obvious speak for itself only after we have said as much as can be said to bring out what is not obvious.

If the present essay has been successful in postponing ultimate taciturnity for a few thousand words, this is the only sort of success its author could realistically have aimed at, always providing that this postponement has not destroyed or signally lessened the final vision. Now of course this provision may not everywhere be vouchsafed: the opponents of objectivism in value-theory would not grant it. But about such a divergence in ultimate vision nothing can be done, save to return constantly to the task of pushing the obvious further back in the hope that somehow in this process agreement will be reached.

This whole appeal to the obvious, to the revelation of what cannot be said, as the *ultimate* arbiter of philosophic disputes may be disconcerting to some prosaic minds. It smacks too much of mysticism. It *is* of course a form of mysticism, but it is mysticism in its most plebeian and I hope unobjectionable garb. There is meant no escape to some ecstatic experience, some high, emotional plane achieved only by the few on rare occasions. The vision appealed to is that which is obvious in all experience, and which is revealed in the sense of our everyday language, a sense that is felt by everyone using that language in everyday situations.

It is hoped that this essay has met this test, that it has not only postponed by some two hundred-odd pages the appeal to the obvious (in this sense), but, resting finally on this appeal, really has retained the obvious, that it has remained true to our feelings for everyday language in pushing back into the unsayable but seen an answer to the question, What is value?

This sensitivity to everyday language, in this case the language of normatives as embedded in our total language which also embraces declaratives, seems to the author to make the following demands: (1) Value is in nature simple, it is irreducible to any form, however complex, of factuality. (2) Value is not a positive quality, however apprehended. (3) Value is in some sense relational. But it is not an empirical relation, like simultaneous with, whose exemplification can be directly observed. (4) It is relational rather in the vague sense in which exemplification is relational. (5) What it relates is always some particular or particulars and some quality or empirical relation. Only particulars have value. But they have it only with respect to some quality or relation. (6) Value includes fact in some sense. It is the exemplification of some quality or relation by some particular or particulars that is valuable. (7) Yet value is independent of fact. That some exemplification of a quality or relation is valuable or ought to be the case is independent of whether that exemplification is the case.

How these demands are satisfied by the view suggested in this essay must be left to the reader's insight. Put incorrectly, that view would have value, like fact, be a way in which particulars are united with their properties, a way revealed by the structure of our normative sentences. Such sentences assert what ought to be the case; they correlate with and in some vague intentional fashion include corresponding sentences declarative of fact; they may be legitimate in the sense of asserting of what actually ought to be that it ought to be; but when not legitimate, they may be so in either of two ways depending on whether an incompatible ought obtains or there is in reality no ought in the matter at all. But the reader must, to grasp this view, discount all this incorrect language used in its formulation. Moreover, even after the position is actually seen, it may be seen to be impossible or without sufficient grounds. And certainly, to make it at all acceptable, it is necessary to associate it with a tenable answer to another question, How can value be known? Corresponding to the question, How are descriptive sentences verified?, is the even more difficult question, How are normative sentences justified? How can we ever establish or even make probable the legitimacy of a normative sentence? *This* question the present essay has left entirely aside. This attempt to divide the territory, to explore it in segments, may have been a fatal mistake. It may be found that by exploring further we are led to put aside entirely the position so vaguely indicated in the present essay. But even if so, it is important not to lose sight of the fact that this essay is trying to do something worth doing: to answer an extremely difficult but also an extremely basic and eminently sensible question, the question, What is value?

INDEX OF PROPER NAMES

SUBJECT-MATTER INDEX